THE DOLOMITES OF ITALY

THE
DOLOMITES
OF ITALY
A TRAVEL GUIDE

James and Anne Goldsmith
with
Giovanni Rizzardi
Gernot Mussner
Paolo Pompanin

A & C BLACK
LONDON

HUNTER PUBLISHING INC.
EDISON, NJ, U.S.A.

A PRODUCTION OF BAY TREE VENTURES, INC.
MILL VALLEY, CA, U.S.A.

THE DOLOMITES

THE DOLOMITES

Tre Cime di Lavaredo (Drei Zinnen)

ACKNOWLEDGEMENTS

This guide to the Dolomites is in large part the result of a cooperative effort between our many valued Italian and American colleagues. They have helped us immeasurably along the way. Profiles of each of them can be found at the back of the book.

Principal Photography:
James Goldsmith
George Charles Hampton
Wayne Hanson

Design and Illustrations:
George Charles Hampton

Map-diagram design:
James Goldsmith
George Charles Hampton
Paolo Pompanin

Published in the United Kingdom by:
A & C Black (Publishers) Limited
35 Bedford Row, London WC1R 4 JH
England

ISBN 0-7136-3128-7

Published in the United States and Canada by:
Hunter Publishing Inc.
300 Raritan Center Parkway
Edison, NJ 08818, U.S.A.

ISBN 1-55650-162-5 (paperback)   ISBN 1-55650-190-0 (hardcover)

Distributed in Italy by:
Edizioni Dolomiti s.n.c.
Corso Italia 21
32046 San Vito di Cadore, (BL) Italia

ISBN 88-85080-05-7 (paperback)   88-85080-06-5 (hardcover)

A Production of:
Bay Tree Ventures, Inc.
100 Shoreline Drive, Suite 225
Mill Valley, CA 94941, U.S.A.

All inquiries concerning bulk sales should be addressed to Bay Tree Ventures, Inc.

Copyright © 1989 by Bay Tree Ventures, Inc.

Library of Congress Catalog Card Number: 88-71743

A CIP catalogue record for this book is available at the British Library.

Printed in Italy by A. Mondadori

Front Cover: Val di Funes (Villnösstal)

Back Cover: Selva, Val Gardena

DEDICATION

For our many wonderful friends in the Dolomites.

INTRODUCTION

During the summer of 1984, Jim and Anne Goldsmith, along with their family, holidayed for the first time in the Dolomites. Although the Goldsmiths had traveled and hiked in many mountain regions in the United States, Europe, and Nepal, the Dolomites seemed to offer unparalleled recreational opportunities for people of all ages and interests. That summer, Jim had the opportunity to renew an old friendship with Giovanni Rizzardi of Rome, and, while on a walk together in the Sesto, they thought of collaborating on this book.

AUTHORS' COMMENTS

It is our intention to acquaint you with the spectacular Dolomite mountains in northeastern Italy—their year-round recreational possibilities, hospitable people, diverse culture, and charming villages. If you are a hiker, we aim to show you one of the premier walking areas in the world; and if your passion is skiing, we want to present an area to rival any other part of the Alps. We hope our suggestions will be an aid in planning your mountain holiday and that this guide will also prove to be a valuable companion during your visit, regardless of whether you spend one day or two months.

We have walked every walk and hiked every hike in the book. We have alpine skied and cross-country skied in nearly all the thirty areas featured. Almost every road in the Dolomites has been explored in over 3000 kilometers of driving. More than 6000 photos have been taken during our research.

Our book does not profess to be an authority on such aspects as geography, natural sciences, or history. If you are interested in any of these subjects, we encourage you to refer to the bibliography. Helpful pamphlets and booklets can be found in the tourist offices in the major villages of the Dolomites and bordering cities.

Some specific details in any guidebook become outdated, such as skiing facilities, hotel lists, and transportation information. It is wise, therefore, to contact the local and regional tourist offices and to purchase some of the excellent maps and other publications which are constantly being updated.

Elevations have been included on the map-diagrams in the book—space permitting. It is not uncommon, particularly in travel writing about mountain regions, to find minor variations among maps regarding elevations, trail numbers, and the names of geographical features. We have found this to be the case in checking our various sources. There may be minor differences between elevations we show and those indicated in other sourcebooks.

Many mountains, towns, and geographical features in the Dolomites are known locally by at least two names; one Italian and the other German. In most cases, we have used the Italian names, recognizing that the Dolomites are in Italy. In many instances we have used both names for those locales where that usage is typical, putting the German name in parentheses.

We have divided the Dolomites into five districts to help us detail some of the cultural and recreational features. We recognize that many criteria, such as historical, political, and/or geological demarcations, can be used for classifying an area into sections. Our book is for the traveler so we have relied upon the excellent road network, geography and common geology to aid us in these delineations. For simplicity, we only discuss the Dolomites in terms of the high seasons—summer and winter while obviously the area's charms are manifold year-round.

TABLE OF CONTENTS

ABOUT THE DOLOMITES

THE DOLOMITES IN SUMMER

TABLE OF CONTENTS

THE DOLOMITES IN WINTER

TRAVELERS' INFORMATION

TABLE OF CONTENTS

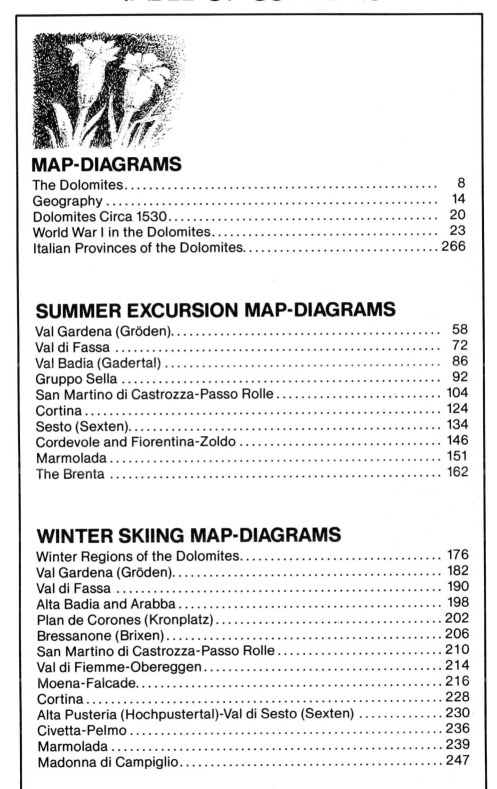

MAP-DIAGRAMS

SUMMER EXCURSION MAP-DIAGRAMS

WINTER SKIING MAP-DIAGRAMS

THE DOLOMITES

Village of Sesto, Val di Sesto

The spectacular Dolomite mountains of northeastern Italy are a major part of the great alpine chain of Europe. They are sandwiched between the Austrian border on the north and the vast Venetian plain on the south. They were formed eons ago when sedimentary rocks under ancient seas were forced upward 3,000 meters by the titanic mountain-building forces which shaped the Alps. Enormous rock walls explode to startling heights above the pastoral green countryside. Indeed, many have said these Dolomites, with their stunning shapes and dramatic brilliant colors, are unsurpassed in appeal and beauty by any mountain system in the world.

The drama of towering Dolomite peaks and spires is contrasted with storybook scenes. Peaceful valleys are sprinkled with lively villages and hamlets while whitewashed farmhouses dot the terraces above. In the summer, the lush velvet meadows are covered with wildflowers and the air is filled with the music of tinkling cowbells as dairy cattle meander along the roads to the higher pas-

THE DOLOMITES

Relaxing above Cortina, Antelao in distance

February in Selva, Val Gardena

tures, prodded on by herdsmen. On the hillsides, farmers tend their crops of hay, with entire families lending a hand for cutting and stacking. A change of scenery comes with the first snows, and the Dolomites turn into an enchanting winter playground.

The cultures of Italy and Austria meet here in the Dolomites. Both are manifested in the food, architecture, and language. Few mountain regions offer so much at such a low altitude—requiring little time out for acclimatization. The area is a premier walking and hiking region in the summer. The Dolomites also offer every sport and recreation in the winter. Accommodation is plentiful and varied—from deluxe hotels to rooms

for rent with local families. There are castles, historic museums, and old churches to see. Chic boutiques are side-by-side with wood-carving studios where craftsmen continue their generations-old art.

These beautiful mountains are easy to reach. Bordered by the efficient inter-European superhighway network, they are less than a four-hour drive from international airports. There is also convenient train and bus service to the Dolomites.

Whether you are a mountain climber or walker, skier or skater, photographer or botanist, or if you just want to relax, there is enough to bring you back again and again to this extraordinary part of the world.

LOCATION

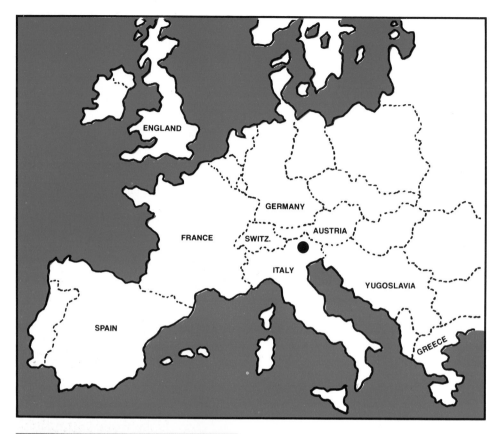

LOCATION AND LOGISTICS

The Dolomites lie in the north Italian regions of Trentino-Alto Adige and Veneto, and within the provinces of Bolzano, Trento, and Belluno. Except for the Brenta Dolomites, a separate district west of Trento, they are generally bordered on the north by Austria; on the west by the Valle Isarco; on the east by the Val di Sesto and Piave River; and on the south by a line that runs approximately from Belluno to Trento.

ARRIVAL BY AIR

For most travelers visiting the Dolomites from points outside Europe, the two major international airports of Milan and Munich are closest and are served by many international airlines. The Venice airport is also convenient, as are the two small regional airports at Innsbruck and Verona.

Travel times by car from the airports are about 4 hours from Milan, 3½ hours from Munich, 2½ to 3 hours from Venice, and 2 hours from Verona and Innsbruck. Train and bus service from the airports is good; schedules are more frequent during the popular tourist months.

ARRIVAL BY TRAIN

There is convenient train service from European cities to the large towns border-

Sassolungo, Val Gardena

LOCATION

ing the Dolomites. Major lines run through the Valle Isarco, over the Brenner Pass, and connect Italy with countries to the north. The main train stations for the Dolomites are at Trento, Bolzano, and Bressanone, with smaller ones at Chiusa, Ora, and Mezzocorona. The Fortezza station is convenient for visitors wishing to travel to the northern parts near the Val Pusteria. East-west trains in the Val Pusteria stop at Brunico, Dobbiaco, and San Candido. It is possible to rent a car or arrange for local bus or taxi service from any of these larger towns to your final destination.

ARRIVAL BY CAR

Using the efficient superhighway system throughout Europe is an easy way to arrive in the Dolomites. Frankfurt, Munich, Vienna, Zurich, Milan and Rome are within a day's drive.

A superhighway in Italy is called an *autostrada*, a tollroad with fees collected at various points. The A22 is strategic to the Dolomites and connects Austria, Germany, and north-central Europe over the Brenner Pass to Italy. Exits from A22 for travel to many parts of the Dolomites are found at Bressanone, Chiusa, Bolzano, and Trento.

There are other important superhighways south and east of the Dolomites. The heavily traveled Milan-to-Venice A4 is on the south. The A23, east of Cortina, connects central Austria (Salzburg) with Venice and Trieste. Both have exits feeding local roads providing convenient access to points in the southern and eastern Dolomites.

TRAVEL WITHIN THE DOLOMITES

Once in the Dolomites, you will find a dense network of local roads—remarkable for such a mountainous region. It is easy to move around by car. Travelers without cars can use taxis or the excellent public bus systems that interconnect villages and important local points.

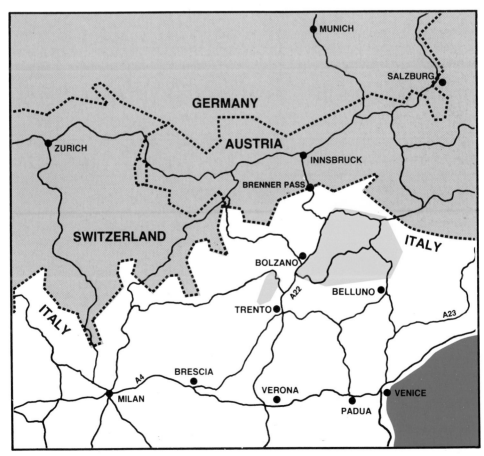

THE DOLOMITES

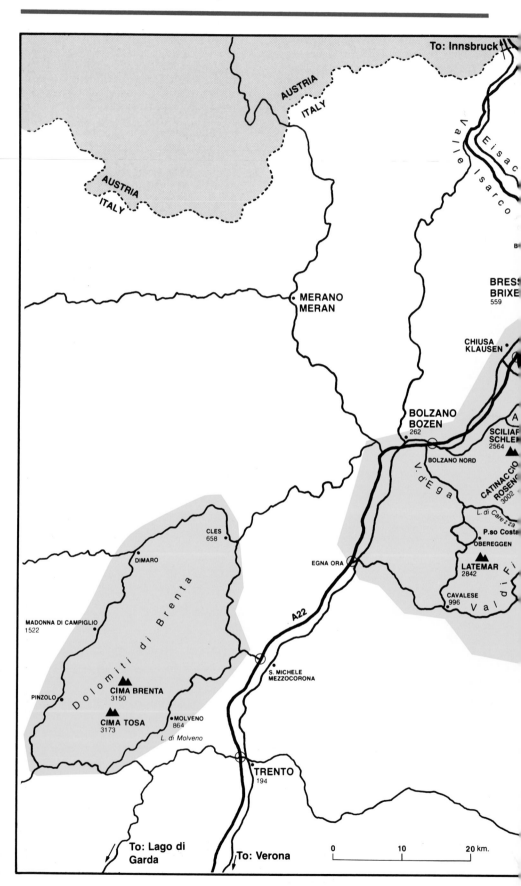

To: Innsbruck

AUSTRIA
ITALY

AUSTRIA
ITALY

Eisac Valle Isarco

MERANO
MERAN

BRESS
BRIXE
559

CHIUSA
KLAUSEN

BOLZANO
BOZEN
262

BOLZANO NORD

SCILIAR
SCHLE
2564

V. d'Ega

CATINACCIO
ROSENG
3002

L. di Carezza

P.so Costa
OBEREGGEN

CLES
658

DIMARO

EGNA ORA

LATEMAR
2842

Val di Fi

MADONNA DI CAMPIGLIO
1522

A22

CAVALESE
996

Dolomiti di Brenta

PINZOLO

CIMA BRENTA
3150

S. MICHELE
MEZZOCORONA

CIMA TOSA
3173

MOLVENO
864

L. di Molveno

TRENTO
194

To: Lago di
Garda

To: Verona

0   10   20 km.

THE DOLOMITES

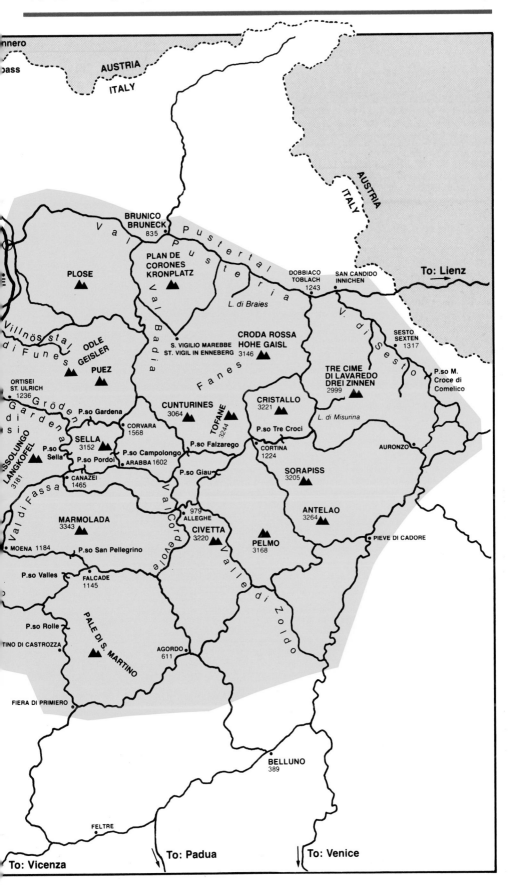

GEOLOGY

GEOLOGY

Prof. Dott. Alfonso Bosellini

The fantastic scenery of the Dolomites is a result of their geology, which is unusual when compared with the rest of the Alps and many other mountains of the world. The principal distinguishing feature of this geology is the juxtaposition of two rock types of different composition, dolomitic and volcanic. Pale towering peaks of dolomitic rock stand above the green gentle slopes of valleys, plains, and high plateaus of dark-brown volcanic rock.

The name *dolomite* is derived from its discoverer, Deodat de Dolomieu (1750-1801), a French chemist and mineralogist who, while traveling to Rome in 1789, collected an unusual carbonate rock in the Valle Isarco (Eisack). A subsequent test proved the rock to be made of a yet unidentified mineral: calcium magnesium carbonate, $CaMg(CO_3)_2$. The term dolomite is now scientifically applied to both the mineral and the rock made of it. The entire region, where these rocky outcroppings are so spectacular, came to be known as the "Dolomites."

Not all the mountains of the region are made of dolomite. The Latemar and Marmolada (highest peak in the Dolomites), for example, are made of limestone $(CaCO_3)$—a slightly different rock with similar origins. When all these rocks were first formed they were limestone—the dolomitization process occurred later and the Latemar and Marmolada were not affected, probably because they were covered by volcanic rocks.

To understand how these mountains were formed, it is necessary to examine two different aspects of their geological history. First, the process of rock formation—when and how the various sedimentary and volcanic rocks were deposited. Second, the process of mountain building—when and how they were uplifted to their present heights and sculptured by weathering and erosion, glaciation, running water, rockfalls, slides, and mass wasting.

Process of Rock Formation: The Dolomites are mountains made largely of sedimentary rock of Triassic age (some 210-240 million years ago), deposited in an ancient, now vanished, warm tropical sea. The major groups of the western Dolomites—Catinaccio, Latemar, Sciliar (Schlern), Sassolungo (Langkofel), Odle (Geisler), Putia (Peitler), Pale di San Martino, the Marmolada, and the lower part of the Gruppo Sella—represent ancient

(Triassic) shallow-water banks and islands, similar in some way to the present-day Maldives or Bahama archipelagos. A prolific community of algae, corals and other marine invertebrates inhabited these banks, and many of their fossil remains can now be found as molds embedded in the massive rock. Since the last century, geologists have considered that the occurrence of these fossils suggests that the Dolomite mountains were formed in a classic "reef" environment. A principal rock from this period is the *Sciliar Dolomite*.

Also, during this Triassic time, two major volcanoes near Predazzo and the Monzoni erupted huge masses of lava which flowed into the sea, partly filling in the deep-water basins that separated the various reefs. Today, this dark brown volcanic rock is visible on the Alpe di Siusi (Seiser Alm) in the Val Gardena (Gröden), above Campitello in the Val di Fassa, and from Passo Pordoi along the Viel del Pan to Porta Vescovo above Arabba. Further evidence can be seen on the Pralongia plateau, the Buffaure above Canazei, and around Predazzo.

This varied and dynamic paleogeographic setting was typical of the Middle Triassic time. Later, toward the end of the Triassic, the entire region became a vast tidal-flat, accumulating bed by bed an enormous

GEOLOGY

thickness of a well-stratified dolomite, the so called *Dolomia Principale* which is best represented in the eastern part of the Dolomite region. The famous mountains surrounding Cortina d'Ampezzo (Tofane, Cristallo, Pomagagnon, Cinque Torri, Croda da Lago, Averau), the Tre Cime di Lavaredo (Drei Zinnen) in the Sesto (Sexten), and Pelmo and Civetta near Alleghe are mountains largely constituted of Dolomia Principale. It also forms the upper part of the Sella edifice and the two small outliers on top of the Sciliar (Schlern) plateau. A typical fossil clam is commonly found in this rock.

The Sciliar Dolomite of the Middle Triassic overlays a varied sequence of older rocks which are spectacularly exposed on the Catinaccio (Rosengarten), the Seceda, on the northern side of the Odle (Geisler) and Putia (Peitler) groups, at Passo Rolle and Passo Valles. These older rocks include Permian and Early Triassic sediments: the red *Gardena Sandstone,* fluvial in origin; the white gypsum beds of the *Bellerophon Formation,* lagoonal and coastal in origin; and the varicoloured shale, sandstone and marly limestone of the *Werfen Formation,* from a shallow marine environment. At the base of these sedimentary successions is a thick slab of red volcanics (quartz porphyries now quarried near Bolzano and Trento), an even older metamorphic rock.

Process of mountain building: The dolomitic and volcanic rocks formed in Permian and Triassic time (some 200-265 million years ago) remained undisturbed for more than 100 million years—buried under huge piles of other marine sediments. During the Tertiary Period (between 60 and 5 million years ago), the collision of the African and European continents deformed, crumpled and uplifted the intervening marine sediments. The Alps, and the Dolomites with them, were born during this time.

Not all the Dolomites reacted the same during the mountain building process. The western Dolomites, probably because of the underlying thick and rigid Permian porphyries, were uplifted as a relatively undeformed block. The eastern Dolomites, however, not being underlain by Permian porphyries, were severely compressed and folded. These different processes account for the fact that the older rocks (e.g. the Sciliar Dolomite) outcrop more extensively in the western Dolomites then in the eastern, where Dolomia Principale prevails.

Glaciers and rivers carved valleys and gorges, and eroded the post-Triassic sedimentary cover, transporting the fine detritus southward to fill the Po Valley. Finally the dolomite rocks of the Triassic were uncovered and returned "to see the sunlight" as magnificent towering peaks and edifices.

Dr. Bosellini is Professor of Geology, Istituto di Geologia, Università di Ferrara, Ferrara, Italy.

GEOLOGICAL TERMS AND NAMES OF ROCKS

English	Italian
Geological Divisions:	
Western	Occidentali
Eastern	Orientali
Names of Rocks:	
Dolomia Principale	Dolomia Principale
Raibl Formation	Formazione di Raibl
San Cassiano Formation	Formazione di San Cassiano
La Valle Formation	Formazione di La Valle
Sciliar Dolomite	Dolomia dello Sciliar
Livinallongo Formation	Formazione di Livinallongo
Serla Dolomite	Dolomia del Serla
Werfen Formation	Formazione di Werfen
Bellerophon Formation	Formazione a Bellerophon
Gardena Sandstone	Arenarie di Gardena
Quartz Porphyries	Porfidi Quarziferi
Basal Conglomerate	Conglomerato Basale
Crystalline Basement	Basamento Scistoso-cristallino

GEOLOGY

GEOLOGICAL CHART TERMS

MILLION YEARS AGO	ERA	PERIOD	SUMMARY OF EVENTS
0	Cenozoic	Tertiary	**Mountain Building** Dolomites stand magnificently eroded by glaciers and rivers
50			Dolomite rocks are deformed and uplifted
100	Mesozoic	Cretaceous	Collision of European and African continents
			Africa and Europe start to converge.
150		Jurassic	Africa and Europe are still far apart
200		Triassic	**Rock Formation** Sediments and volcanics that form the rocks of the Dolomite mountains were deposited in a tropical sea separating the European continent to the north from the African continent to the south.
250	Paleozoic	Permian	

GEOLOGY

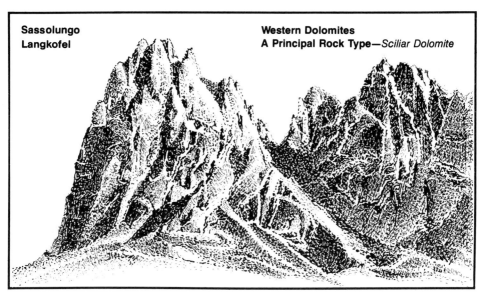

Sassolungo
Langkofel

Western Dolomites
A Principal Rock Type—*Sciliar Dolomite*

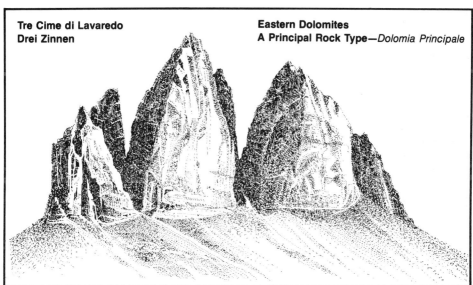

Tre Cime di Lavaredo
Drei Zinnen

Eastern Dolomites
A Principal Rock Type—*Dolomia Principale*

ROCK NAMES

Dolomia Principale
Raibl Formation
San Cassiano Formation
La Valle Formation
Sciliar Dolomite
Livinallongo Formation
Serla Dolomite
Werfen Formation

Bellerophon Formation
Gardena Sandstone
Quartz Porphyries
Basal Conglomerate
Crystalline Basement

GEOGRAPHY

The great alpine chain of Europe forms a giant crescent of some 1200 kilometers beginning on the west near the Côte d'Azur in France and ending in Yugoslavia south of Vienna, Austria. The Italian Dolomites, one of the largest regions in this mountain system, cover an area of more than 90 kilometers (north-south) by 100 kilometers (east-west). They are at an approximate latitude of 46.30° north (about the same as Zermatt, Switzerland) and between 11° and 12° longitude east (about the same as Munich, Venice, Rome and the alpine resorts of Innsbruck and Garmisch).

The Dolomites consist of more than 14 distinct mountain massifs—each with at least one 3000-meter peak. These massifs are separated by rivers, valleys and passes. The major river systems are the Isarco and Adige on the west; the Rienza on the north; the Piave on the east; and the Avisio and Cordevole running north-south through the Dolomites. The only massif west of the Adige is the Brenta which forms a large oval surrounded by valleys.

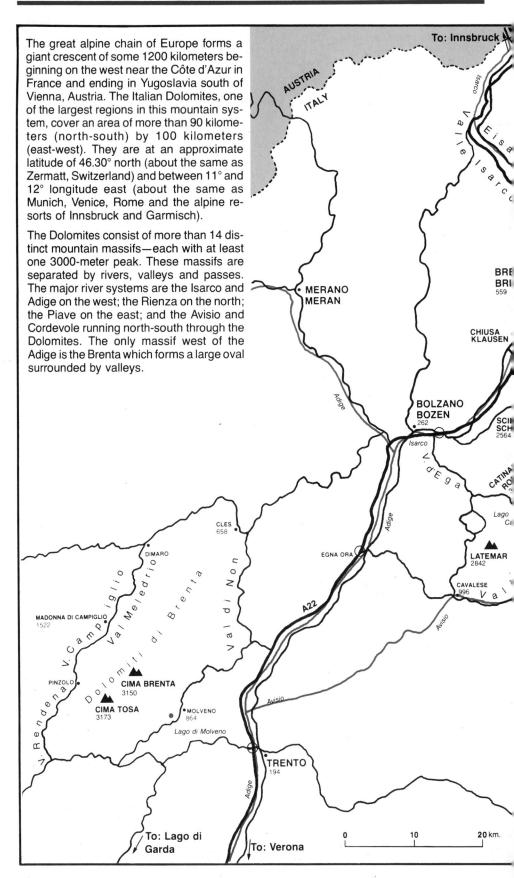

GEOGRAPHY

CLIMATE

CLIMATE

The Dolomites are usually warmer and receive less precipitation than the more northern alpine regions of Austria, Switzerland and France. Stormtracks approach from the south and southwest. Winds from the north are harbingers of fair weather. On rare occasions some of the bitterest winter storms arrive from the northeast across Russia. As in any mountain area, weather can change suddenly and it varies locally between regions within the Dolomites. As a rule, the southeastern and southwestern parts may have more foggy days because they are close to the warm Venetian plain and Adriatic Sea. The northern sections near the Val Pusteria get less precipitation from storms coming from the south because moisture is lost as these storms travel over the mountains.

In summer, from mid-June to early August, days are pleasant with cool nights and only an occasional storm. Later in August the days become warmer and there can be frequent afternoon thunderstorms. September tends to be clear and fairly warm with good consistent weather often continuing well into October. Frequent snowfalls occur from the end of January through March. While the Dolomites generally do not receive as much snow as other regions of the Alps, the snow tends to last and the quality usually remains good.

FLORA

Wildflowers spring back to life in the Dolomites from the moment the snows begin to melt until late in summer. Hundreds of species flourish here for the Dolomites are on the southern reaches of the Alps, relatively low in altitude, and there is virtually no perpetual snowline. Most importantly, the soil in these limestone mountains drains well and is excellent for plant life. In addition, above the deeper valleys there are vast upland meadows, *alps*, where moisture and terrain are ideal for wildflowers.

In early spring, crocuses sprout from under the snow, and by the end of June and early July, the green valleys and slopes above are carpeted with vivid colors—the yellows of the arnicas, poppies, trollios (golden buttons); the blues of the gentians and campanulas; and the pinks and reds of primulas, rhododendrons and azaleas. Higher alpine flora can also be a source of wonder although usually it is not until late July when the edelweiss, *stella alpina,* and tiny lilies can be seen on ledges and in the more inaccessible native rock gardens. Even late in summer and into September,

lavender and white ranunculi pop up after the haymaking. By October, the wildflowers are gone but the hillsides turn golden as the larch trees change colors.

Three vegetation zones are found here: Mountain (800-1800 meters); Subalpine (1800-2400 meters); and Alpine (above 2400 meters). Trees of the Mountain Zone include beech, red and white fir, and an occasional pine, with a lush undergrowth of heather, juniper and myrtle. The Subalpine Zone forests of larch, fir, and cembro pine have colorful rhododendrons and fragrant daphne and roses. Blue sesleria and king-of-the-alps (a dwarf forget-me-not) are also well-known wildflowers in this zone. Common at the Alpine Zone are mugo pines growing in broad bushy thickets, with an isolated fir and cembro pine. Flowers in the higher alps and passes of this zone may vary according to the substrata but species of ranunculi, orchids, primulas, gentians, veronicas, campanulas, asters, and lilies are all represented.

Many species of wildflowers are protected—picking them is prohibited. There are small pocket guides and larger books to help you with identification as well as trips with naturalists organized by local tourist offices.

Mushrooming is a popular pastime in the Dolomites but it should only be considered if you are a true expert at identification. Days of picking and amounts are regulated by local officials. The rich forest floors abound with countless varieties of *funghi*. These are hunted and collected by devotees who are skilled in identification and find them a real delicacy—particularly the porcini variety.

Gentiana

FAUNA

The wildlife of the Dolomites make their homes chiefly in the natural parks, remote valleys, and in the high recesses of the mountains. Despite the ever-increasing pressures of tourism, expansion of villages and farming, some native animals remain fairly common. Among these are the brown (black in winter) chamois, *camoscio;* marmot; large deer, *cervo;* and the small roe

FLORA AND FAUNA

Wildflowers in the Brenta

deer, *capriolo*. Sometimes on a hike you might see the shy camosci with their young above the Vallunga in the Val Gardena, in the Parco Naturale-Fanes-Sennes-Braies in the Val Badia, or high on the Tofane and Sorapiss in Cortina. Two of the rarer animals you may be lucky to spot are a large wild mountain goat, the *stambecco*, and the alpine brown bear whose habitat is the Parco Naturale Adamello-Brenta.

A rich variety of birds can be seen in these mountains. The magnificent golden eagles often soar among the highest peaks. Above the treeline you may observe crow-like orange-beaked alpine choughs flying in groups over the high ridges. Grouse seek the protective cover of forests, while the white ptarmigan (which turns brown in summer) as well as ravens and alpine accentors will be found in higher open areas. Woodlarks, finches, nutcrackers, woodpeckers, warblers, nuthatches and treecreepers make their home in the lower forests.

Naturally, the most common animals are the domestic ones. The ubiquitous cows with their melodious cowbells graze peacefully in the meadows or wander through the villages on their way to the pastures. Herds of goats and sheep also are seen everywhere in the higher pasturelands.

Grazing camosci (chamois)

17

HISTORY

The Dolomites were seldom united politically although they occupy a relatively small geographic area and share an essentially homogeneous geology. For nearly 1000 years before World War I, the Dolomites were divided between the Austro-Germanic powers to the north and west and the Venetian-Italian powers to the south and east. Today, the linguistic and cultural boundaries throughout the Dolomites differ considerably from the historical-political ones.

8000 B.C.-5500 B.C.
Mesolithic Age

Burial sites, stone instruments and other artifacts found in mountain passes are evidence of seasonal hunting camps in the Dolomites.

5500 B.C.-800 B.C.
Neolithic, Copper
and Bronze Ages

A few traces of small settlements in the main bordering valleys date from 5000 B.C. to 1800 B.C. Some small settlements appear in Dolomite valleys from 1800 B.C. to 800 B.C.

800 B.C.-15 B.C.
Iron Age

About 500 B.C., Celtic invaders populate areas around the Isarco and Adige valleys. The Roman Empire is gradually expanding northward but has not yet reached the Alps. The Romans refer to all the alpine people, including those in the Dolomites, as *Raetians*.

15 B.C.-476 A.D.
The Roman Empire

Roman Legions led by Drusus and Tiberius, stepsons of Emperor Augustus Caesar, complete the conquest of the Alps. The Dolomites become part of the Empire.

The Romansch or Raeto-Roman language, Ladin, has its origins with the integration of the Latin-speaking Roman troops and the early inhabitants of the Dolomites.

5th-6th Centuries
Barbarian Invasions

With the collapse of the Roman Empire, tribes of barbarians—Huns, Heruls, Ostrogoths, Franks—follow each other, sweeping across Italy.

6th Century
Lombards

In the late 6th century, Lombards invade the Dolomites from the south and occupy parts for 150 years—establishing Trento as a duchy.

7th Century
Bavarians

Germanic settlers from Bavaria in the north gradually move into the Dolomites—Val Pusteria and Valle Isarco as well as Bolzano and Merano—Germanizing these areas.

During this time the Latinized inhabitants of the Dolomites retreat into the deeper valleys, preserving their Ladin language and culture—still prevalent today.

774-843
Franks
Charlemagne

Conquests of Charlemagne, the great Frankish king, absorb what is now Italy into the Carolingian Empire — unifying the Dolomites under a single leadership.

After Charlemagne's death in 814, various struggles end the Carolingian Empire. The Treaty of Verdun in 843 splits the Dolomites between the Italian and German kingdoms.

10th Century
German Sovereignty

A new German Holy Roman Empire, created under Otto I, spreads nearly as far as Naples by 962.

11th Century
Episcopal Principalities

Episcopal principalities (bishoprics) are created. Trento and Bressanone are given jurisdiction of much of the northern, northwestern, and western Dolomites, while the southern and eastern areas are given to Feltre and Aquileia.

13th Century
Formation of Great
County of Tyrol
Feudal Vassals

The Counts of Tyrol absorb most of the territories of the Trento and Bressanone bishoprics.

Feudal vassals of Aquileia rule the eastern and southeastern Dolomites (Cadore).

HISTORY

14th-18th Centuries
Hapsburgs
Republic of Venice

In 1363, the powerful House of Hapsburg acquires the Tyrol after the death of the last-remaining member of the Tyrol family. This control lasts, for the most part, until the end of the Austro-Hungarian Empire in 1918.

The Republic of Venice gradually expands toward the eastern Dolomite regions, and in 1420, the Cadore, including Cortina and the Piave basin, are added to its territories.

Conflicts between Venice and the Hapsburg Emperor, Maximilian I, result in Cortina joining the Hapsburg-held Tyrol in 1511.

1788-1789
Discovery of Mineral
Name of Region

French geologist Deodat de Dolomieu discovers an unusual carbonate rock in the Valle Isarco. The new mineral is named *dolomite* after him. Later, the entire mountain region adopts the same name.

1797-1813
Napoleon

Napoleon's conquests, with the aid of Bavarian troops, bring about temporary boundary changes. In 1809, the Tyroleans, led by Andreas Hofer, stage an historic but unsuccessful revolt against the Bavarians.

1815-1914
Congress of Vienna
Unification of Italy
Beginnings of Tourism

Following Napoleon's defeat, the Congress of Vienna peace settlements give all the Dolomites to Austria. For about 50 years the Dolomites are unified.

In 1866, the Dolomites south and southeast of Cortina (Cadore) join the new Kingdom of Italy. Cortina and the northern and western valleys remain with Austria.

Between 1864-1867, a railroad is constructed over the Brenner Pass. Tourism begins to spread as English and other European adventurers and scientists discover the beauty of the Dolomites.

1914-1918 WWI

The border between Austria and Italy, dividing the Dolomites, becomes the scene of bitter fighting after Italy enters World War I against Austria (1915). The bloody conflict in the mountains ends in late 1917.

1919
New Boundaries

In 1919, the Treaty of St. Germain establishes the present border between Austria and Italy. All the Dolomites, including the formerly Austrian-controlled areas, become a part of Italy.

1919-1939
Fascism

The Dolomites are divided among three provinces: Bolzano, Trento and Belluno.

Between the two World Wars, there is a growth of Fascism. Attempts to Italianize the language and customs of much of the Dolomites fail.

1939-1945 WWII

Germans occupy and administer the Dolomites, 1943-1945.

Post War

The 1946 Paris Peace Conference reconfirms for Italy the borders in the region of the Dolomites that existed before the war.

The Trentino-Alto Adige Region — Provinces of Bolzano and Trento — gains administrative autonomy in 1948.

Growth of tourism: Cortina hosts the 1956 Winter Olympics; World Ski Championships are held in the Val Gardena in 1970.

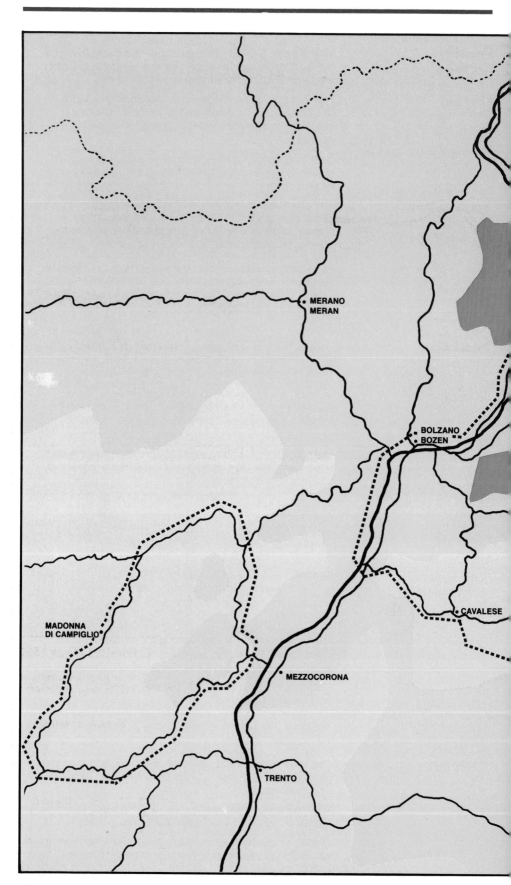

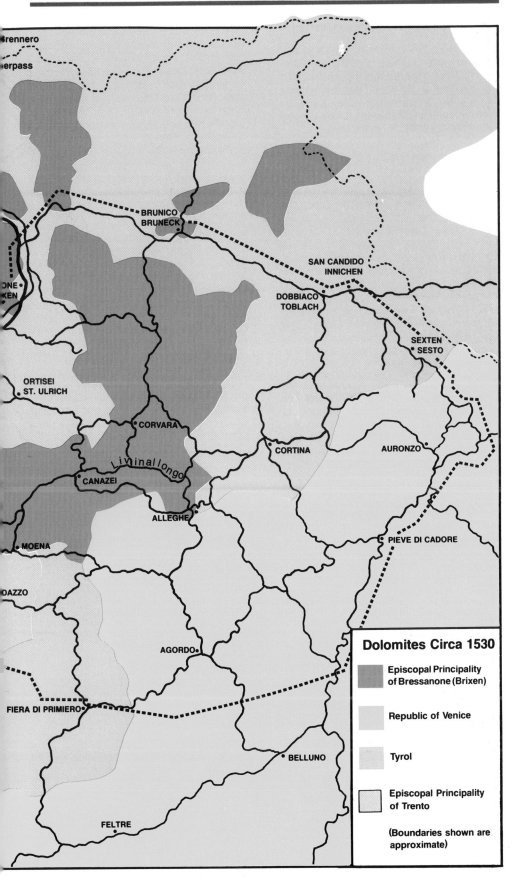

Dolomites Circa 1530

- Episcopal Principality of Bressanone (Brixen)
- Republic of Venice
- Tyrol
- Episcopal Principality of Trento

(Boundaries shown are approximate)

WORLD WAR I

WORLD WAR I IN THE DOLOMITES

World War I, the "war to end all wars," had profound effects on the people of the Dolomites. They were caught up in the bitter fighting on their mountain tops and in their valleys; in some locations the landscape was forever altered. In many cases, citizenships changed following the war.

MAY 23, 1915

For several hundred years before the outbreak of war in 1914, most of the Dolomites were within the Austro-Hungarian Empire. In the initial stages of the war, the Dolomites were not affected because Italy had not formally taken sides and Austria was diverted by its campaign in Russia. On May 23, 1915, Italy declared war against the Austro-Hungarian Empire siding with the allied powers of England, France, Imperial Russia, and later the United States. The war began in the Dolomites because the border between Italy and Austria ran through the mountains.

Austria's forces were too committed to the Russian front to maintain their border with Italy, so they decided to abandon political boundaries in certain locations and retreat to geographically defensible mountain tops and passes. This decision was to impact many areas. For example, Cortina d'Ampezzo and San Martino di Castrozza had been Austrian but were to find themselves behind Italian lines by the summer of 1915.

From late spring 1915 to November 1917, Austria and Italy fought a war of fixed positions and the front line remained essentially stationary. The war was one of survival and attrition for both sides with the object of establishing positions as high as possible, often on mountain tops. Fortifications established in spring, summer and fall were maintained through the harsh winters at great sacrifice. The winter of 1916 was particularly bitter when a record ten meters of snow fell and more than 10,000 men lost their lives from avalanches. On the Marmolada some 400 soldiers died in a single avalanche.

Both sides were ingenious in establishing their positions. Engineers designed and troops built trenches, observation posts, and literally thousands of meters of tunnels or galleries. Often, there would be hand-to-hand combat when opposing forces were only a few meters apart. In some cases troops slept within earshot of their enemy. Both sides exploded mines that changed the face of the landscape. The Col di Lana, in the Val Badia area, was the scene of Italian mine explosions that completely altered the shape of its summit. Mountain walls were marred and pitted and valley lines were reshaped as in the regions around the Croda Rossa di Sesto and Lagazuoi near Cortina.

Austrian troops on Piccolo Lagazuoi, World War I

WORLD WAR I

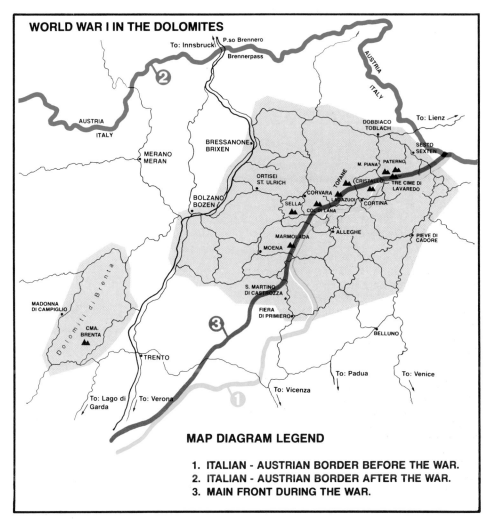

WORLD WAR I IN THE DOLOMITES

MAP DIAGRAM LEGEND

1. ITALIAN - AUSTRIAN BORDER BEFORE THE WAR.
2. ITALIAN - AUSTRIAN BORDER AFTER THE WAR.
3. MAIN FRONT DURING THE WAR.

World War I remnants on Monte Piana

Italian observation post on Averau, World War I

WORLD WAR I

Neither side won this tragic war in the mountains. The Italians were forced to retreat south from the Dolomites after their defeat in the campaign of Caporetto at the end of 1917. The final political resolution of the region took place at the bargaining table, far from the battle zone, and without recognition of the actual events of the war. With the Armistice of 1918, the fighting ceased but the actual transfer of the Dolomites to Italy was a result of the Treaty of St. Germain, signed in 1919 in Paris, between Austria and the Allies.

Many tragic episodes about the war are still remembered:

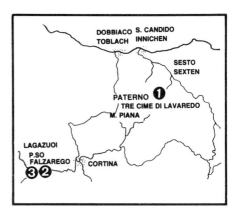

❶ Sepp Innerkofler

At the outbreak of the war, Sepp Innerkofler, a Tyrolean (Austrian), was a highly respected and well known local mountain guide. The Austrian military retained him to advise on strategic matters during the bitter conflict in the Sesto. The Italians held positions on the summit of Mt. Paterno and the Tre Cime di Lavaredo, while the Austrians controlled many of the peaks and pinnacles opposite them. In July, 1915, Sepp scaled the northwest ridge of the Paterno. Near the top, he suffered a mysterious calamity causing him to fall to his death. The Italian soldiers buried him on the summit but after the Austrians regained the summit they reinterred him in the Sesto village cemetery in August, 1918.

It was originally thought that the Italians had dislodged a boulder from above that caused his fall. However, after the war, a thorough investigation of his death began. His exhumed body was found to have wounds, presumably from machine-guns. Veterans of the battles in the area were interviewed. As a result, the most accepted tragic account is that his own Austrian countrymen did not recognize him as he scaled the Paterno and mistakenly shot him.

❷ Il Castelletto

At the west end of the Tofana di Rozes is a small, detached serrated peak called "the tragic rock." This, the Castelletto, was an excellent observation point for watching the action below in the main Travenanzes valley, and a key point for observing the vast terrain to the south. The Austrians were positioned on its crest. The Italians spent from February to July, 1916, tunneling 500 meters or more into the mid-section of the Castelletto from their position at the base of the Tofana. While the Austrians could hear the construction, they apparently were unaware of what was actually taking place. On July 11, 1916, 35 tons of explosives destroyed part of the south towers of the Castelletto and many of the Austrian defenders.

Sepp Innerkofler

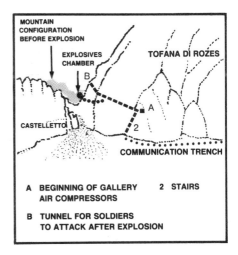

MOUNTAIN CONFIGURATION BEFORE EXPLOSION

EXPLOSIVES CHAMBER

TOFANA DI ROZES

B

A

CASTELLETTO

2

COMMUNICATION TRENCH

A BEGINNING OF GALLERY AIR COMPRESSORS

2 STAIRS

B TUNNEL FOR SOLDIERS TO ATTACK AFTER EXPLOSION

WORLD WAR I

❸ Piccolo Lagazuoi

This mountain, a popular center for hiking excursions in the summer and skiing in the winter, was the scene of both Austrian and Italian mine explosions during the war. In January 1916, an Austrian mine caused only minor damage, but a year later on January 14, 1917, the Austrians exploded a mine that demolished a small part of the Cengia Martini—a ledge midway up the south face of the mountain that had been used by the Italians to approach the Austrian position. The explosion created a gulf between the opposing forces. Later that year, in May, 1917, a devastating mine was again exploded by the Austrians. The resulting crater is nearly 200 meters deep and 136 meters across, changing nearly the entire upper part of the mountain's south face.

The Italians constructed some 1100 meters of tunnels in order to explode a mine on June 20, 1917. (These tunnels are still visible and are quite a tourist attraction). The Austrians apparently expected the explosion and removed their troops; the attack-ing Italian Alpini suffered some casualties later while storming over the crater. On September 16, 1917, the Austrians exploded the most effective mine of all, destroying the middle part of the Cengia. Today, from the Passo Falzarego, you can see two rock slides: the smaller one on the right was caused by the Italian mine explosion; the larger one on the left by the cumulative effects of the four Austrian mines.

Piccolo Lagazuoi was the site of fierce combat during WWI. For 2 years the Austrians defended the top of the mountain while the Italians attacked from their postion on Martini Ledge below. On June 20, 1917, after 6 months of tunnelling 1100 meters into the mountain, the Italians detonated 33,000 kg. of blasting gelatin in order to dislodge the Austrians. However, the Austrians, hearing the construction work, abandoned their position before the explosion. The rock slide on the right in this photo shows the debris from that explosion. The slide on the left is the result of four Austrian mine explosions. There were no winners in this tragic mountain war.

Piccolo Lagazuoi from Passo Falzarego

WORLD WAR I

Today you may wander and hike in the battle zones surrounded by incomparable scenery. Remnants of the conflict are everywhere: trenches, tunnels, barbed wire, shell fragments; bits of boots and uniforms, as well as rubble from logs and bricks used for constructing shelters and kitchens.

Trails through World War I battle zones, Sesto

Italian soldier

World War I cannon, Monte Piana

LADIN

LADIN LANGUAGE AND CULTURE

Ladin is the unusual-sounding native tongue still spoken today in many valleys of the Dolomites, and used side-by-side with Italian and German. It had emerged by the 5th century as a direct result of the earlier Roman expansion into the Alps. As the Romans moved into the recesses of the valleys, their Latin language fused with the native tongue of the mountain people.

Over the ensuing centuries, the great migrations of people destroyed the linguistic unity of Ladin. Today, this ancient Romansch language is heard only in the Dolomites, the Friuli region of Italy, and Swiss Engadine. Several local Ladin dialects have also evolved.

It is not uncommon to find linguistic borders between Dolomite valleys or even within valleys. This is probably a result of their historic isolation and the difficulty of traveling from one valley to the next. Near Ortisei in the Val Gardena, for example, people living in the tiny section of Pontives speak

Ladin while their neighbors a few hundred meters west in San Pietro speak only German.

The Ladin language is usually the preferred tongue within families and among friends, and is taught in the schools along with Italian and German. Ladin families have protected their language and customs despite political pressure to Italianize or Germanize their culture.

The following are a few Ladin words and phrases:

Good morning	Bon di
Good evening	Bona sëira
Thank you	De Gra
Good bye	Assudëi

Presently, about 40,000 people in and around the Dolomites consider themselves Ladins. For the most part, they live in the valleys radiating from the Gruppo Sella—Val Gardena, Val di Fassa, Val Badia, and Livinallongo—but the language is spoken

Traditional dress of the Val Gardena

LAND OWNERSHIP

as far away as Cortina. Ladins constitute approximately 4.3% of the population of the Province of Bolzano. There are Ladin newspapers, two Ladin cultural institutes, and Ladin language broadcasts daily from Bolzano.

LAND OWNERSHIP

Methods of land ownership and control that probably trace their earliest origins to Roman times still exist in the Dolomites. In these early centuries, year-round settlements began to increase. In the summer, farmers would move their cattle to the higher elevations to graze while they cut trees for lumber and firewood. With the onset of winter, they would return to settle in the villages, bringing their livestock and wood with them to await the next summer season.

Beginning in the late Middle Ages, programs were instituted to protect grazing and wood-cutting rights for the common good and to insure that title to family land was passed on from generation to generation. Two systems of land management— *Regole di Cortina d'Ampezzo* and the *Maso Chiuso* in the Province of Bolzano—

are both centuries-old.

The Regole is a governing cooperative that dates from about the 12th century. It is made up of eleven Regole and consists of 800 families. Together, these families administer the property of the Regole—lands that cannot be subdivided or reassigned.

For eight centuries the Regole has been a symbol of autonomy, supervising the grazing of pastures and use of forests. Today, the Regole is recognized by the Italian government as a local power in Cortina and protects the land from over-development and inappropriate land uses. Amazingly, it privately controls far more land than the local government.

The Maso Chiuso is an Austro-Germanic system of primogeniture that originated about the 16th century. Upon the death of the father, the family was prohibited from dividing the *maso*, or farm. Rather, the property passed on to the eldest son. A law in 1929 attempted to abolish this practice, but it was continued voluntarily until it was legalized again in 1954. Presently, it is estimated that there are some 11,500 Masi Chiusi in the Province of Bolzano.

THE REGOLE COATS OF ARMS

Regola Alta di Lareto

Cadin

Campo

Chiave

Fraina

Lareto B

Mandres

Regola di Ambrizola

Pocol

Rumerlo

Zuel

ECONOMY

ECONOMY

A flourishing summer and winter tourist trade probably makes the largest contribution to the economy of the Dolomites and affects nearly every aspect of local life. However, locally made handicrafts, along with agriculture and light manufacturing, are also important contributors to the relatively stable prosperity of this part of the Alps.

Modern tourism began in earnest in the mid 19th century when British scientists and mountain climbers came to explore the Dolomites. Other European hikers and climbers also discovered the scenic appeal of the area and by the 1870s many of the highest peaks had been scaled. The first mountain huts—forerunners of the modern *rifugi*—were built in those early years. Hotels and *garni* soon sprang up to accommodate the growing numbers of visitors. The increasing popularity of winter sports following World War II brought about a dramatic growth in the number of facilities. Then, in 1956, the Winter Olympics in Cortina focused world attention on the Dolomites as a major international skiing area—a reputation that continues to grow. For the most part, development has been low key and architecturally attractive as stringent planning controls have been applied to protect the natural beauty of the environment.

A variety of crafts has developed over the years in different parts of the Dolomites. In the Val Gardena, as early as the 17th century, woodcarvers were producing toys and figurines. Enterprising traders from the valley began carrying them to neighboring countries and by the 1860s over one-hundred companies all over Europe had opened to market the output. These wood crafts now enjoy worldwide sales. Though some craft designs are now fabricated in small workshops, many are original works by noted artists and are prized by collectors.

Master carver, Ortisei

In the Cortina area many exquisitely designed handicrafts are made, such as wooden boxes with inlays of mother-of-pearl, wrought iron reliefs, bowls and plates of hammered brass or copper, and delicate birds and animals sculpted in silver.

Agriculture still contributes to the economic base, as it has for centuries. Herds of dairy cattle supply local markets with milk, butter and cheese. Mountain farm crops are principally hay and grain to maintain the livestock.

For the most part, light industry is keyed to local needs and resources. Snow-cats are produced in Ortisei. Skis are manufactured in Cortina. Wooden chairs and other household furniture are manufactured in both Cortina and Moena.

All of these activities result in a fairly balanced economy, and give the Dolomites an air of prosperity and well-being.

Summer haymaking, Val Gardena

LEGENDS

A rich body of Dolomite folklore has been passed down by word of mouth from generation to generation. In the 19th century, these legends and fairytales were collected and recorded by a local writer, Karl Felix Wolff. One of these is about the evil sorcerer of Lago di Carezza.

THE MAGNIFICENT COLORS OF
LAGO DI CAREZZA

Adapted from the story
by Karl Felix Wolff

While other lakes in the Dolomites appear blue, green or black, Lago di Carezza glows with aquamarine and red, separated by bands of golden yellow. Some think that precious stones buried in the lake cause these wonderful colors, but this is not true; a rainbow once fell in Carezza.

Long, long ago, a beautiful water nymph lived in the lake. By day she sat on the shore and sang, but when anyone approached, she disappeared. In a forest nearby, toward the Latemar, there lived an evil sorcerer. One day he caught a glimpse of the nymph and decided she must be his. Each day he came to the lake, but the nymph instantly vanished when she saw him. This made him so angry that he caused thunderstorms and hurled lightning bolts to frighten her, but she only laughed at him.

After a time, the sorcerer saw that his actions were in vain, and as he was a magician, he changed himself into an otter. At noon, when the nymph was on shore he crept from the forest, thinking to himself, "You will never escape me." But on that day, great flocks of birds perched in the trees to listen to the songs of the nymph. When they saw the malicious otter approaching they began to chirp loudly to warn her. The nymph, on hearing the birds, fled into the lake. The otter followed, but fast as he swam, she was even faster. The sorcerer was so furious with the birds that he thought of cutting down the trees. However, he quickly realized that without their protective cover, the nymph would see him even sooner.

Full of disappointment, the sorcerer told a witch of his misfortunes and asked her advice. She laughed and said, "You are a magician and cannot deal with this? You are a foolish child, not a sorcerer!"

This made him more angry since he had already asked two other magicians who had not been able to help him. The witch continued to laugh, but she gave him a plan.

"The nymph has never seen a rainbow," she said. "Go to the top of the Latemar towers and build a rainbow. Then, stand it on its base so it mirrors in the lake. When the nymph sees its colors, she will be very curious. Now, transform yourself into an old trader with a long white beard and a bag full of golden clips and spangles. Then, walk through the forest with sure, convinced steps to show the nymph you apparently have no bad intentions. When you see the rainbow, take hold of it and speak aloud: 'Oh, look! This is just what I want—the fine fabric from which jewels are made.' Cut off a piece of it and put it in your bag. As you do so, let some of the clips and spangles fall out.

"The nymph by now will be even more curious for she does not have such beautiful things, and she will come out of the water and try to talk to you. Be very calm and say that a beautiful princess has ordered jewelry from you and that you are taking the golden clips and spangles to show her. At this point, the nymph will not be able to contain herself. She will come very close to see them and you can catch her."

The sorcerer was convinced this scheme would work, and so that very afternoon he went up to the Latemar and built a wonderful rainbow which spanned the forest and ended in the lake. The nymph swam up to watch, just as the witch had said.

When the sorcerer saw her admiring the rainbow, he forgot everything and raced down to the lake—not even remembering to transform himself into an old trader. Of course, he so frightened the nymph that she once again vanished.

When he realized what had happened, the sorcerer flew into a rage, chopping down trees and hurling giant stones around the shore. Finally, in his anger, he grabbed the rainbow and threw it into the lake. Then, he went back into the mountains and was never seen again.

But as the rainbow melted, its magnificent colors rose to the surface and spread out across the lake. And to this very day, the colors of the rainbow float on Lago di Carezza.

VILLAGE LIFE

VILLAGE LIFE

The village is the center of commerce, social, and religious activities for the people of the Dolomites. Each day residents flow into the *centro* to market, bank, and visit with friends.

Baskets in hand, people move from one shop to the next, completing their daily visits to the *alimentari* for groceries, *panificio* for bread, *macelleria* for meat, and an occasional small supermarket. In summer, outside stalls display tempting fresh fruits and vegetables. The giant hardware store is nonexistent, so electrical items are sold in one store, plumbing equipment in another. Often the proprietor may also be the village repairman.

There are clothing and gift stores of every description: boutiques with the latest fashions; shoe stores with everything from leather sandals to hiking and climbing boots; and sport shops with hiking pants, dirndls, tennis and ski fashions. Craft shops feature many traditional items, often handmade locally, such as wood carvings and table linens.

A stop at a café is routine. Though they vary in size and decor, they offer a complete list of snacks and drinks from coffee to alcoholic beverages. Stop for a *toast*, hot sandwich; a *panino*, roll with cheese or ham; or strudel with whipped cream. If you are in a hurry, just pause and order an *espresso* or *cappuccino* at the stand-up bar. In summer, relax at an outside table and watch the *passeggiata*, the afternoon stroll. While the stores generally close from noon to three, the cafés are always open.

The church dominates the skyline of most villages. Some are small whitewashed buildings with bulbous Tyrolean steeples; others are large Italian-gothic structures with adjoining campaniles. Interiors are often richly adorned with paintings, frescoes, and elaborate wood carvings. On Sunday the shops are closed and families dress up to attend early Mass and enjoy a day of rest together. On special "feast days" or holidays you may see people in their native costumes and hear groups of local musicians in the town square.

Village of Fiè, Sciliar in background

HOTELS AND RESTAURANTS

HOTELS

Hotels, *alberghi* in Italy, are currently classified into five categories which are identified by stars. Deluxe is the most luxurious, with five stars. The most modest accommodation has one star. The starred category is clearly posted outside all hotels. *Pensioni* are more moderately priced and less formal than hotels. There are also the popular and even less expensive *garni* — the Italian version of the bed and breakfast. Their rooms range from small to rather spacious and some have private baths. In many villages, apartments are available for rent, as are rooms in homes. These vary in quality but generally are neat and clean.

Many of the hotels and pensioni offer two plans: pension, with all meals included, and demi-pension, with two meals included. Rates fluctuate during the year and are the most expensive during the popular "high seasons" of July and August, February and March, and during peak holiday periods such as Christmas and Easter. At these times many hotel rooms and apartments are rented only by the week. In winter, it sometimes can be difficult to find a single night's lodging. If you arrive without reservations, it is helpful to check with the *Azienda di Soggiorno,* the village tourist office, which maintains an up-to-date list of available accommodation. Hotels for the major villages, and the addresses of the *aziende* are listed in the Travelers' Information section. Your travel agent and other travel books also will be helpful.

HOTEL CATEGORIES

Deluxe	★★★★★
First	★★★★
Second	★★★
Third	★★
Fourth	★

RESTAURANTS

Every village, large or small, has a wide selection of restaurants, cafés, and bars, as well as the typical pizzeria and rosticceria. More formal restaurants are found in the larger villages and many are located in the hotels. The pizzeria and rosticceria are less formal and serve pizza baked crisp in wood-burning ovens, as well as a variety of other tasty foods. Pasta, soups, grilled meats, vegetables, and salads are all listed on the menu. Italians love their ice cream and it is on menus in cafés and bars everywhere.

In the province of Bolzano, menus are in both German and Italian. Throughout this area you may find yourself sharing a table with others in some of the more informal restaurants during the peak season.

Tips are generally included in *il conto,* the bill, but you may want to leave a few extra lire as an additional gratuity.

San Pietro, Val di Funes

33

FOOD AND WINE

FOOD

Cuisine in the Dolomites, depending on where you happen to be, is Italian, or a unique blend of Tyrolean and Ladin specialties. Frequently, it is a combination of all three. Generally the farther north you are the greater the accent on Tyrolean and Ladin, "alpine" foods. As you travel south, west and east, the menu becomes more Italian. Whether it's the Trentino specialties in the Brenta, the more Venetian-influenced dishes in Cortina, or the Tyrolean fare in the Val Gardena, meals are beautifully prepared and moderately priced.

Tyrolean dishes include *knödel suppe,* a clear broth with large bread dumplings; *spaetzli*, a small flour dumpling served with meat sauces; *wienerschnitzel*, a breaded and sauteed veal cutlet; veal stew and goulash. A real favorite is *stinco,* a roasted shank of *maiale*, pork, or *vitello*, veal. Popular desserts include apple strudel, and a sweet crepe with *mirtilli*, wild bilberries, sprinkled with powdered sugar. The breads, such as thick wheat and sweet milky brioche with currants, are especially delicious. Be sure to try a *krapfen,* a round doughnut filled with jam or whipped cream.

Ladin names for popular local specialties include *pan da paur,* a rye, cracker-like bread; *panicia,* a filling barley soup; and *crafuncins,* a delicious thin spinach ravioli with a light sauce of melted butter and grated parmesan cheese.

Italian cuisine covers a wide range. First courses will list a variety of soups, pasta with tomato or meat sauce, risotto with vegetables and *funghi,* mushrooms. Indeed, in the fall the wild mushrooms are a delicacy and these will be added to all types of sauces and often served with polenta. Salads are usually simple combinations of lettuce and tomatoes served with small bottles of wine vinegar and olive oil. This is the *insalata verde* while the *insalata mista* will include a few cooked vegetables.

Other tempting foods are available on menus throughout the Dolomites. Chicken, deliciously and simply roasted, meat sausages with cabbage, and local game such as the small deer, *capriolo*, commonly served with a brown sauce and polenta, are three popular selections. Mountain trout is the only fish found with any regularity and is usually grilled. A popular choice to accompany grilled dishes is inevitably *patate fritte*, french fries, made from the very tasty locally-grown potatoes. Salad bars where you can choose your own combinations are growing in popularity and present an array of fresh vegetables and lettuce as well as pasta and potato salads. Fresh produce and fruits, though seldom mountain grown, are readily available from the gardens and orchards of villages near the Dolomites. Local dairy products are delicious, and you will taste some of the best cheeses, milk and yogurt found anywhere.

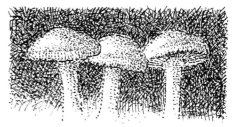

Outdoor produce market, Moena

FOOD AND WINE

MEAL CUSTOMS

The typical continental breakfast of a roll with butter and jam, and hot beverage— tea, hot chocolate, black coffee, *normale*, or with milk, *caffè latte*–is usually included in your room charge. For a few extra lire, you can sometimes select from an à la carte menu that will include yogurt, assorted fruit juices and fresh fruits, choices of hot or cold cereals, breads, eggs, small packages of cheese, and even cold cut meats. If you order your breakfast the night before, you may have it served in your room, or you may join other guests in the dining room for either regular table service or a tempting buffet.

Lunch, as in other parts of Italy, is the largest meal of the day and is served anytime between noon and 2:00 p.m. Dinner is also a large meal and both can include several courses. The first course or *primo piatto* is pasta or soup. The second course, *secondo piatto,* features meat or fish with potatoes, vegetables, and salad. Finally, there are the choices of sweets, *dolci,* fruit, *frutta,* or cheeses, *formaggi.* Coffee is served at the very end of the meal. Menus may include a fixed-price meal but you can always choose à la carte.

WINES

The local wines are reasonably priced and are typically light and clear, often with a hint of sparkle. Nearly all restaurants offer a house wine by the carafe, *caraffa,* as well as wine lists. Most of these wines come from the lower elevations of Trentino-Alto Adige (Provinces of Bolzano and Trento) or from the Friuli region. Two of the local labels are St. Magdalener, a red wine, and Sylvaner, a white. While travelling in the Brenta you will taste reds such as Merlot del Trentino and Pinot Nero del Trentino.

MENU

PRIMI PIATTI
Rice and pasta dishes
Erste Gänge
    Spaghetti con melanzane
      Spaghetti with eggplant
      Spaghetti mit Auberginen
    Risotto con funghi
      Risotto with mushrooms
      Reis mit Pilze-Sauce

SECONDI PIATTI
Main Course
Hauptgerichte
    Vitello con funghi
      Veal in mushroom sauce
      Kalbsfleisch in Pilze-Sauce
    Stinco di vitello
      Roast shank of veal
      Kalbschackse

Casunziei all'ampezzana
    Casunziei (ravioli) a la ampezzana
    Casunziei (ravioli) auf ampezzaner Art
Canederli al formaggio
    Cheese dumplings
    Käseknödel
Gnocchi di spinaci
    Spinach gnocchi
    Nocken mit Spinat

Stinco di maiale per 2 persone
    Roast shank of pork for 2 persons
    Schweinehackse für 2 Personen
Capretto in brodetto
    Roast kid with brodetto sauce
    Kitzbraten mit brodetto Sauce
Cosciotto di capriolo con salsa di mirtillo
    Leg of roebuck with cranberry sauce
    Rehkeule mit Preiselbeersauce

CONTORNI
Vegetables
Beilagen
    Patate al forno
      Roast potatoes
      Röskartoffeln
    Spinaci al burro
      Buttered leaf-spinach
      Blattspinat

Insalata di stagione
    Vegetables of the season
    Salat nach Jahreszeit
Funghi alla griglia
    Grilled mushrooms
Polenta e salsicce
    Polenta and sausages

DESSERT
Tiramisú
Gelato della casa
Macedonia fresca

RIFUGIO

One of the pleasures for the walker or hiker in the Dolomites is the *rifugio*. These small inns, sprinkled liberally throughout the mountains, provide access to the most magnificent panoramas. You reach many by lifts; others by foot after a walk on a pleasant path; and a few by car.

There are more than a hundred rifugi in the Dolomites, so comfort, sociability and shelter from the onset of inclement weather are never far away. Most are owned and managed by the Club Alpino Italiano, C.A.I., though some are private enterprises. Vary-ing from old timbered huts to commodious stucco and stone lodges, all are efficiently operated for the convenience of those who have come to enjoy the higher elevations of the mountains.

A rifugio can be a destination for a half-day excursion or an all-day hike. It is quite possible to plan a several-day hiking itinerary from rifugio to rifugio. Trail signs are excellent, and distances and hiking times between points are indicated on signposts, boulders, and other prominent land features. You will also find that the owners or managers are helpful in giving advice on any facet of your itinerary.

Along with reasonably priced meals and snacks, *rifugi* offer modest overnight accommodations. Kitchens operate from

Rifugio Lagazuoi, Cortina

RIFUGIO

dawn to well after dark turning out amazingly varied menus, considering that supplies must be brought up by lifts, mechanical hoists, or even, in some cases, by helicopter. Soups, salads, pasta and meats are available as well as a wide selection of beverages from beer and wine to a steaming, delicious cappuccino. Self-service is typical but meals are often served at your table. Postcards, stamps, and small souvenirs can be purchased, and telephone calls, if necessary, can often be made.

An overnight stay is highly recommended. Sunset and sunrises offer spectacular technicolor shows in these high mountains. Accommodation varies. Most rifugi have rooms with four beds, and large dormitories with eight or more. A few have rooms with two beds.

During the crowded summer, and for the rifugi on more heavily traveled trails, it is a good idea to write in advance or phone ahead for reservations—especially if you wish one of the less common semiprivate rooms. The nights in the mountains can be quite cold so it is advisable to bring long underwear or the equivalent. Bedding is provided and includes a comforter or blankets. While electricity is adequate and candles are provided, extra matches and a flashlight are handy to have. The quality of the WC varies and can be quite primitive. Newer rifugi and those nearer popular trails and lifts generally have modern WCs. Showering is rarely possible. However, in some rifugi, hot water is provided in basins in your room. Continental style breakfasts are served early. It is advisable to settle your bill in the evening instead of waiting until morning when everyone is anxious for an early start.

Guidebooks and directories of the rifugi are found in local villages. These list the type and size of accommodation, phone numbers and schedules, and quite often trail numbers, distances, and hiking times between a particular rifugio and other important nearby points. This information is also included on some of the area maps.

Rifugio Vicenza, Val Gardena

Papaver alpinum

Rifugio Catinaccio, Val di Fassa

THE DOLOMITES IN SUMMER

THE DOLOMITES IN SUMMER

SUMMER

Traditionally, the summer season in the Dolomites begins in mid-June when many cable cars, gondolas, and chairlifts begin operating to take you to the higher elevations. However, this timing varies from district to district and valley to valley. Some major lifts do not begin operation until July. In the Val Gardena and the Val Badia, the major lifts and hotels tend to be open through September. In Cortina, Alleghe, San Martino di Castrozza, and Madonna di Campiglio, many lifts and hotels begin closing by mid-September. You will need to plan accordingly as the inability to use lifts is certainly a limiting factor for some walks and hikes. However, by driving or taking buses or taxis, access to many starting points is still possible.

From about mid-June, for several months, wildflowers are glorious and snow is still visible in the higher mountains. If you are planning walks or hikes you must consider the possibility of encountering both snow and ice. By mid-July, the flowers are in full bloom, the snow has all but disappeared and village life buzzes in shops, hotels, cafés, and restaurants. Farmers are at work everywhere and local artisans are busy with their crafts. You will feel most welcome as you become an integral part of the alpine way of life.

Spring and fall can be pleasant seasons in the Dolomites, but there are a few drawbacks. Hotels, pensioni, and garni may be closed as many local people use these months for their own vacations.

The weather in spring, as in any mountain area, varies from year to year. It is often unsettled with periods of snow and rain. The melting snow can make touring difficult, and before the appearance of flowers and leaves on the trees, the landscape appears rather bleak.

Early autumn, however, tends to be quite lovely with the changing colors in the forests and meadows. The weather is usually clear and crisp until mid-October.

During the summer there is an inexhaustible list of things to do in the Dolomites. Sporting and recreational activities abound. Tennis, swimming, bicycling, walking, hiking, and fishing are nearby as are the more challenging hang-gliding and mountain climbing.

Hobbies and special interests can be pursued: wildflower identification, drawing, painting, and photography are just a few possibilities. The unusual and dramatic shapes of the Dolomites stimulate an interest in geology. Even novices will enjoy discovering fossils, the remains of a prehistoric time when the entire area was covered by seas. In the natural parks, plants and animals are protected and can be easily observed. Sightseeing is rewarding, too, for not only are there museums and noteworthy old churches and castles to explore, but the large towns and villages bordering the mountains are also of historical and cultural interest.

Window box on pensione

SUMMER

Colfosco, Val Badia

Village of Colle Santa Lucia

SUMMER

OUTINGS AND EXCURSIONS

In this summer section, easy rambles, excursions by car, and rides on major lifts are listed. These outings will help you plan your time and enjoy the villages, valleys, and mountain panoramas. They require, at most, a leisurely stroll and take you to a spot to sit on the grass, or to a rifugio or hotel for the view and to enjoy the passing scene. You do not need hiking boots; comfortable walking shoes are fine. Driving excursions are short and normally can be done within a couple of hours.

WALKING AND HIKING

Perhaps nowhere in the Alps is there a wider range of opportunities for walking and hiking. You can stroll on a completely level path or hike an extremely steep and exposed trail. Within a half hour from a village or rifugio at the top of a lift station you will

find yourself in a meadow of wildflowers, surrounded by spectacular mountains and wide panoramas. Such an experience is often reserved for only the most adventuresome hiker in other mountain regions.

Veronica fruticans

Hikes are suggested throughout this section. They are briefly described and are positioned on map-diagrams. Hikes are, for the most part, along well-marked trails so that with map in hand, plus some study before undertaking the hike, there should be no difficulty in following a particular route.

There are also at least six *Alte Vie* in the Dolomites. These are high level, hut-to-hut walking routes criss-crossing the mountains, each requiring several days to complete.

Lifts that operate during the summer season can be a wonderful aid to your hiking programs and include: a *funivia,* tram or cable car; an *ovovia*, gondola; a *seggiovia*, chairlift.

Walking beneath the Odle, Val Gardena

SUMMER

GRADING OF HIKING ROUTES

Hikes in this book have been judged according to their degree of difficulty. Quality of footing, steepness and exposure are all considered. (Exposure is a characteristic of portions of trails bordered by unprotected sheer drops. A trail can be steep and not exposed, or level with good footing and exposed. Exposure is usually greater when hiking parallel to the contour and perpendicular to the slope line of a hill.) A standard walking pace has been assumed: about two km/hour uphill and about four km/hour downhill or on flat terrain. Remember, with poor visibility, and/or a storm, an *Easy* grade level hike can become an *Intermediate* grade challenge! In bad weather all hikers should avoid *Difficult* and *Expert* grades.

Easy: Essentially a flat level path with good safe footing and without steepness or exposure. Suitable for families and younger children. These are usually short itineraries of 1 to 3 hours.

Moderate: Some uphill and downhill but normally not more than a maximum single uphill gain in elevation of 250 meters.

Intermediate: For the more experienced hiker. Up and down portions with a maximum gain in elevation of 500 meters. Some steepness and some exposure.

Difficult: For the seasoned hiker who is sure-footed, not afraid of heights or exposure. Some experience on snow is required. Up and down portions are common and the maximum uphill stretch can be around 1000 meters.

Expert: A route that has portions of narrow exposed and steep hiking with some scrambling required. Minor experience in climbing can be useful. Sudden changes in weather are possible. The use of a compass and route-finding skills are important. Up and down portions are common and the uphill vertical gain can exceed 1000 meters.

METRIC CONVERSION TABLE

Meters (m.)	Feet (ft.)
1	3.28
500	1640
1000	3280
1500	4921
2000	6562
2500	8202
3000	9842

1 Centimeter (cm.) = 0.3937 Inches (in.)
1 Inch (in.) = 2.54 Centimeters (cm.)

1 Kilometer (km.) = 0.62 Miles (mi.)
1 Mile (mi.) = 1.61 Kilometers (km.)

1 Kilogram (kg.) = 2.2 Pounds (lb.)
1 Pound (lb.) = 0.45 Kilogram (kg.)

HIKING CODE

Enjoy and respect nature.
Avoid unnecessary noise.
Destroy nothing.
Do not leave litter.
Do not pick wildflowers or plants.
Do not disturb wildlife.
Re-close gates.
No fires.
Stay on the footpath.
Respect and observe local custom.

GENERAL POINTERS

1. Study your route before the hike.
2. Try to get a current weather forecast. (Check barometers in front of hotels.)
3. Carry your own water or drink bottled water in the rifugio.
4. Leave word of your route and, in particular, your estimated time of return with the rifugio or friends.
5. Use the lifts when possible to save time and endurance.
6. Start your return early—especially with the onset of bad weather.

SUMMER

MOUNTAIN CLIMBING AND THE VIA FERRATA

There is a rich tradition of mountain climbing in the Dolomites. Many of the great climbing routes in the Alps are found here, and the Dolomites continue to be the home of some world-famous mountaineers. Climbing is not discussed in this book but for those interested, there are excellent climbing schools and guides throughout the Dolomites. You may inquire at local tourist and visitor centers for information and suggestions on these services. Travelers will enjoy watching the climbers from vantage points at rifugi and even from the road while touring. Popular climbing areas include the Cinque Torri, the Tre Cime di Lavaredo, and the south walls of the Gruppo Sella and the Tofana.

You will also see and hear about the *Via Ferrata,* the "iron way", and find them marked on maps and along trails. These are quite extraordinary technical climbing routes that have been laid out with fixed climbing aids such as wire cables, pegs, and iron ladders. A fit hiker, with some climbing training and skills, can utilize these devices with a simple harness, carabiners, and a short climbing rope, and thus do routes that otherwise would require normal mountaineering equipment and climbing partners. The Via Ferrata should not be attempted without a full knowledge of the route and its condition, and the ability to climb. Via Ferrata routes have not been included, but, for the qualified, they should be researched because they are fun and unusual. On some Expert routes there are a few stretches with fixed iron cables provided for added support.

WHAT TO WEAR

The key to comfort for any mountain hiking excursion is preparation for cold and dampness. Layers of clothing are the rule. The same common sense regarding safety, clothing, weather, and health pertains as much to the Dolomites as to any other mountain region. A warm clear day can be transformed by a hail storm. Within an hour, considering the wind-chill factor, temperatures can drop 15°C!

When there are rifugi available, your need to tote many items can be greatly reduced. If you are going to ride an open lift, remember that it can be quite cold and windy so dress accordingly. Also remember to remove any daypack first and have it comfortably positioned in front of you so that you can get on and off the lift without becoming entangled.

CLOTHING

Jacket
Comfortable boots
Liner socks, heavy socks
Loose fitting hiking pants (trousers)
 (Shorts not a good idea)
Long-sleeve shirt
Sun hat

ADDITIONAL ITEMS

Sun protection
Lip protection
Money
Maps
Compass
Multi-purpose pocketknife
Snacks
Sunglasses
Umbrella
Camera and binoculars (optional)
Phrase book and dictionary (optional)
Notepad (optional)

CARRY IN DAY PACK

Extra liners, heavy socks
Sweater or equivalent
Wool hat
Gloves
Wind and rain wear
Water container/water
Whistle (good idea)
Minimum first-aid supplies

SUMMER

MAPS AND TRAIL MARKINGS

There are excellent maps of the Dolomites which show trails, topography, and important land features. These are regularly updated and improved, and any serious walker is encouraged to invest in them. Generally, 1:50,000 scale should be adequate and easiest to read. All maps are oriented toward magnetic north (magnetic declination in the Dolomites is minimal). They often have their own marking system indicating the degree of difficulty for a particular trail or portion of a trail. These can be very helpful in assessing a hike.

Occasionally you will find minor variations in elevation for certain geographic features between maps drawn by different cartographers and even between different scaled maps by the same cartographer. For the most part these will be only a few meters. You may also find similar minor discrepancies between maps you are using and the map-diagrams in this book. Since two and sometimes three languages are common to many parts of the Dolomites, these same maps may vary in the use of the Italian name, German name, or at times both, for villages, rifugi, or topographic features.

The district, region, summer excursion, and hiking maps in this book are really *map-diagrams* for planning. There is no substitute for toting a good topographic map. According to your need, you may choose maps from the following:

- 1:50,000 (2cm=1km; 1¼in=1mi)
  Tabacco Series for all the Dolomites
  Kompass Series covers most of the Dolomites
  F&B series covers some of the Dolomites
- 1:25,000 (4 cm=1km; 2½in=1mi)
  Tabacco covers most of the Dolomites
  Geo covers most of the Dolomites

WAYMARKING AND SYMBOLS

Trails are usually clearly marked by red and white stripes of paint applied to posts, prominent rocks, or other terrain features. Some markings and signs show the trail numbers and have arrows pointing to a particular destination. Others guide you toward the nearest rifugi as well. If you are hiking and do not encounter an appropriate mark or sign within 10 minutes or so, it may be best to double back to make sure you are on the right route. It is also a good idea to stop from time to time to check the trail behind you because there may be clearer markings showing from the other direction.

Trail signs

Near Passo Sella, Marmolada in the distance

THE FIVE DISTRICTS

In this book the Dolomites have been divided into five districts to facilitate your travel planning. Using the passes and valleys that separate the mountain groups and massifs, you may drive or walk from one district to the other with relative ease. You will not find these district demarcations on commercial maps.

While the districts have similar geology, they are quite different scenically and culturally. In general, the Tyrolean-Austrian flavor of the north becomes progressively more Italian as you travel south. This distinction is manifested in the language, architecture, and cuisine. You may often have the feeling of being in two different countries when traveling between villages in neighboring districts separated by just a few kilometers.

Nine travel areas are highlighted in this summer section. Two of these center on mountains—the Marmolada and Gruppo Sella—the others focus on valleys. All of these travel areas have been chosen for their extraordinary scenery, range of things to do and see, facilities, and accessibility. Each has been named for a well-known

APPROXIMATE DRIVING TIMES BETWEEN MAJOR CENTERS AND THE NEAREST POINT IN THE DOLOMITES
(Assumes normal traffic and weather conditions)

	Hours
Milan	3½
Munich	3
Salzburg	3
Innsbruck	1½
Lake Garda	2
Venice	2½
Verona	2
Florence	4
Rome	7
Vienna	5½
Zurich	5½
Frankfurt	6
Amsterdam	9

Once arriving there can be an additional 2 hours of driving depending on your destination.

geographic feature; boundaries may extend to include parts of neighboring valleys. For example, the Val Gardena travel area includes the nearby Val di Funes. Drives, excursions, walks, and hikes are suggested for each of the areas.

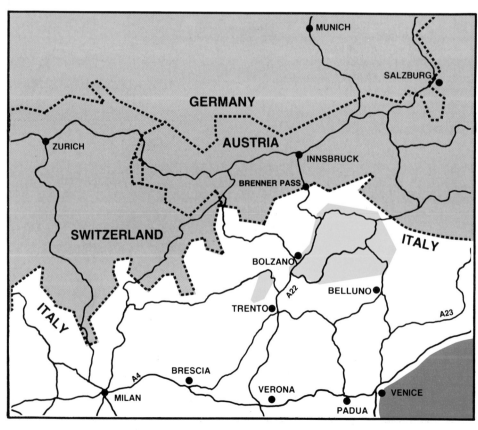

THE FIVE DISTRICTS

SUMMER DISTRICTS AND TRAVEL AREAS

Northwest
Val Gardena (Gröden)
Val di Fassa
Val Badia (Gadertal)
Gruppo Sella

Southwest
San Martino di Castrozza - Passo Rolle

Northeast
Cortina and the Sesto (Sexten)

Southeast
Cordevole and Fiorentina-Zoldo
Marmolada

West
The Brenta

MAP DIAGRAM LEGEND

⌒	Roads	🚠	Cable Cars
⌇	Private, Restricted, and/or Unpaved Roads	⬗	Gondolas
○	Autostrada Exits	⬗	Chairlift
⌇	Passes	❶	Route Number
▲	Mountains	⌒	Trail
■	Rifugio	⤍	Alternate Trail
•	Top Lift Station	←	Direction of Travel on Trail

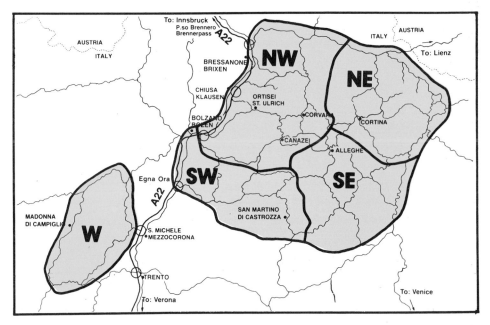

47

NORTHWEST

The peaceful Val di Tires, near Val di Fassa

NORTHWEST

Four travel areas are within the district. The **Val Gardena (Gröden)** is closest to the autostrada; it has several charming Tyrolean villages, large open alps to explore and spectacular mountains to view. The **Val di Fassa** can be easily reached from the north or south. Several small Italianate villages line the flat valley floor; there are interesting and popular walks and hikes in its surrounding mountains. The **Val Badia (Gadertal)** has an old-world Tyrolean charm of its own and is set in a sunny wide expanse, ringed by mountains. The **Gruppo Sella** is a mountain massif popular for all types of walks and hikes and is accessible from roads that surround it.

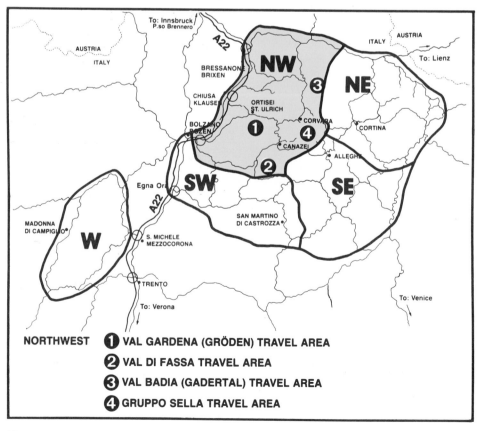

NORTHWEST   **❶** VAL GARDENA (GRÖDEN) TRAVEL AREA
            ❷ VAL DI FASSA TRAVEL AREA
            ❸ VAL BADIA (GADERTAL) TRAVEL AREA
            ❹ GRUPPO SELLA TRAVEL AREA

Summit plateau of Gruppo Sella, Val Badia in distance

IMPORTANT FEATURES

Region: Trentino-Alto Adige (Südtirol)
Provinces: Bolzano (Bozen), Trento
Valleys: Gardena (Gröden), Fassa, Badia (Gadertal)
Villages: Ortisei (St. Ulrich), Santa Cristina (St. Christina), Selva (Wolkenstein), Canazei, Moena, Corvara
Mountains: Sassolungo (Langkofel), Gruppo Sella, Catinaccio (Rosengarten), Sciliar (Schlern)

VAL GARDENA (GRÖDEN)

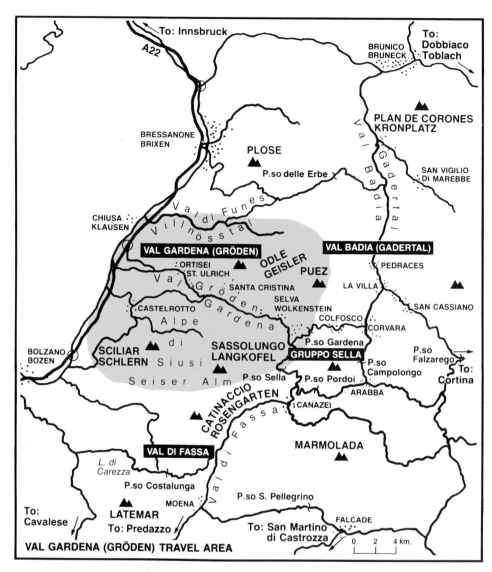

VAL GARDENA (GRÖDEN) TRAVEL AREA

HIGHLIGHTS

The Val Gardena is one of the most popular destinations in all the Dolomites. In no other major valley is the variety of Dolomite scenery more apparent. It is also sunnier here than in some of the narrower valleys. The soft green alpine pastures contrast with the stark, vertical gray rock of the mountains. Wildflowers bloom everywhere from May through July. In June, you can wade through a sea of color on the Alpe di Siusi.

Tourism blends harmoniously with the everyday life of local farmers and artisans. The charming Tyrolean villages have a complete range of modern tourist facilities—from modest inns and garni to deluxe hotels and apartments. Unlike many tourist centers in the Alps, the Val Gardena experiences a year-round economy as the centuries-old industries of agriculture and woodcarving continue to thrive. Italian, German, and ancient Ladin are spoken here, and you will see signposts using all three languages to indicate villages and important geographic features.

MAJOR VILLAGES	Population	Elevation
Ortisei (St. Ulrich)	5,000	1236m
Santa Cristina (St. Christina)	1,500	1428m
Selva (Wolkenstein)	2,300	1563m
Castelrotto (Kastelruth)/Siusi (Seis)	2,800	900m-1100m

PRINCIPAL LANGUAGES: German, Italian, and Ladin

50

VAL GARDENA (GRÖDEN)

HOW TO ARRIVE

By Air:
International airports at Munich, Milan, Venice or smaller airports in Verona and Innsbruck.

By Rail:
Nearest stations: Bolzano, Bressanone, and Chiusa. Then transfer by bus or car.

By Bus:
Direct service from Milan and Munich to the Val Gardena in high season.
Local service from Bolzano, Bressanone, and Chiusa to the Val Gardena.

By Car:

From West, North, South:	Exit A22 at Chiusa. Follow the signs to the Val Gardena. Chiusa to Val Gardena: 30 min.
From East:	Use local roads in the Dolomites from Cortina over the Passo Falzarego to San Cassiano, continuing over the Passo Gardena to the Val Gardena. Cortina to Val Gardena: 1¼ hrs.

MAJOR ROAD PASSES INTO THE AREA

Passo Gardena (Grödner Joch)	2121m
Passo Sella (Sellajoch)	2244m

Selva and Santa Cristina

VAL GARDENA (GRÖDEN)

APPROACHES

The easiest and most scenic approach to the Val Gardena is from the autostrada exit at Chiusa. If possible, take this drive in the afternoon to see the most dramatic light on the mountains. From the east (Cortina), drive over the Passo Gardena, or from the south, use the Passo Sella. You will have a sweeping westerly view of the valley before descending into Selva. All the primary and most secondary roads are good and only during part of the winter are the Passo Gardena and Passo Sella likely to be closed.

SETTING

The scenery in this V-shaped valley is both soothing and dramatic as the lush green alps and meadows give way with astonishing abruptness to the craggy, awe-inspiring mountains. Near the upper end of the valley the Sassolungo seems literally to explode from the meadows that surround it. The compact giant massif of the Gruppo Sella, with its uneven summit plateau, frames the eastern end of the valley and appears to block further travel. These peaks are over 3000 meters above sea level (1500 meters directly above the valley floor) and are always visible from the major villages. Rising above the valley to the north, are the jagged rocky spires of the Odle and the block-like Puez. Charming hamlets perch on terraces at the entrance to the valley, while larger villages line the valley floor. The slopes surrounding the hamlets and above the villages are carpeted with meadows and sprinkled with tidy white villas and rustic farmhouses.

One of the most important natural features of the Val Gardena is the Alpe di Siusi. This essentially flat upland alp is the largest in the Dolomites and one of the largest in Europe. It rises about 500 meters above the valley floor, encompasses an area of nearly 55 square kilometers, and borders the entire length of the valley. In summer, it is ideal for pleasant walking as many species of wildflowers bloom in every conceivable color and there are unobstructed views of the Sassolungo and Sciliar.

HISTORY

There is evidence from four or five thousand years ago, that people ventured into the Val Gardena in summertime for hunting. During the last millenium before Christ, there must have been active trading because an ancient mountain path that still exists—*Troi Paian*—connected Laion to the Passo Gardena. Apparently this served as a link between the iron mines to the east and the commerce moving north-south in the Valle Isarco. Many bronze and iron implements, dated about 400 B.C., have been found above Ortisei and are on display in the local museum.

About 15 B.C., the Romans began to exert control over the people in the Dolomites. Their ways fused with local customs until a distinct culture and an independent Romansch language, Ladin, emerged. Many people of the Val Gardena still speak this ancient tongue and continue to observe many age-old traditions. Even today, you can see families in their traditional costumes strolling through the village centers listening to local musicians play folk songs.

During the Middle Ages, permanent settlers came into the heart of the Val Gardena. These were mountain farmers who inhabited the southern slopes and whose livelihood depended upon both dairy cattle and crops of oats, barley and potatoes. Over the succeeding centuries, farming grew in importance and continues today to be a major factor in the local economy.

As part of the South Tyrol region of the Austro-Hungarian Empire, the Val Gardena enjoyed relative tranquility for nearly six centuries until World War I when the Dolomites became the scene of heavy fighting between Austria and Italy. During the war years of 1916 and 1917, a narrow-gauge railway was built here by 12,000 men including 8,000 Russian prisoners of war. It was used to supply the front lines high in the mountains and linked Plan at the upper end of the valley with the Valle Isarco. The railway continued to operate for commercial and tourist purposes until 1960 when it became unprofitable. The valley, as well as what is now the Trentino-Alto Adige, was ceded to Italy at the end of World War I.

Carved figurine

VAL GARDENA (GRÖDEN)

ECONOMY

In the 17th century, the woodcarving industry began—a major economic turning point for this valley. This craft, using the plentiful local pine, provided a needed balance to the hard, agriculture-based life of the farmers. By the early 19th century, there were over 300 carvers in the valley and small, allied industries and skills such as barrel-making, cabinetry, and gilding gradually developed. In 1872, the first woodcarving schools opened in Ortisei and made a major contribution to the development of this local craft which is now known throughout the world.

Today, it is estimated that about 3,000 people in the Val Gardena are involved in woodcarving, either full or part-time. Homes often double as studios, and in factories carved pieces are made both in assembly-line fashion or started by machine and finished by hand. A few pieces are made entirely by hand and are authenticated by a metal stamp. The selection of articles includes wooden toys, nativity scenes, collectible figurines such as musicians, comics and animals, and large sculptured scenes in wood relief. Some woodcarving companies are known worldwide, such as ANRI in Santa Cristina.

Tourism began in the late 19th century and is now a major economic factor both summer and winter. The valley has a superb range of tourist facilities, and is the site of annual World Cup ski racing in December.

Hamlets of the Val Gardena

GEOGRAPHIC FEATURES

Mountain Groups and Their Major Peaks: Summit Height

Sassolungo (Langkofel)	3181m
Sasso Piatto (Plattkofel)	2958m
Gruppo Sella	
Piz Boè	3152m
Sciliar (Schlern)	
M. Pez	2564m
Odle (Geisler)	
Sass Rigais	3025m
Furchetta	3030m
Gruppo Puez	
Punte del Puez	2913m
Seceda	2518m

Other Features:
Val di Funes (Villnösstal)
Alpe di Siusi (Seiser Alm)

VAL GARDENA (GRÖDEN)

GEOLOGY

A classic section of the oldest rocks of the Dolomites is exposed on the cliffs below the top lift station of the Seceda. The red strata, Gardena Sandstone, are Paleozoic sediments while the overlying white gypsum beds were formed in an ancient lagoon. The Sciliar, with its table-like summit plateau and two adjoining, yet detached peaks is another important geological landmark. Its steep exposed northern flanks—as well as the stark walls of the Sassolungo—contain some of the best examples of the ancient reefs that once fringed deep-water sea basins. These basins are now represented by the soft dark rocks of the Alpe di Siusi. The nearby Vallunga is an ideal example of a flat U-shaped glacial valley and is easy to see and explore. It is about 10 kilometers long and begins northeast of Selva.

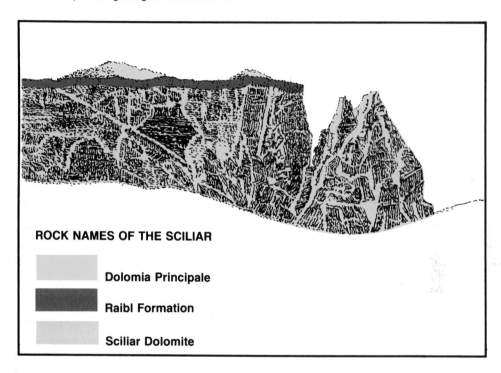

ROCK NAMES OF THE SCILIAR

Dolomia Principale

Raibl Formation

Sciliar Dolomite

Sciliar from Alpe di Siusi

VAL GARDENA (GRÖDEN)

MAJOR VILLAGES

Ortisei (St. Ulrich), with a population of 5,000, is the largest village in the Val Gardena. It has a charming main street and central piazza. An amazing array of shops, such as food and meat markets, pharmacies and bakeries, plus fashionable boutiques for clothing and sporting goods are located here. Hotels and cafés, where you can have a coffee, tea, ice cream or snack, are plentiful. You can join in the *passeggiata* or meander east or west and above the piazza onto residential streets, among schools, and small churches. As you walk higher you will note the transition from town to small farms where families keep their livestock and tend their crops.

The Museo della Val Gardena in the village center is a must for the history buff. It is a small, well organized museum with collections of prehistoric relics, as well as local paintings and woodcarvings from the past 300 years. There are also displays on geology and natural history.

Santa Cristina (St. Christina), population 1,500, is a smaller village a few kilometers east of Ortisei. Its main street, also the thoroughfare for the valley, is on an upward slope and is lined with boutiques, gift and sport shops. Above the village on the residential streets, are some of the best views of the Sassolungo.

Selva (Wolkenstein), population 2,300, higher still and also on the main road through the valley, nestles in a small sunny bowl. The western walls of the Sella massif form a magnificent backdrop for Selva, and the Sassolungo can also be seen from most parts of the village. Shops and stores tend to be grouped in the village center. Hotels and restaurants are clustered here but are also found along the gentle slopes rising north and east above the village.

Castelrotto (Kastelruth), Siusi (Seis), Fiè (Völs), Laion (Lajen), and **San Pietro (St. Peter)** are smaller, but equally charming, villages in this travel area. They are well worth visiting as are the villages in the Val di Funes.

THINGS TO DO AND SEE
Museums, Churches, Buildings
Ortisei:
Congress Hall and Permanent Exhibition of Handicrafts.
Church of St. Anthony, 1673-1676, in the town square.
Museo della Val Gardena (Cësa di Ladins).
Church of St. Jakob, above Ortisei.

Ponte Gardena:
Trostburg Castle, 12th Century.

Santa Cristina:
Fischburg Castle, Mid-14th Century.

Selva:
Wolkenstein Castle, ruins dating from about the 13th Century, in the Vallunga.
Stations of the Cross: wood sculptures by local artisans.

Natural Parks
Sciliar - includes a portion of the Alpe di Siusi
Puez - Odle

Characteristic Old Houses/Villages
Castelrotto (Kastelruth)
Laion (Lajen)
San Pietro (St. Peter)

Other Summer Activities
Indoor and outdoor swimming • Indoor and outdoor tennis • Minigolf • Cinema • Mountain climbing schools • Fishing • Indoor ice skating • Horseback riding • Concerts • Camping • and more.

VAL GARDENA (GRÖDEN)

OUTINGS AND EXCURSIONS

The following are a few suggestions, from among many possibilities, for touring the Val Gardena. They can be combined in various ways to suit your plans for any specific day. In certain cases Italian names are used with the German names in parentheses.

Half-day Drives

Ortisei-Castelrotto-Siusi-Alpe di Siusi: Small Tyrolean villages, pastoral country, mountain views of Sassolungo, Sella, and Odle.

Val di Funes (Villnösstal): Idyllic small villages and hamlets in pastoral meadows, mountain views of Odle.

Ortisei-San Pietro-Laion: Small rural villages of the Val Gardena, mountain views of Sella, and Sassolungo.

Around Gruppo Sella and over the four passes of Gardena, Campolongo, Pordoi and Sella: A variety of panoramic valley and mountain views. Best to start in the morning as there can be traffic.

View Panoramas

Passo Gardena, Passo Sella, Alpe di Siusi

Santa Cristina

Rambles

Around Selva and Ortisei to enjoy the charm of these villages.

Selva along the river, through woods, towards Plan de Gralba to see quiet charm of village life.

Between Selva and Santa Cristina for a walk among houses and gardens.

Selva Stations of the Cross walk: Hand-carved scenes of the Passion of Jesus Christ exhibited along a wooded path.

Selva: Vallunga, a rather level walk in a cliff-sided valley.

Using Lifts

Alpe di Siusi lift: Ortisei to Alpe di Siusi. Ideal for viewing the vastness of this alp.

Seceda lift: Ortisei north to Odle. Excellent for close-ups of these rocky towers and spires and for panoramas of the Val Gardena.

Col Raiser lift: Santa Cristina towards Odle. Vistas of Selva, Sassolungo, and Sella.

Ciampinoi lift: Selva towards Sassolungo. Views of Val Gardena and close-ups of Sassolungo.

Dantercepies lift: Selva to Passo Gardena. Scenes west of Val Gardena, and of the north and west walls of the Sella.

Bullaccia lift: From center of Alpe di Siusi. Sweeping easterly views of the Val Gardena and towards the Sella.

Forcella Sassolungo lift: Passo Sella to the forcella. Exciting views into the Sassolungo and across to the Sella.

VAL GARDENA (GRÖDEN)

Dramatic peaks, Gruppo Sella in distance

Pastoral countryside near Selva

APPROXIMATE DRIVING TIME TO MAJOR CENTERS

Milan	3½ hrs
Munich	3 hrs
Salzburg	3 hrs
Innsbruck	1½ hrs
Lake Garda	2 hrs
Venice	3 hrs
Verona	2 hrs
Florence	4 hrs
Rome	7 hrs
Cortina	1½ hrs

VAL GARDENA (GRÖDEN)

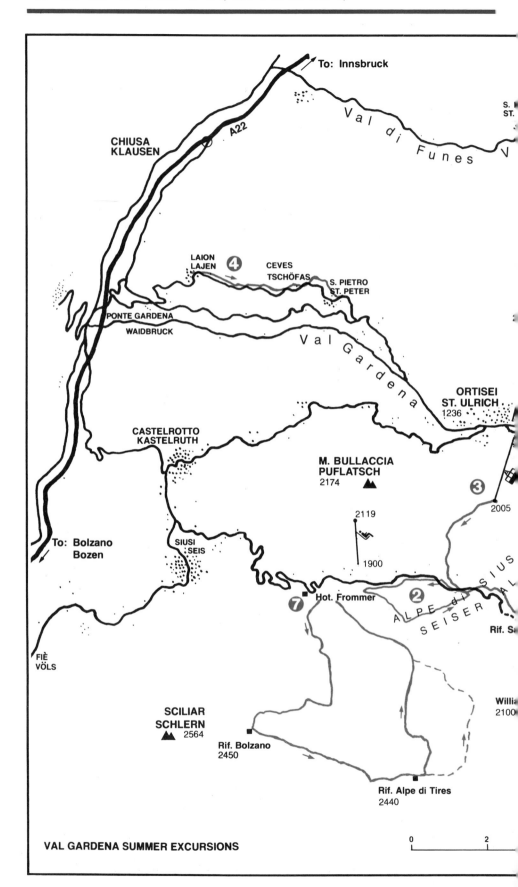

To: Innsbruck

V a l   d i   F u n e s

S. ST.

CHIUSA KLAUSEN

A22

LAION LAJEN ④ CEVES TSCHÖFAS S. PIETRO ST. PETER

PONTE GARDENA WAIDBRUCK

V a l   G a r d e n a

ORTISEI ST. ULRICH 1236

CASTELROTTO KASTELRUTH

M. BULLACCIA PUFLATSCH 2174

③ 2005

2119

1900

To: Bolzano Bozen

SIUSI SEIS

⑦ Hot. Frommer

② ALPE di SIUS SEISER AL

Rif. S

FIÈ VÖLS

SCILIAR SCHLERN 2564

Rif. Bolzano 2450

Willi 2100

Rif. Alpe di Tires 2440

VAL GARDENA SUMMER EXCURSIONS

0   2

58

VAL GARDENA (GRÖDEN)

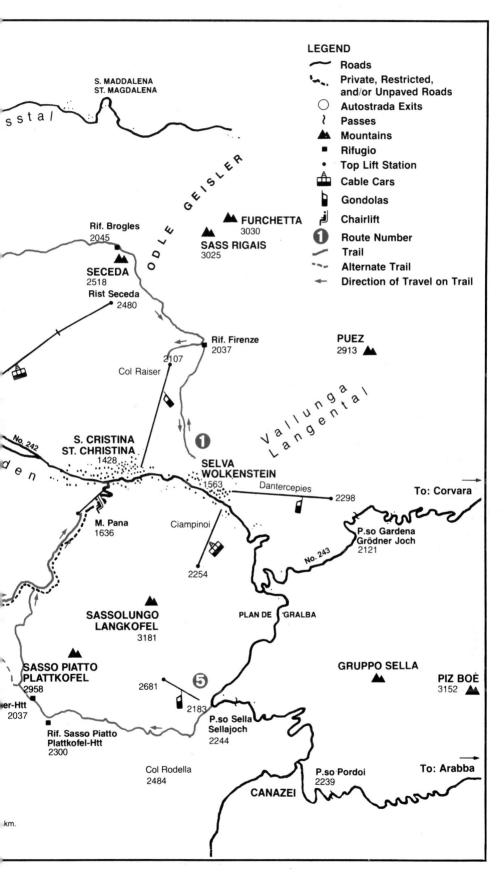

LEGEND

Roads
Private, Restricted, and/or Unpaved Roads
Autostrada Exits
Passes
Mountains
Rifugio
Top Lift Station
Cable Cars
Gondolas
Chairlift
Route Number
Trail
Alternate Trail
Direction of Travel on Trail

S. MADDALENA
ST. MAGDALENA

s s t a l

ODLE GEISLER

Rif. Brogles
2045

SECEDA
2518
Rist Seceda
2480

FURCHETTA
3030

SASS RIGAIS
3025

Rif. Firenze
2037

PUEZ
2913

Col Raiser
2107

V a l l u n g a
L a n g e n t a l

No. 242

d e n

S. CRISTINA
ST. CHRISTINA
1428

❶

SELVA
WOLKENSTEIN
1563

Dantercepies
2298

To: Corvara

M. Pana
1636

Ciampinoi

P.so Gardena
Grödner Joch
2121

2254

No. 243

SASSOLUNGO
LANGKOFEL
3181

PLAN DE GRALBA

SASSO PIATTO
PLATTKOFEL
2958

2681

❺

GRUPPO SELLA

PIZ BOÈ
3152

2183

...er-Htt
2037

Rif. Sasso Piatto
Plattkofel-Htt
2300

P.so Sella
Sellajoch
2244

Col Rodella
2484

CANAZEI

P.so Pordoi
2239

To: Arabba

km.

VAL GARDENA (GRÖDEN)

WALKS AND HIKES

A few of the many walks and hikes of varying type, length, and difficulty in the Val Gardena are highlighted. Routes 1 through 4 can easily be accomplished in a half day or less. Some itineraries can be completed without using a lift.

Maps: 1:50,000: Tabacco #2, Kompass Sellagruppe #59; 1:25,000: Tabacco #05, Geo Le Odle #5, Geo Val Gardena #7, Wanderkarte Grödner Tal #22.

ROUTE ❶ — SELVA TO RIFUGIO FIRENZE
A gradual ascent over meadows through woods with views of valley, pastoral country, and peaks of the Sassolungo, Sella, and Sciliar.

Distance: About 3½ km one way.
Time Required: About 2 hrs to Rifugio Firenze.
Grade: Moderate.
Special Considerations:
1. **Verify rifugio schedule.**
2. **You can return the same way by foot in about 1 hr, or by lift to Santa Cristina, then walk or take the bus back to Selva.**

Starting Point: Take trail #3 from the Larciunëi section of Selva (which is north and a bit west of the village center) near Station 1 on the Stations of the Cross walk.

You begin among chalets and farmhouses, move through open woods, surrounded by pleasant views, and arrive first at the tiny Rifugio Juac which is tucked among meadowed knolls. From here, staying on trail #3, there is a gradual descent before you resume the easy ascent along a meandering creek to the rather large and well-equipped Rifugio Firenze. This is a lovely spot to have lunch or a snack and has a longer season than many of the other rifugi in the area. You can return the same way or vary somewhat using trail #4 and then the service road towards Santa Cristina.

Sassolungo from trail to Rifugio Firenze

ROUTE ❷ — A WALK ON THE ALPE DI SIUSI
Pleasant walking over open pastureland with sweeping vistas of the Sassolungo and Sciliar.

Distance: 2 to 8 km, depending on your choice of routes.
Time Required: 1 to 4 hrs.
Grade: Easy to Moderate.
Special Considerations: The Alpe di Siusi is accessible by both car and lift.

VAL GARDENA (GRÖDEN)

Starting Point: Drive to the main hotel/commercial complex on the Alpe di Siusi. Using your map, choose any route you wish, staying on roads or marked trails.

The vast trail network on the Alpe di Siusi takes you among farmlands with placid grazing cattle set against a mountain backdrop. Nearly all trails are on turf-like terrain with soft footing. Since the Alpe di Siusi is an absolutely immense open area, it is hardly possible to get lost. There are rifugi everywhere for food, beverages, and resting. One possible itinerary is shown.

Alpe di Siusi with Sassolungo

ROUTE ❸— ALPE DI SIUSI HIKE USING LIFT FROM ORTISEI

A gradual descent over the pastoral Alpe di Siusi to Monte Pana and Santa Cristina.

Distance: 9 km one way.
Time Required: 3½ to 4 hrs.
Grade: Moderate.
Special Considerations:
1. **Check to see if the lift is operating between Monte Pana and Santa Cristina. If not, arrange for a taxi. (Returning by foot to Santa Cristina from Monte Pana requires about 1 additional hr.)**
2. **You end in Santa Cristina so you must make some arrangement to return to your beginning point.**
3. **Signs on the Alpe di Siusi show directions and names of the rifugi but often omit trail numbers.**

Starting Point: Top of lift. From the rear deck of the lift station, take trail #6.

There are some spectacular views from the upper lift station, including the Tofane group near Cortina. Take trail #6 and then #3 to your initial destination: Rifugio Saltria. The way is level at first through woods and then gradually downhill over the vast open pastureland of the Alpe di Siusi. Farmers' huts and rifugi are sprinkled everywhere. Take a break at Rifugio Saltria, an important center for activities on the Alpe di Siusi. After leaving Saltria, head towards Monte Pana on the unpaved road (trails #3 and #525). You walk alternately through woods and clearings, with glimpses of Sassolungo and distant peaks. After a few kilometers, you reach the small complex of hotels and lifts at Monte Pana where there are spectacular views of Sassolungo towering above you. The lift down to Santa Cristina is easy to find. Alternatively it is possible to hire a taxi, although the hour-long walk down to Santa Cristina is rather pleasant.

VAL GARDENA (GRÖDEN)

ROUTE ❹ — LAION, CEVES, AND SAN PIETRO

A fairly level country ramble between picturesque, rural villages with the Sassolungo, Sella, and Sciliar in the distance.

Distance: 4 to 8 km depending on route. Laion to San Pietro: 4 km one way.
Time Required: 2 to 4 hrs.
Grade: Easy.
Special Considerations: You can make a loop between the villages or plan a one-way trip by dropping off a car or making other arrangements for your return.

Starting Point: You can plan your own route as the roads and trails between the villages are clearly marked. A one-way itinerary from Laion toward San Pietro is suggested.

Trails parallel the road and, since there is little traffic, it is also pleasant to wander on the road. Laion is the largest of the villages with some quaint shops and cafés. There are traditional old farm houses with flower gardens along the way and the walking is easy with good vistas east of the Val Gardena, Sassolungo and Sella.

Near Ceves, Val Gardena

VAL GARDENA (GRÖDEN)

ROUTE ❺ – PASSO SELLA TO ZALLINGER HÜTTE TO MONTE PANA
A scenic level walk on the flanks of the Sasso Piatto followed by a gradual descent over the pastureland of the Alpe di Siusi.

Distance: About 11 to 12 km one way.
Time Required: About 6 hrs—3 hrs to Zallinger and 3 hrs to Monte Pana.
Elevation: Starting point 2180m; Zallinger 2037m; Monte Pana 1636m.
Change in Elevation: Gain of about 200m; Loss of about 700m.
Grade: Intermediate.
Special Considerations:
1. **Your starting and ending points are quite far apart so plan accordingly.**
2. **From Monte Pana you can return to Santa Cristina on foot (about an extra 1 hr), take the lift or call a taxi.**
3. **Verify that rifugi are open for lunch breaks.**

Starting Point: From Rifugio Passo Sella, about ½ km before the actual Passo Sella look for trail #594.

From Rifugio Passo Sella, start towards the Col Rodella on trail # 594, heading for Rifugio F. August. Take time to be sure you are on the right trail and going in the right direction as there is a maze of trails and activity at Rifugio Passo Sella. For the first half hour, you walk gradually up on the Passo Sella plateau below the Sassolungo. There are also views of the Gruppo Sella, Marmolada, and you can even catch a glimpse of the great north wall of Civetta in the distance. After perhaps 45 minutes you begin your trek west along the southern flanks of Sasso Piatto. You are on the popular F. August Weg. The trail is quite wide, and, at each bend, your views ahead, behind, and to the left are dramatic. After about two hours of gentle walking you arrive at Rifugio Sasso Piatto. Now, you start down and the environment becomes more pastoral as you move onto the Alpe di Siusi towards Zallinger Hütte. Perhaps 100 meters before reaching Zallinger Hütte, you will see trail #7 (your route) branching right towards Monte Pana. You may choose to take a break now at Zallinger Hütte for it is full of atmosphere and has pleasant decks where you can relax and enjoy the vista. The trail to Monte Pana is delightful over meadows and through woods and always beneath the Sassolungo.

Alternatives: There are many other trails from Zallinger Hütte, but study your map well before starting an alternate route. The Alpe di Siusi is huge and it always takes longer than you think to walk from one point to another. One alternative is to walk down trail #7a (or take the lift from Williamshütte), to reach a central point on the Alpe di Siusi where there are both rifugi and new hotels. From this point it is possible to make your way to Santa Cristina or to the major hotel and shopping complex on the Alpe di Siusi near the Sporthotel. Taxis are available on the Alpe di Siusi and can be called to take you to any of the villages in the Val Gardena. When the lifts are running, the possibility for variations are even broader. For example, it is quite possible after making your way to the hotels below Williamshütte, to hike up to the cable car station and ride the lift to Ortisei.

Alpe di Siusi from high above Zallinger Hütte

VAL GARDENA (GRÖDEN)

The Odle from near Forcella Pana

ROUTE ⑥ — RASCIESA LIFT FROM ORTISEI: HIKE TO RIFUGIO BROGLES THEN TO RIFUGIO FIRENZE ENDING IN SANTA CRISTINA
A somewhat strenuous hike with an extraordinary variety of terrain and environments. There are close-up views of the Odle, plus superb vistas of the Sella, Sassolungo, and Alpe di Siusi.

Distance: About 11 km if you use the Col Raiser lift to return to Santa Cristina.
Time Required: About 5 hrs not including lift rides.
Elevation: 2093m top of lift from Ortisei; 2447m at Forcella Pana;
   2037m Rifugio Firenze.
Change in elevation: Gain of about 520m; Loss of about 400m.
Grade: Difficult.

VAL GARDENA (GRÖDEN)

Special Considerations:
1. **Verify that lifts and rifugi are open.**
2. **The ascent from Rifugio Brogles is steep, with some exposure so be sure that snow and ice are not present and visibility is good (ask at Rifugio Brogles). Attempt only if you are sure-footed.**
3. **An easier route from Rifugio Brogles takes you back to the Seceda lift (and Ortisei).**
4. **You begin at Ortisei but your ending point may be in Santa Cristina.**

Starting Point: In Ortisei follow directions to the Rasciesa lift, northwest of the main piazza. At the top of the lift you take trail #35 to Rifugio Brogles.

After the rather long lift ride from Ortisei (wear warm clothing), trail #35 ascends gradually through woods. You break into the clear and follow the contour of the ridge on its southern flanks with splendid expansive vistas of the Val Gardena, Sassolungo, and Sella. This first part of the hike is on trails with easy turf footing. At Rifugio Brogles, you have alternatives depending on the weather, trail conditions, and your energy. You can either continue on the prescribed course to the Forcella Pana or take the easier trail #3 to the southwest which leads to the middle station of the Seceda lift and a return to Ortisei (a gradual descent of 4 kilometers reducing the grade of the hike to Intermediate). The switchback hike up to Forcella Pana from the rifugio is very dramatic, but the footing is good, largely over rock and scree with fixed iron cables for support. At the forcella there is a typically Dolomitic surprise view: the Val Gardena, all the surrounding mountains and the Alpe di Siusi unfold before you. The gradual descent down the Seceda's grassy slopes to the Rifugio Firenze is through open pastureland. The large Rifugio Firenze is well equipped to serve you before you proceed the short way to the Col Raiser lift and back to Santa Cristina.

Alternatives: You can return by foot to Ortisei from the top of the Col Raiser lift which adds about 6 km or 2½ hrs to your trip.

ROUTE ❼ – TWO DAY HIKE: ALPE DI SIUSI TO SUMMIT OF SCILIAR WITH OVERNIGHT IN RIFUGIO BOLZANO.

A diversified experience: first walking over the meadows of the Alpe di Siusi, then steeply up the side of the Sciliar and finally across the flat table-like summit plateau to the rifugio. The return is a ridge walk, then over the alp.

Distance: About 5 km to Rifugio Bolzano with a 12 km return.
Time Required: 5 to 6 hrs to the rifugio, and 5 to 6 hrs the next day to return.
Elevation: Starting point 1705m; Rifugio Bolzano 2450m.
Change in Elevation: Gain of about 1000m; Loss of about 1000m.
Grade: Intermediate to Difficult.
Special Considerations:
1. **It is a good idea to make overnight reservations at the rifugio. Telephone number is (0471)72952.**
2. **The ascent to the summit is rather steep, but without serious exposure.**
3. **Check on the weather forecast. In fog and clouds, the summit plateau has little variation in terrain so finding the trail can be difficult.**

Starting Point: Albergo Frommer on Alpe di Siusi. Take trail #5 which parallels the lift.

Begin on trail #5 gradually ascending across meadows, then descending into a gully, crossing a stream and finally starting a switchback climb to the summit plateau of the Sciliar. You cross the huge, flat, table-like summit and at last, see in the distance the large Rifugio Bolzano. There are 360° views from the rifugio and the mountain landscape that surrounds it is fun to explore.

The next morning, take the rather flat trail #4 towards Rifugio Alpe di Tires. (Be careful not to take the trail which branches to your left as it is a Via Ferrata, albeit not an extremely difficult one.) There are some spectacular vistas of the steep walls of the Catinaccio along the way. Just beyond Rifugio Alpe di Tires, turn north using trail #2. The first stretch is up and then steeply down, before reaching the Alpe di Siusi. Views across the Alpe di Siusi are expansive and the walk back is long but pleasant.

Alternatives: You will be tempted to take alternative trails along the Alpe di Siusi portions of your program—both going to Rifugio Bolzano, and returning from Rifugio Alpe di Tires. Ask at the rifugi for suggestions. For a gentle return route, stay on trail #4 from Rifugio Alpe di Tires, head towards Rifugio Molignon, finally using a service-type road across the Alpe di Siusi. This adds 30 to 45 minutes to your program.

VAL DI FASSA

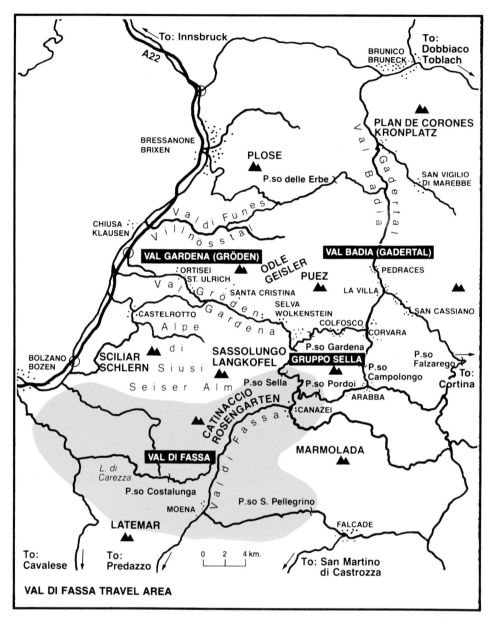

To: Innsbruck

A22

To: Dobbiaco Toblach

BRUNICO BRUNECK

PLAN DE CORONES KRONPLATZ

BRESSANONE BRIXEN

▲ PLOSE

P.so delle Erbe

SAN VIGILIO DI MAREBBE

Val di Funes

Villnösstal

Val Badia / Gadertal

CHIUSA KLAUSEN

VAL GARDENA (GRÖDEN)

ODLE GEISLER

VAL BADIA (GADERTAL)

ORTISEI ST. ULRICH

▲ PUEZ ▲

PEDRACES

SANTA CRISTINA

Val Gröden

LA VILLA

▲

CASTELROTTO

SELVA WOLKENSTEIN

SAN CASSIANO

Alpe

Gardena

COLFOSCO

di

CORVARA

BOLZANO BOZEN

▲

SCILIAR SCHLERN

Siusi

SASSOLUNGO LANGKOFEL

P.so Gardena

GRUPPO SELLA

P.so Falzarego

To: Cortina

Seiser Alm

P.so Sella

P.so Pordoi

P.so Campolongo

ARABBA

CATINACCIO ROSENGARTEN

Val di Fassa

CANAZEI

VAL DI FASSA

MARMOLADA

L. di Carezza

P.so Costalunga

Val di Fassa

P.so S. Pellegrino

MOENA

▲ LATEMAR ▲

FALCADE

To: Cavalese

To: Predazzo

0   2   4 km.

To: San Martino di Castrozza

VAL DI FASSA TRAVEL AREA

HIGHLIGHTS

The Val di Fassa is a key starting point for drives or hiking and climbing excursions into the nearby Catinaccio (Rosengarten) and Latemar massifs. It is one of the Dolomite valleys where the Ladin culture and language is still preserved and is a popular area for visitors, offering a wide variety of moderately-priced accommodations. The valley itself is rather flat with terraced green slopes rising on its western side below the Catinaccio and Latemar, while smaller forested valleys fan out to the east. Italianate villages line the valley floor from Moena in the south to Canazei at the northern end.

MAJOR VILLAGES	Population	Elevation
Canazei	1,700	1465m
Campitello	700	1442m
Vigo di Fassa	950	1382m
Moena	2,600	1184m

PRINCIPAL LANGUAGES: Italian, German, and Ladin

VAL DI FASSA

Canazei, Marmolada in background

HOW TO ARRIVE

By Air:
International airports in Munich, Milan, or Venice, or smaller airports in Verona and Innsbruck.

By Rail:
Nearest stations: Bolzano and Ora, then transfer by car or bus.

By Bus:
Direct service from Milan and Munich to the Val di Fassa in high season. Local service from Bolzano and Trento.

By Car:

From West, North, South:
Exit A22 at Bolzano Nord and follow signs to the Val d'Ega (which begins on the east side of the autostrada). Take the road through this valley. It leads to the Passo Costalunga, then to Vigo where it connects with No. 48. Turn north here and drive to Canazei. Bolzano Nord exit to Canazei: about 1 hr.

From East:
From Cortina use local roads over Passo Falzarego to Passo Pordoi and then to Canazei. Cortina to Canazei: about 1 hr.

Or use local roads from Cencenighe over Passo San Pellegrino to Moena. Cencenighe to Moena: about 40 min.

MAJOR ROAD PASSES INTO THE AREA

Passo Costalunga (Karerpass) 1745m
Passo Sella (Sellajoch). 2244m
Passo Pordoi 2239m
Passo San Pellegrino 1918m

VAL DI FASSA

Peaks of the Catinaccio

APPROACHES

You can reach the Val di Fassa from four directions. From the north you drive over the Passo Sella or Passo Pordoi. The Passo Sella route is the more scenic of the two, particularly in the morning when early light bathes the eastern slopes of the Catinaccio and Sassolungo. If you choose the Passo Pordoi, giant peaks of the eastern Dolomites may be seen in the distance before you begin your descent into the Val di Fassa.

The route from the west is over the Passo Costalunga to Vigo di Fassa—midpoint of the Val di Fassa. Panoramic views from the passo contrast meadows and forests with the stark mountain forms of the Latemar, Catinaccio, and more distant peaks.

The route from the east over Passo San Pellegrino to Moena is less traveled and more rural. From the south, a busy road leads from the A22 through the Val di Fiemme reaching the Val di Fassa at Moena.

SETTING

The 29-kilometer-long Val di Fassa is one of the most typically V shaped of all Dolomite valleys. The valley floor along the Avisio River is delightful for walking because there is only a slight change in elevation. At the northern end is a sunny amphitheater with the village of Canazei and its two small neighbors, Campitello and Alba. Other small villages are on both sides of the road south to Moena.

The Catinaccio is the dominating geographical feature. When viewed from below, it appears like a continuous north-south ridge with clusters of soaring spires and towers. It is easy to explore this fascinating massif from various points above the valley by using the lifts operating in the summer, jeep roads or trails. Access is also possible from its western side along the road connecting the Passo Costalunga and Tires. You can take the lift from near the passo to Rifugio Paolina to enjoy the view of the Catinaccio's steep vertical western flanks.

The Latemar, seen from the north, looks like a concave ridge of continuous spires resembling giant organ pipes. The best views of the ridge are just west of the Passo Costalunga. You may wish to take a brief detour from here and visit the small beautifully-situated Lago di Carezza at the base of the Latemar. It is particularly pretty in the spring and early summer.

HISTORY

Discoveries of stone age sites in 1968 near Mazzin, and others in 1970 near Campitello, support the belief that the Val di Fassa was, like other Dolomite valleys, the scene of seasonal prehistoric settlements. From the beginning of the 11th century, the valley was controlled by the bishopric of Bressanone and later became a part of the Tyrol region of the Austro-Hungarian Empire. During the Napoleonic period the valley was briefly included in the Kingdom of Italy but was returned to Austria in 1815. It was ceded to Italy at the end of World War I.

VAL DI FASSA

The Val di Fassa was a base for the first ascents of the Marmolada and has been a favorite rendezvous of summer hikers and climbers since the late 1800s. After World War II there was a rapid expansion of accommodations and facilities in the valley, and today tourism is its most important industry.

Beginning in Renaissance times, important trails through the Dolomites passed through the Val di Fassa. Today, a portion of this route is the well-known Dolomite Road, a marvel of engineering and construction. It runs from Bolzano though the Val di Fassa to Cortina and is the most traveled route through the Dolomites.

GEOLOGY

The mountains of the Val di Fassa are largely represented by the so-called Triassic reefs—Catinaccio and Latemar. These are separated by huge piles of dark volcanic rocks (Buffaure above Pozza, Val Duron near Campitello, Viel del Pan east and above Canazei). One interesting geological phenomenon is the greater presence here than in other nearby valleys of volcanic rocks and peaks. The rock succession—geological profile—of this valley is typical of the western Dolomites.

MAJOR VILLAGES

Canazei, population 1,700, is the most strategically located village in the valley. It is on the main road to the important Sella and Pordoi passes. This village is an enjoyable place to explore. It has an abundance of shops, a piazza and side streets where you will find interesting old buildings. Drive east of the village for a splendid view of the Marmolada.

Campitello, population 700, a few kilometers west of Canazei, has some well-preserved old farm houses nestled above the village.

Vigo di Fassa, population 950, is the popular access point for initiating excursions to the sunny Ciampedie bowl and the Catinaccio. The village is built along a gentle slope rising above the valley. There are picturesque churches and chapels to visit.

Moena, population 2,600, is an attractive village situated in a sunny open bowl. The river meanders through the center, and there are numerous side lanes to wander. Moena has all the amenities for the traveler with many shops, cafés, and a variety of tourist accommodations. The old churches of St. Vigilio and St. Volfango are especially interesting.

THINGS TO DO AND SEE

Museums, Churches, Buildings
Vigo di Fassa: St. Giuliana sanctuary, nearby baroque chapel.
Moena: St. Vigilio and St. Volfango churches.

Characteristic Old Houses/Villages
Campitello
Moena

Other Summer Activities
Indoor swimming • Tennis • Minigolf • Cinema • Mountain climbing schools • Fishing • Indoor ice skating • Horseback riding • Concerts • Camping • Music festivals • and more.

GEOGRAPHIC FEATURES

Mountain Groups and Their Major Peaks:

Summit Height

Catinaccio (Rosengarten)
Catinaccio d'Antermoia 3002m
Torri del Vajolet 2813m
Latemar 2842m

Other Features:
Avisio River
Lago di Carezza (Karersee)

VAL DI FASSA

OUTINGS AND EXCURSIONS

The following are a few suggestions for touring the Val di Fassa. They can be combined in various ways to fit your plans for any specific day.

Half-day Drives
Vigo-Passo Costalunga-San Cipriano/Tires: Scenic pass and countryside drive with small hamlets.

Vigo-Lago di Carezza-Nova Levante: Lovely mountain lake and village.

Canazei-Lago di Fedaia: You can see the Marmolada from the lake.

View Panoramas
Passo Pordoi, Passo Sella, Passo Costalunga

Val di Fassa towards Gruppo Sella

Rambles
Around Canazei, Campitello, Vigo and Moena.

Along the river between Canazei and Campitello.

Campitello: Stations of the Cross walk above the village.

Walks along Lago di Carezza and Lago di Fedaia for views of mountains.

Using Lifts
Canazei-Pecol-Belvedere lift: Excellent for sweeping views of the Val di Fassa and the surrounding mountains.

Vigo di Fassa-Ciampedie lift: Best for close-up views of Catinaccio.

Campitello-Col Rodella lift: Panoramic views of Val di Fassa, Gruppo Sella, Sassolungo.

VAL DI FASSA

WALKS AND HIKES

The Catinaccio (Rosengarten) is truly one of the premier hiking areas in the Dolomites with trails that vary in degree of difficulty. The trail network is well marked and offers many alternatives so that you may alter your plans while hiking and also choose from different return routes to the roads below. It is wise to study these possibilities before starting and plan your return to the point of departure in the event you do make a change.

Those portions of trails that traverse the Catinaccio tend to be steep and quite challenging. Many areas get little sun so some trails will have snow and ice when little is seen or expected elsewhere. Except for Route 2, the suggested itineraries are in the Catinaccio. Routes 1, 2, and 3 can be done in a half day; the others are longer.

Maps: 1:50,000: Tabacco #2, Kompass Sellagruppe #59; 1:25,000: Tabacco #06, Geo Val Gardena #7, Geo Marmolada #6, Geo Latemar #8, Wanderkarte Dolomiti di Fassa.

Near Rifugio Vajolet and the Catinaccio

ROUTE ❶—RIFUGIO GARDECCIA TO RIFUGIO VAJOLET AND RETURN
A gradual ascent between the vertical cliffs of the Catinaccio.

Distance: About 1½ km one way; 3 km round trip.
Time required: About 1½ hrs to Rifugio Vajolet and the same for return.
Grade: Intermediate.
Special Considerations:
1. There are rocky, but well-marked switchbacks near the Rifugio Vajolet.
2. The trail can still have some snow in early summer.

Starting Point: Take a taxi to Rifugio Gardeccia, then follow the well-marked trail #546 north to Rifugio Vajolet.

In the beginning the trail is wide and heavily traveled. You pass through a lovely forest with the Catinaccio walls on your left. After emerging from the forest, the trail continues up a narrowing rocky valley with a few easy switchbacks before reaching the large Rifugio Vajolet which sits on a rocky plateau. Views of the surrounding mountain walls are striking. You can explore the area but be aware that the trails leading off in different directions get steep quickly. Your return walk along the same path is equally splendid.

VAL DI FASSA

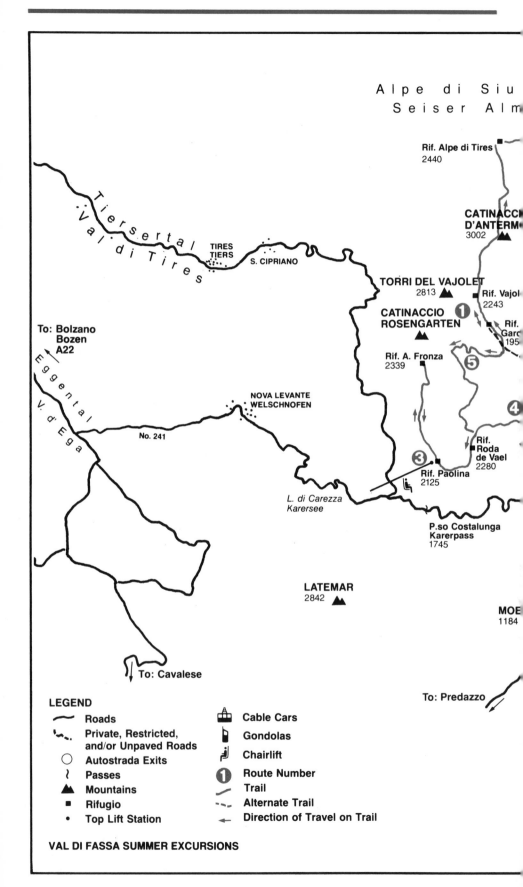

Alpe di Siu
Seiser Alm

Rif. Alpe di Tires
2440

CATINACC
D'ANTERM
3002

TORRI DEL VAJOLET
2813

Rif. Vajol
2243

CATINACCIO
ROSENGARTEN

1

Rif.
Gard
195

Rif. A. Fronza
2339

5

4

Rif.
Roda
de Vael
2280

T i e r s e r t a l
V a l d i T i r e s

TIRES
TIERS

S. CIPRIANO

To: Bolzano
Bozen
A22

E g g e n t a l
V. d' E g a

NOVA LEVANTE
WELSCHNOFEN

No. 241

3

Rif. Paolina
2125

L. di Carezza
Karersee

P.so Costalunga
Karerpass
1745

LATEMAR
2842

MOE
1184

To: Cavalese

To: Predazzo

LEGEND

〜 Roads

ᔗ Private, Restricted,
and/or Unpaved Roads

◯ Autostrada Exits

ʃ Passes

▲ Mountains

■ Rifugio

• Top Lift Station

🚠 Cable Cars

📱 Gondolas

ʃ Chairlift

1 Route Number

— Trail

–·– Alternate Trail

← Direction of Travel on Trail

VAL DI FASSA SUMMER EXCURSIONS

72

VAL DI FASSA

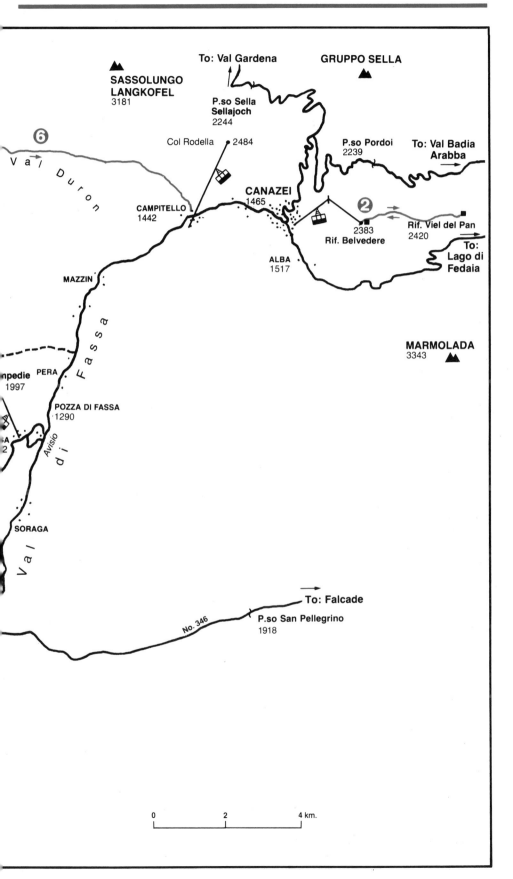

VAL DI FASSA

Marmolada from trail to Rifugio Viel del Pan

ROUTE ❷—LIFT FROM CANAZEI TO BELVEDERE: RIDGE WALK TO RIFUGIO VIEL DEL PAN

A truly spectacular and easy ridge walk with magnificent views of the Marmolada.

Distance: About 3 km one way to Rifugio Viel del Pan (6 km round trip). You can continue another 2 km with very little change in elevation.
Time: About 1½ hrs to Rifugio Viel del Pan and the same to return.
Grade: Moderate.
Special Considerations: This trail can also be reached by an easy one-hour hike along a service road from near the Passo Pordoi.

Starting Point: From the top lift station follow the broad path towards Rifugio Belvedere.

After you reach Rifugio Belvedere, the Marmolada looms closer every few meters. You may even see skiers on the upper glacier. Less than a half-hour later you join the main trail #601, known as the Viel del Pan, one of the most popular in this part of the Dolomites and a portion of the Alta Via #2 (one of the high level hiking routes through the Dolomites). You soon reach the Rifugio Viel del Pan which has a spacious deck and splendid views across to the Marmolada. Time permitting, you can continue along the trail, or take one of several small unmarked trails parallel and above, with even more expansive views. On your return you enjoy panoramas of the Catinaccio, Sassolungo and, towards the end, the Gruppo Sella.

ROUTE ❸—SHORT CATINACCIO HIKE USING LIFT TO RIFUGIO PAOLINA

Mostly level walk below the west walls of the Catinaccio.

Distance: About 3 km one way or 6 km including the return.
Time Required: About 1½ hrs each way.
Grade: Intermediate.

Starting Point: Take the long lift 1 km west of the Passo Costalunga which you can reach along the main road to Nova Levante. Be sure that you take the lift to Rifugio Paolina as there are several lifts in the same area.

After reaching Rifugio Paolina at the top of the lift, take trail #552 north along the flanks of the Catinaccio to Rifugio A. Fronza (Rosengarten Hütte). This flat rocky path is well-traveled so you should have no trouble finding it. The precipitous Catinaccio walls are on the right and below are expansive views of alpine meadows and valleys. On your return from Rifugio A. Fronza the Latemar looms directly ahead of you.

VAL DI FASSA

Latemar from near Rifugio Paolina

In the Catinaccio

VAL DI FASSA

ROUTE ❹—LIFT FROM VIGO DI FASSA: HIKE TO RIFUGIO PAOLINA
A nearly level, dramatic hike around the southern flanks of the Catinaccio.

Distance: About 5 km one way.
Time Required: 3 to 4 hrs not including lifts.
Elevation: Starting point 1997m; Rifugio Roda de Vaèl 2280m; Rifugio Paolina 2125m.
Change in Elevation: Gain of about 350m; Loss of about 150m.
Grade: Intermediate to Difficult.
Special Considerations:
1. **Verify lift schedules.**
2. **Use normal precautions if you encounter snow or ice.**
3. **Plan your return to the starting point as there are several different trails from which to choose.**

Starting Point: Take the lift from Vigo di Fassa to Rifugio Ciampedie. Use the well-marked trail #545 from the lift station towards Rifugio Roda de Vaèl.

The first part is a gradual, sunny ascent. As you near Rifugio Roda de Vaèl, the trail becomes steeper while the views become strikingly more dramatic. For the strong hiker there is a worthwhile side trip from the rifugio. Take the steep trail up approximately 300 meters to the Masare where there is a breathtaking panorama. This ascent increases the hike's grade to Expert and the round trip adds 2 hours to the itinerary. From Rifugio Roda de Vaèl, your walk around the southern slopes of the Catinaccio to Rifugio Paolina is a reward for your efforts as the valley vistas in all directions are varied and expansive. The return by lift from Rifugio Paolina or down the alternate trails towards the Passo Costalunga affords views of the Latemar and the pastoral countryside near Nova Levante.

ROUTE ❺—RIFUGIO GARDECCIA TO RIFUGIO PAOLINA
A demanding one day adventure for the strong hiker.

Distance: About 8 km one way to Rifugio Paolina.
Time required: About 6 hrs.
Elevation: Starting point 1950m; Highest point 2630m.
Change in Elevation: Gain of about 700m; Loss of about 850m.
Grade: Difficult to Expert.
Special Considerations: Same as Route 4.

Starting Point: Take a taxi to Rifugio Gardeccia, then follow the short trail south to Rifugio Catinaccio. There, connect with trail #550 heading steeply west towards the Catinaccio itself. The trail may also be marked towards Rifugio A. Fronza (Rosengarten Hütte.)

When you near the mountain walls, you meet a main north-south trail #541, turn left (south) and hike to your first goal—Rifugio Roda de Vaèl. You will have some steep but dramatic hiking through a rocky pass, around and between cliffs. The balance of the itinerary to Rifugio Paolina is described in Route 4.

ROUTE ❻—TWO-DAY CATINACCIO HIKE: RIFUGIO GARDECCIA TO CAMPITELLO WITH OVERNIGHT IN RIFUGIO ALPE DI TIRES.
A classic mountain excursion between the vertical walls of the Catinaccio.

Distance: About 7 km to Rifugio Alpe di Tires. The next morning 10 km return to Campitello.
Time Required: 5 to 6 hrs to Rifugio Alpe di Tires; 4½ to 5½ hrs to Campitello.
Elevation: Starting Point 1950m; High point 2599m; Rifugio Alpe di Tires 2440m; Campitello 1442m.
Change in Elevation: First day—Gain of about 1000m; Loss of about 500m. Second day—Loss of about 1000m.
Grade: Difficult to Expert depending upon presence of snow or ice.
Special Considerations:
1. **Your beginning point is many kilometers from your ending point so plan to use the excellent bus system or a taxi.**
2. **Make overnight reservations at Rifugio Alpe di Tires. Telephone number: (0471) 71590.**
3. **This route, over boulder and rock, has a high probability of snow and ice. You should inquire about conditions at the rifugi on route.**

VAL DI FASSA

4. There can be poor visibility at times due to fog and clouds but the trail is popular and well marked.
5. It is advisable to begin your hike early in the morning when the weather is generally more reliable.

Starting Point: From Rifugio Gardeccia take trail #546 north to Rifugio Vajolet.

Rifugio Alpe di Tires

You head to Rifugio Vajolet on #546 as in Route 1. At the rifugio continue north on #584 up a gentle rocky slope to the Passo Principe. This narrow pass is just below the highest peak of the Catinaccio. On your right, you will see other hikers on trails leading steeply up and around a dramatic cliff. Check here at Rifugio Principe on the conditions ahead which may include snow and ice. The way continues on trail #554 down beside precipitous rock walls for a descent of some 300 meters. You are then rewarded with views west towards Rifugio Bergamo and the less populated valleys below. Now you must zigzag up rather steeply to reach another rewarding view point—the Passo Molignon. Ahead is your destination, the small rather new Rifugio Alpe di Tires. In the distance is the Alpe di Siusi and Sassolungo. Continue down from the passo to the rifugio.

The next morning you can select one of several trails leading from Rifugio Alpe di Tires either into the Val di Fassa or the Val Gardena. One way is a downward trek through the gentle and peaceful Val Duron ending at Campitello in the Val di Fassa. The first part of this route is straight, and seems a bit long, before entering the woods above the village. Another interesting route, on trail #2, is over a small rise onto the Alpe di Siusi where you may either proceed to the Passo Sella or towards the villages of the Val Gardena. If lifts are operating and the weather is cooperative you can walk to the lift station above Ortisei for a welcome ride down to the Val Gardena.

VAL BADIA (GADERTAL)

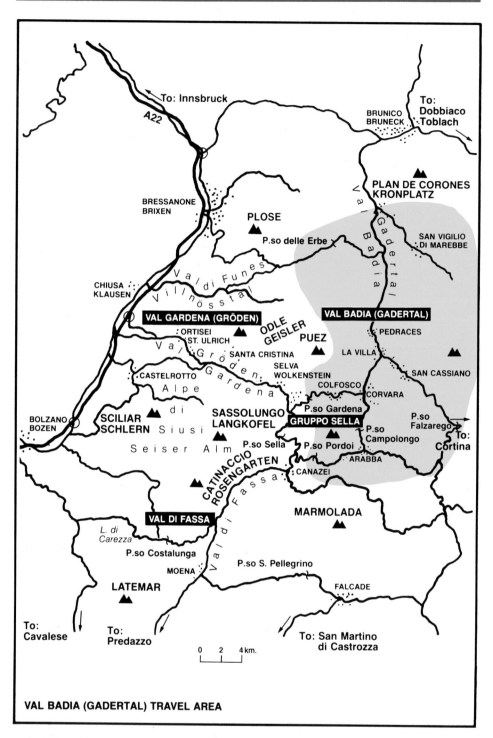

VAL BADIA (GADERTAL) TRAVEL AREA

HIGHLIGHTS

The open and sunny Val Badia has a pastoral countryside that appears unchanged over the centuries. The meadowed slopes above the spotless white Tyrolean villages and just below the mountains are dotted with colorful old farmhouses and barns. There are many small hamlets to explore in the picturesque lateral valleys. The Ladin culture and language probably predominate here more than in any other valley—although both German and Italian are spoken and signs are often in all three languages. Tourism is a vital part of the economy and while there are a few large hotels, every village has countless smaller pensioni, garni and apartments.

VAL BADIA (GADERTAL)

MAJOR VILLAGES	Population	Elevation
Corvara...700.............1568m		
Colfosco (Kolfuschg)...............................500.............1645m		
La Villa (Stern)......................................850.............1450m		
San Cassiano (St. Kassian).........................650.............1550m		
Pedraces (Pedratsches)..........................1,150.............1400m		
San Vigilio di Marebbe (St. Vigil in Enneberg)..........1,200.............1201m		
Arabba..350.............1602m		

PRINCIPAL LANGUAGES: German, Italian, and Ladin.

Colfosco, Gruppo Sella in background

HOW TO ARRIVE

By Air:
International airports at Munich, Milan, Venice or smaller airports in Verona and Innsbruck.

By Rail:
Nearest stations: Brunico (Bruneck), then transfer by bus or car.

By Bus:
Direct service from Milan and Munich in high season. Local service is very convenient from cities bordering the Dolomites.

By Car:

From West, North: Exit A22 at Bressanone. Take No. 49, following signs to the Val Pusteria. Near Brunico turn right (south) on No. 244 to the Val Badia and Corvara. Bressanone exit to Corvara: about 1 hr.

From South: Val di Fassa over the Passo Pordoi and north at Arabba to Corvara. Canazei in the Val di Fassa to Corvara: about ¾ hr.

From East: In the Val Pusteria, take No. 49 from Dobbiaco to near Brunico then south to Corvara. Dobbiaco to Corvara: about 1½ hr.

From Cortina drive over Passo Falzarego to La Villa to Corvara. Cortina to Corvara: about 1 hr.

VAL BADIA (GADERTAL)

APPROACHES

A 30-minute drive from Brunico will take you to the main "hollow" of the Val Badia near Pedraces. A few kilometers farther, at La Villa, the road divides. The left-hand branch leads up the Valle San Cassiano towards Passo Valparola and Cortina; the right leads to Corvara.

From the west—Val Gardena—drive over the Passo Gardena, a spectacular trip. You descend many gradual hairpin turns over a wide meadowed slope between the walls of the Gruppo Sella and Puez. As you pass the village of Colfosco, the entire sweep of the central Val Badia stretches before you. After a few more turns you are in Corvara.

If you are in the Val di Fassa, drive over the Passo Pordoi. This is also a beautiful drive with views towards the eastern Dolomites. You first reach the village of Arabba which is tucked into a small sunny bowl; from here take the road north and you will arrive in Corvara in 45 minutes.

From points east, such as Cortina, take the road over the Passo Falzarego towards La Villa and branch left to Corvara.

MAJOR ROAD PASSES INTO THE AREA
Passo Gardena (Grödner Joch) 2121m
Passo Falzarego 2105m
Passo Pordoi 2239m
Passo Campolongo 1875m

Central Val Badia and Pralongia plateau

SETTING

The Val Badia begins in the north as a narrow gorge along the Gadera River and continues to the southern ridge of the Pralongia plateau above Livinallongo. Near Pedraces the valley bursts into a huge triangular-shaped hollow circled by a seemingly unbroken rim of mountains. The Puez and Gruppo Sella are on the west, and the Sasso della Croce, Cunturines and Fanes groups are on the east.

In the center of this hollow, rising an average of 500 meters above the surrounding valleys, is the large undulating Pralongia plateau. While its average elevation is about 2000 meters above sea level, the plateau has a few higher peaks reaching between 2300 and 2500 meters. One of these, the Col di Lana (2452m), was the site of fierce fighting during World War I. The Italians exploded two mines near the summit in an attempt to destroy Austrian positions and the shape of the summit was forever changed to a *col*, saddle or small pass. One hundred soldiers were buried alive—which accounts for the peak's second name, the Col di Sangue.

VAL BADIA (GADERTAL)

Rustic farm in the Val Badia

HISTORY

There have been important prehistoric discoveries in the Val Badia. As recently as the fall of 1987, remains of bears dating from about 80,000 years ago were uncovered in a cave above the Passo Valparola in the Cunturines group. These are among the oldest bones yet found in the Dolomites. Stone implements discovered near the Fanes and the Sella indicate that there were human inhabitants in the valley centuries before Christ.

Romans entered the valley in 15 B.C., ruling for five centuries. The Ladin language that emerged from Roman times still exists here as strongly and in as pure a form as anywhere in the Dolomites. According to the 1981 census, Ladins comprise 96% of the valley population.

After the Romans the valley's political and cultural history paralleled that of most of the northwestern Dolomites. Between about 1025 and 1800 control of the valley was divided — the western part was generally under the Bressanone bishopric and the eastern under local lordships. Thereafter it was administered by the Hapsburgs and the Austro-Hungarian Empire. The valley's people fought on the Austrian side during World War I. However, after the war, Val Badia was ceded to Italy.

The valley has been engaged in vital economic activities throughout its history. In the 16th century iron brought in from other nearby areas, was forged into arms for Venice and much of Europe. During the 18th century the timber industry prospered because lumber was in demand for markets in the Venetian Republic.

Today, when touring in this valley, you will see evidence of historic forms of land management—an old form of cooperative land ownership called *vile* is unique to the Val Badia. These are clusters of rustic farmhouses where facilities such as drinking troughs and ovens for baking are still shared.

GEOGRAPHIC FEATURES

Mountain Groups and their Major Peaks: Summit Height

Col di Lana	2452m
Sasso della Croce	2907m
Fanes	2989m
Cunturines	3064m
Gruppo Sella	3152m
Sassongher	2665m

Other Features:
Parco Naturale Fanes-Sennes-Braies
Gadera River
Cordevole River
Pralongia Plateau

VAL BADIA (GADERTAL)

GEOLOGY

The Val Badia is located in an important geological position. A north-south line through the valley, along the Gadera River to the Cordevole River, divides the Dolomites into two geological zones—the eastern, *orientali,* and the western, *occidentali.* Each zone has a distinctly different geological profile.

Strata, very rich in fossils, the so-called San Cassiano Formation, extensively outcrop in the "alta" Val Badia (south of Pedraces). The study of this formation helped scientists piece together the geological history of the Dolomites.

On the way to Corvara

MAJOR VILLAGES

Sunny **Corvara**, at the base of the Sassonger, with a population of 700, is a delightful valley village. It has shops and hotels dispersed in two small districts. A handsome modern church as well as a smaller and older one are in the main district. On the slopes above is a mixture of new and old houses interspersed with many farms. Dozens of new two and three-story whitewashed hotels, garni, and pensioni have sprouted up everywhere. There is one to suit each budget.

Above Corvara, towards the Passo Gardena is **Colfosco (Kolfuschg)**, population 500, an enchanting village that has re-

VAL BADIA (GADERTAL)

tained much of its old-world charm despite recent tourist development. An imposing white Tyrolean church with a bulbous steeple sits proudly in the center. Some of the most charming old farmhouses and barns in any of the valleys are found here. Views of the sheer walls of the Gruppo Sella are truly awe-inspiring.

La Villa (Stern), population 850, is well located for access to the Pralongia plateau and has a small selection of tourist accommodations.

San Cassiano (St. Kassian), population 650, is another village worth a visit. It extends along both sides of the road and there is pleasant walking on the slopes above. There is a good selection of tourist facilities.

Pedraces (Pedratsches), population 1,150, along the main road, and quaint **San Leonardo**, adjoining on the east and above, are also centers for touring. The chairlift, leaving from San Leonardo, takes you right over the rural countryside and gives access to some lovely excursions above the valley. There is an excellent assortment of small alberghi, and you are just a short drive from the shopping in Corvara.

Tucked away at the end of a small valley, 30 minutes by car from Corvara, is **San Vigilio di Marebbe (St. Vigil in Enneberg),** population 1,200. In an idyllic setting, this village is a mixture of old and new. You can spend many hours exploring and wandering in the surroundings.

Arabba, population 350, an important ski center, is also popular in the summer. It is small, quiet and somewhat secluded with limited accommodation.

Church in Colfosco

THINGS TO DO AND SEE

Museums, Churches, Buildings
Churches in Corvara and Colfosco.
Unusual handmade wooden crucifixes and Stations of the Cross above Pedraces.

Characteristic Old Houses/Villages
Colfosco
S. Leonardo
La Valle
Pieve di Marebbe

The Val Badia offers one of the best opportunities in the Dolomites for drives and walks in small villages and remote hamlets, some seemingly untouched for centuries.

Other Summer Activities:
Indoor and outdoor swimming • Indoor and outdoor tennis • Minigolf • Cinema • Mountain climbing schools • Fishing • Ice skating • Horseback riding • Camping • and more.

VAL BADIA (GADERTAL)

OUTINGS AND EXCURSIONS

The Val Badia has a wealth of outings and excursions and is also centrally located in the Dolomites so that you may easily tour neighboring valleys such as the Val Gardena, Val di Fassa and Cortina.

Half-day Drives
Corvara-Colfosco: Two pastoral Tyrolean villages with old churches and farmhouses.

San Martino in Badia-Antermoia and Passo delle Erbe: Rural life is unchanged in these remote hamlets perched on high green alps.

Val Badia-San Vigilio di Marebbe: An isolated valley with a charming Tyrolean village.

View Panoramas
Passo Pordoi
Passo Valparola
Passo Gardena

Hamlets above the Val Badia

Rambles
Around the small villages of Corvara and Colfosco.

Visit La Valle, a picturesque hamlet with pleasant mountain and valley views.

Above Colfosco, to see weathered old farmhouses and alpine views.

Using Lifts
Col Alto lift: Corvara to Pralongia plateau. Good views of mountains encircling the Val Badia.

Pradat lift: Colfosco. Views of Colfosco below and across to the massive Gruppo Sella.

Pedraces lift: San Leonardo. From the top walk up to nearby Abbazia S. Croce to see a tiny church in a dramatic setting. There are gentle walks throughout this entire area. Along the trail you pass some of the most interestingly designed crucifixes seen anywhere in the Dolomites.

VAL BADIA (GADERTAL)

Corvara, Sassongher in background

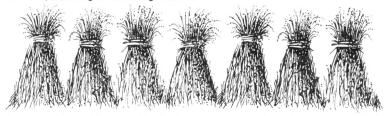

VAL BADIA (GADERTAL)

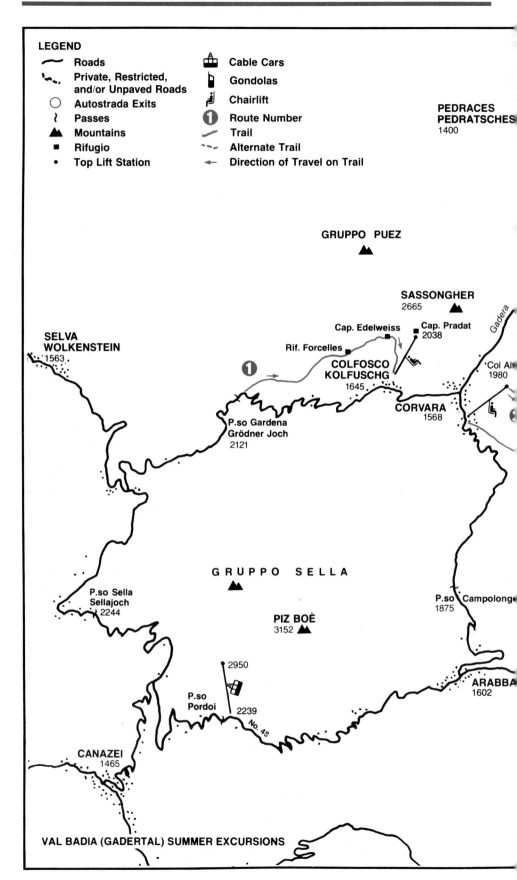

LEGEND

∿	Roads	🚠	Cable Cars
⌇	Private, Restricted, and/or Unpaved Roads	📱	Gondolas
○	Autostrada Exits	🪑	Chairlift
⟩	Passes	①	Route Number
▲	Mountains	⌒	Trail
▪	Rifugio	⌁	Alternate Trail
•	Top Lift Station	←	Direction of Travel on Trail

PEDRACES
PEDRATSCHES
1400

GRUPPO PUEZ
▲▲

SASSONGHER
2665 ▲▲

Gadera

Cap. Edelweiss
Cap. Pradat
2038

SELVA
WOLKENSTEIN
1563

Rif. Forcelles

① →

Col Al
1980

COLFOSCO
KOLFUSCHG
1645

CORVARA
1568

P.so Gardena
Grödner Joch
2121

GRUPPO SELLA
▲▲

P.so Sella
Sellajoch
2244

PIZ BOÈ
3152 ▲▲

P.so Campolong
1875

2950

P.so
Pordoi
2239

No. 48

ARABBA
1602

CANAZEI
1465

VAL BADIA (GADERTAL) SUMMER EXCURSIONS

86

VAL BADIA (GADERTAL)

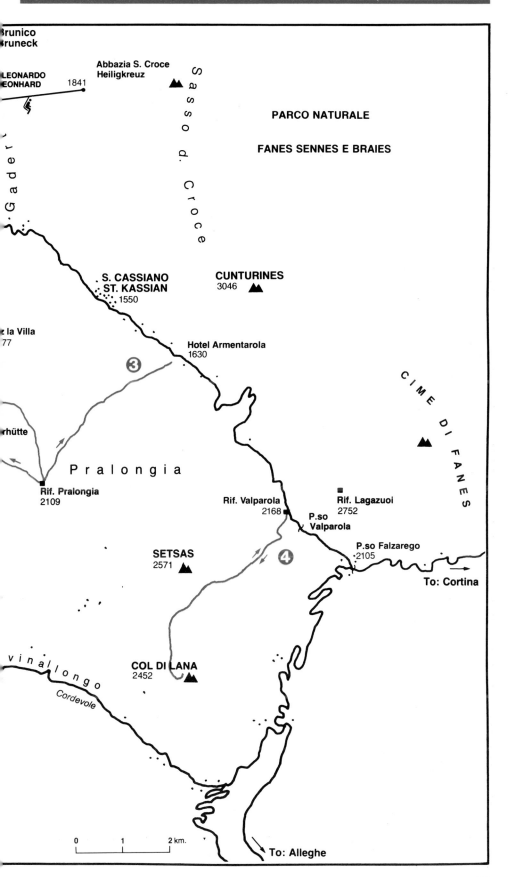

Brunico
Bruneck

Abbazia S. Croce
Heiligkreuz

LEONARDO
LEONHARD   1841

Sasso d. Croce

PARCO NATURALE

FANES SENNES E BRAIES

Gader

S. CASSIANO
ST. KASSIAN
· 1550

CUNTURINES
3046

la Villa
77

Hotel Armentarola
1630

③

CIME DI FANES

rhütte

Pralongia

Rif. Pralongia
2109

Rif. Valparola
2168

Rif. Lagazuoi
2752

P.so
Valparola

SETSAS
2571

④

P.so Falzarego
·2105

To: Cortina

vinallongo

COL DI LANA
2452

Cordevole

0   1   2 km.

To: Alleghe

VAL BADIA (GADERTAL)

WALKS AND HIKES

Walking excursions in the Val Badia are generally on gentle terrain within sight of villages and hamlets and can easily be done in half a day if you wish. Longer mountain itineraries take you from the valley into the surrounding mountain groups. Some of these are all-day hikes and generally not crowded.

Maps 1:50,000: Tabacco #2, Kompass Sellagruppe Marmolada #59; Kompass Cortina #55, 1:25,000: Tabacco #07, Geo Le Odle #5, Geo Marmolada #6.

Trail entering Colfosco

ROUTE ❶—PASSO GARDENA TO COLFOSCO

An undulating downhill walk over meadowed terrain with views of the Sella walls and Puez cliffs.

Distance: About 5 km one way.
Time Required: About 2½ hrs.
Grade: Moderate.
Special Considerations:
This is a one-way route (however, the return hike up is gradual and would take about the same time). It is possible to take a bus or hire a taxi from Colfosco back to the Passo Gardena.

Starting Point: About 100 meters down from the Passo Gardena, on the Corvara side, you will see a bend in the road. Walk to this point where you will find a sign pointing towards Colfosco and Rifugio Malga Cir. Follow this trail. Alternately, you can join the route by hiking down from the top of the Dantercepies lift.

You begin this popular walk on a level contour above the road, and then meander over rolling meadows. Shortly you leave the sights and sounds of cars and proceed gradually down towards Colfosco. On your right are the awesome towering cliffs and buttresses of the Sella and, on your left the less imposing but still dramatic and close-by walls of the Puez. Near the end, sunny Colfosco appears as you approach the peaceful valley—Edelweisstal.

VAL BADIA (GADERTAL)

Pralongia plateau from Gruppo Sella

ROUTES ❷ AND ❸ —WALKS ON THE PRALONGIA PLATEAU
The Pralongia is one of several flat-meadowed plateaus in the Dolomites that are ideal for walking, wandering, and exploring. There is easy access to the Pralongia from the valleys and villages that surround it. You can use lifts, if they are operating, or hike up. Trails are everywhere—they are not always marked. Much of the terrain looks the same, so it is a good idea to have a map and ask directions. You can wander without a prescribed plan and alter your itinerary as you go, visiting one of several rifugi on the way. Local buses or taxis connect the villages surrounding the base.

Distance and time required: Itineraries can be 2 to 12 km and can be loops or one-way routes.
Elevation: Once on the plateau you walk at an average elevation of 2000m with flat and rolling stretches that vary 100 to 200m in elevation gain and loss.
Grade: Generally Easy to Intermediate.
Special Considerations: Hikes require more time than would appear. For example, from Col Alto to the Col di Lana is about 10 km and requires a steady pace for 3½ hrs.

Starting Points to the Pralongia plateau:
Take Col Alto lift from Corvara.
Take the lift from La Villa.
From just north of the Passo Campolongo walk up towards the Rifugio Cherz.

ROUTE ❷ —COL ALTO LIFT. HIKE TO RIFUGIO PRALONGIA TO NEGERHÜTTE TO CORVARA
A one-way meadow walk of 4 hrs with wide open vistas. Grade: Moderate.

ROUTE ❸ —COL ALTO LIFT: HIKE TO RIFUGIO PRALONGIA TO ARMENTAROLA
A 3 to 4 hr one-way plateau jaunt with a gentle descent in front of the walls of the Cunturines group to a large, prettily situated hotel. Grade: Easy.

ROUTE ❹ —RIFUGIO VALPAROLA TO COL DI LANA AND RETURN
A 5 hr challenging but rewarding round trip to the Col di Lana. You will see the devastating effects of the World War I mine explosions. There are some magnificent views of the Marmolada and Civetta.

Exposure on the last part of this hike upgrades it from Intermediate to Expert. It should be attempted only in clear weather.

GRUPPO SELLA

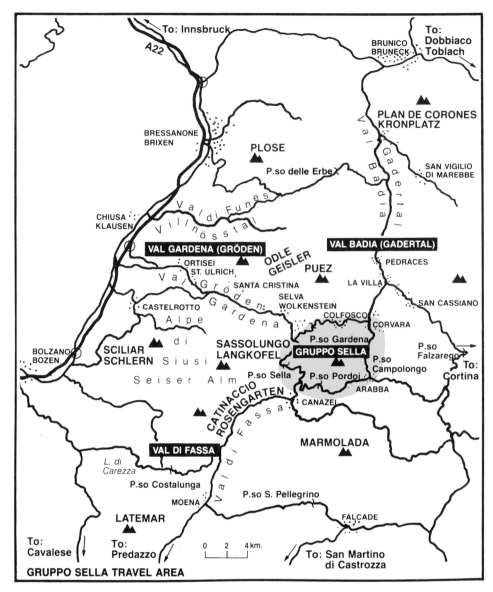

GRUPPO SELLA TRAVEL AREA

HIGHLIGHTS

The fortress-like Gruppo Sella (summit—Piz Boè, 3152m) is uniquely positioned in the Dolomites. It sits apart from other massifs and stands as a seemingly impregnable terminus to four principal valleys. From most vantage points its colossal form appears symmetrical. It is easily approached via four highway passes and can be circled in a 50-kilometer drive.

This massif is a popular destination for hikers and mountain climbers in the summer and for skiers in the winter. For the hiker the reward awaits after an arduous climb to the summit. From this desolate plateau—a lunar-landscape of scoured pinnacles and towers—there are unending panoramas of the surrounding pastoral countryside and distant Dolomite peaks.

APPROACHES

The only lift access to the summit plateau of the Gruppo Sella is from the Passo Pordoi; otherwise you must hike up. The ride on the cable car is a thrilling airy trip. If you are touring by car, there are many ways to approach the Sella and each is dramatic. From the west you may drive through the Val Gardena and over the Passo Gardena; from the south via the Val di Fassa and over the Passo Sella or Passo Pordoi; and from the north and east by way of the Val Badia or Livinallongo over the Passo Campolongo or Passo Pordoi.

Minuartia verna

90

GRUPPO SELLA

GEOLOGY

The Gruppo Sella, located in the middle of the Dolomites, is of much geologic interest. It is constituted largely of two different dolomitic rocks. The lower one is not stratified, measures 300 to 500 meters in thickness, and was an atoll in the ancient sea that once covered this area. The upper one, horizontally bedded, is the Dolomia Principale, the same formation which constitutes major parts of the mountains around Cortina (e.g. Tofane, Cristallo). These two dolomite rocks are separated by a continuous ledge of soft marly sediments—the Raibl Formation (non-dolomitic).

NEAREST MAJOR VILLAGES AND VALLEYS
Selva (Wolkenstein) in the Val Gardena (Gröden)
Canazei in the Val di Fassa
Corvara in the Val Badia (Gadertal)
Colfosco (Kolfuschg) in the Val Badia (Gadertal)
Arabba (Livinallongo)

Gruppo Sella from Val Gardena

OUTINGS AND EXCURSIONS

Drives
A drive around the Gruppo Sella is the best way to view the stark vertical walls of this mountain. There are many curves and traffic is frequently heavy, so allow several hours for your tour.

View Panoramas
Passo Gardena
Passo Campolongo
Passo Pordoi
Passo Sella

Using Lifts
Take the Sass Pordoi lift (cable car) from Passo Pordoi to the summit plateau for one of the finest panoramic views in the Dolomites.

GRUPPO SELLA

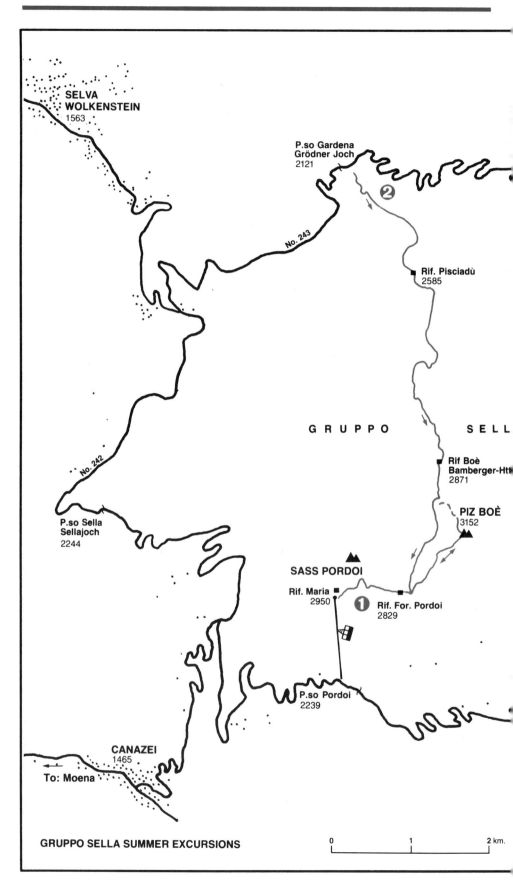

SELVA
WOLKENSTEIN
1563

P.so Gardena
Grödner Joch
2121

No. 243

②

Rif. Pisciadù
2585

No. 242

G R U P P O   S E L L

Rif Boè
Bamberger-Htt
2871

P.so Sella
Sellajoch
2244

PIZ BOÈ
3152

SASS PORDOI

Rif. Maria
2950

① Rif. For. Pordoi
2829

P.so Pordoi
2239

CANAZEI
1465

To: Moena

GRUPPO SELLA SUMMER EXCURSIONS

0   1   2 km.

GRUPPO SELLA

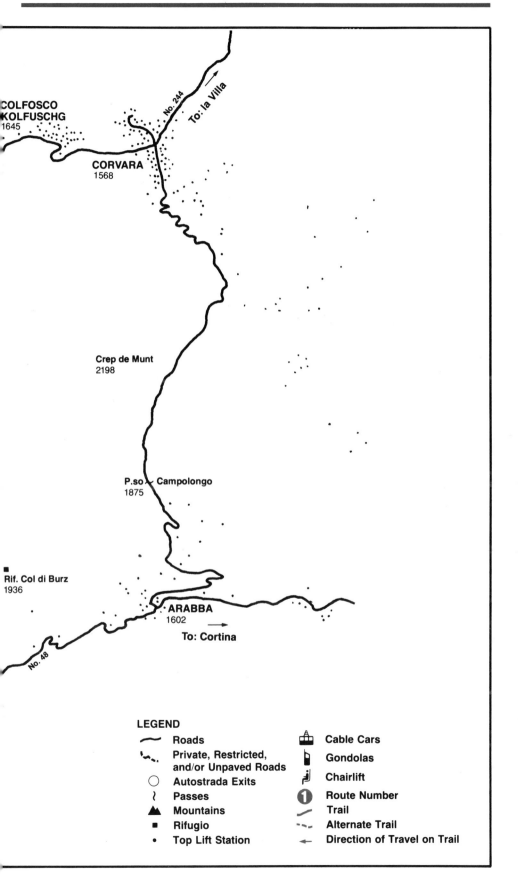

COLFOSCO
KOLFUSCHG
1645

No. 244

To: la Villa

CORVARA
1568

Crep de Munt
2198

P.so Campolongo
1875

Rif. Col di Burz
1936

ARABBA
1602

To: Cortina

No. 48

LEGEND

⌢	Roads	🚠	Cable Cars
〰	Private, Restricted, and/or Unpaved Roads	🚡	Gondolas
◯	Autostrada Exits	🚡	Chairlift
⌇	Passes	❶	Route Number
▲	Mountains	╱	Trail
▪	Rifugio	〰	Alternate Trail
•	Top Lift Station	←	Direction of Travel on Trail

GRUPPO SELLA

WALKS AND HIKES

Amazingly, trails have been constructed in the few possible places where the hiker can ascend onto the summit plateau. One of these routes is described below. If you wish to avoid the rigors of this 800-meter climb, take the Sass Pordoi lift to the summit. Once on the top, trails crisscross and pass two handsome stone rifugi, conveniently spaced to suit most hiking itineraries.

If you wish more information regarding climbing or hiking routes contact any village tourist office or climbing school in the Val Gardena, Val di Fassa or Val Badia.

Maps 1:50,000: Tabacco #2, Kompass Sellagruppe-Marmolada #59; 1:25,000: Tabacco #05, #06, or #07, Geo Marmolada/Gruppo di Sella #6, Wanderkarte Dolomiti di Fassa.

Catinaccio seen from summit plateau of Gruppo Sella

ROUTE ❶—LIFT FROM PASSO PORDOI: HIKE TO SUMMIT OF GRUPPO SELLA (PIZ BOÈ)

A gradual ascent over the rocky summit plateau to the highest point on the Sella.

Distance: About 2 km one way.
Time required: About 2 hrs one way, 3¼ hrs round trip.
Elevation: Starting point 2950m; Piz Boè 3152m.
Change in Elevation: Gain of about 300m; Loss of about 300m.
Grade: Intermediate.
Special Considerations:
1. **The entire way is over rock and scree, with some scrambling over boulders.**
2. **This high trail is subject to wind and weather changes. It should only be attempted when skies are fairly clear and there is no snow or ice.**

Starting Point: At the top of lift, take the only well-marked trail north to the summit.

When you get off the lift, you will have astounding views of the Marmolada, Sassolungo, and the Val di Fassa. Pause to enjoy this vista now, and again after your hike, perhaps while sipping a drink in the large restaurant at the upper lift station. The first part of your hike is rather level before you descend to the Forcella Pordoi. From the forcella you ascend and soon will see distant mountains and valleys. You approach a trail fork with the left branch heading to Rifugio Boè. Bear right and follow the obvious trail towards the summit. The awe-inspiring 360° panorama from the top includes the Tofane near Cortina, Civetta, the Marmolada and many other peaks. The return poses no problem. However, go slowly for you are on rock and, while not difficult, the way can be slippery and you may be tempted to look at the scenery instead of your footing.

GRUPPO SELLA

Summit plateau of Gruppo Sella

ROUTE❷—FROM THE PASSO GARDENA UP TO THE SUMMIT PLATEAU OF THE GRUPPO SELLA
A strenuous day hike to explore the high mountain environment of the Gruppo Sella.

Distance: About 8 km.
Time Required: 5¼ to 6 hrs.
Elevation: Starting point 2143m; Rifugio Boè 2871m; Sass Pordoi lift 2950m.
Change in Elevation: Gain of about 850m; Loss of about 150m.
Grade: Expert.
Special Considerations:
1. **You begin in a shady gully with steep switchbacks over scree. Ask to be sure there is not a great deal of snow and ice on the upper portions of the gully as this could make the way hazardous.**
2. **Snow and ice remain on the summit plateau much of the year so you may need an ice axe. Ask in village tourist offices.**
3. **Be sure rifugi are open and the Sass Pordoi lift is operating for your descent at the end of the hike. You will finish on the other side of the Sella and must plan your return from Passo Pordoi.**
4. **Carry water and a nutritious snack.**
5. **While the trail is generally well-marked, be aware that it is more difficult to see the trail and markings across rocky tundra.**
6. **Although not a Via Ferrata, parts of the ascent and a few portions of the way across the summit plateau have fixed iron cables for added support.**
7. **In bad weather or poor visibility do not attempt this route.**

Starting Point: From Passo Gardena look towards the Gruppo Sella for trail #666 (Alta Via #2). It will be to the south and above you.

After several switchbacks, you traverse the north flank of the Sella before starting to climb a steep gully between two towering buttresses. You leave the soft green valley below and increasingly have the sensation of a high mountain ascent. As you near the top of the gully, watch for snow and ice. Footing over the last part is good but can be slippery in spots. You can also use fixed iron cables to help your final scramble onto the vast rocky summit plateau. It is a relief to finally reach a fairly level stretch and see friendly signs to the attractive Rifugio Pisciadù.

GRUPPO SELLA

Rocky tundra around Rifugio Pisciadù

Adjacent to the rifugio is a small pond that gives some contrast to the otherwise barren landscape. Towers and buttresses are your companions as you start your trek across the plateau towards Rifugio Boè. Footing is good but be careful as you are on rock the entire time. As you near Rifugio Boè, the view opens up and you can see the summit of the Sassolungo on your right and the Val di Fassa below. Take the trail branching to the left, which goes up a bit, before descending to the rifugio. An alternative trail to the right appears level; however it has some exposure, fixed cables and requires sure-footedness.

At the Rifugio Boè, take trail #627(still on Alta Via#2) and soon you must decide if you want to take a detour to the summit, Piz Boè. It adds about 1½ to 2 hours to the itinerary and there is some scrambling near the top.

If you choose to save the summit visit for another occasion, the trail from Rifugio Boè is rather flat before you descend to the Forcella Pordoi. There you will be startled by valley views between steep cliffs. The restaurant at the Pordoi lift is wonderfully sited so take time to enjoy a refreshment and bask in the satisfaction of the adventure just completed.

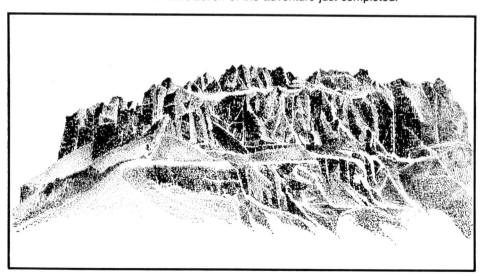

GRUPPO SELLA

Approaching Gruppo Sella from Passo Gardena

SOUTHWEST

San Martino di Castrozza, Val Cismon

SOUTHWEST

The Southwest district is bordered on the west by the A22 with convenient exits at Bolzano and Ora. It includes two important valleys, the Val Cismon and Val di Fiemme. The **San Martino di Castrozza-Passo Rolle** travel area is located in the Val Cismon. San Martino is a small resort village at the base of the Pale di San Martino, a magnificent ridge of spires and peaks. There are spectacular walks and hikes in and around the Pale. The Val di Fiemme is a major commercial valley with two large villages, Cavalese and Predazzo.

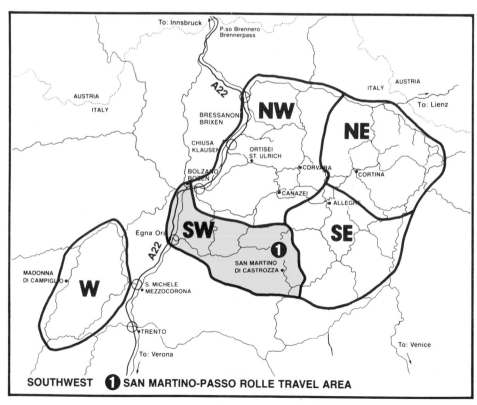

SOUTHWEST ❶ SAN MARTINO-PASSO ROLLE TRAVEL AREA

SOUTHWEST

Hikers, Pale di San Martino

IMPORTANT FEATURES

Region: Trentino-Alto Adige
Province: Trento
Valleys: Val Cismon, Val di Fiemme
Villages: San Martino di Castrozza, Fiera di Primiero, Cavalese, Predazzo
Mountains: Pale di San Martino

SAN MARTINO DI CASTROZZA

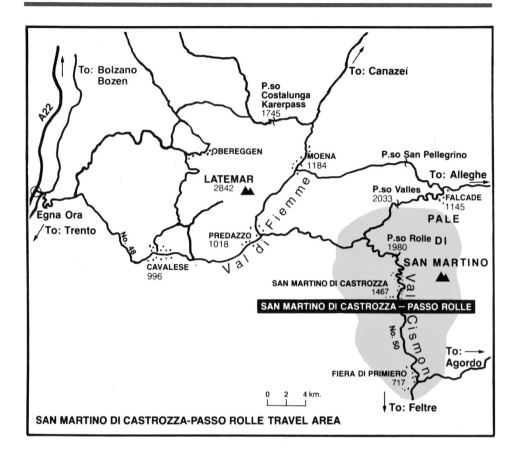

SAN MARTINO DI CASTROZZA-PASSO ROLLE TRAVEL AREA

HIGHLIGHTS

San Martino is dramatically situated below one of the most breathtaking of all Dolomite mountain groups, the Pale di San Martino. This ridge of jagged peaks and spires, part of the western (Occidentali) Dolomites, can be seen from virtually every point. There are a wealth of walks, excursions, hikes and climbs in the Pale itself, across from the Pale on the Tognola side of the Val Cismon, and near the Passo Rolle at the north end of the valley.

Tourism is the primary business in this resort area, particularly in San Martino, which offers both summer and winter recreation. Considering its relatively small size, San Martino has an impressive selection of new and grand old hotels, as well as recently constructed apartments and condominiums. The village is small and rather confined so it is easy to wander and explore. Fiera di Primiero, at the southern end of the valley, is at a low elevation and sunny; a delight to visit summer or winter.

Cimon della Pala

MAJOR VILLAGES	Population	Elevation
San Martino di Castrozza	600	1467m
Fiera di Primiero	2,400	717m
PRINCIPAL LANGUAGE: Italian		

SAN MARTINO DI CASTROZZA

HOW TO ARRIVE

By Air:
International airports in Munich, Milan, Venice, or smaller airports in Verona and Innsbruck.

By Rail:
Nearest stations: Feltre, or if you are coming from the west, Ora or Trento.

By Bus:
Direct frequent service from Venice and, in high tourist season, at least twice a week from Milan.

By Car:

From West and North:
Exit A22 at Ora. Take route No. 48 following the signs to Cavalese (Val di Fiemme) and Predazzo. At Predazzo take No. 50 over the Passo Rolle to San Martino. Ora to San Martino: about 2 hrs.

From South and East:
Take the A27 north and local roads to Belluno. Then use highway No. 50 through Feltre and north to San Martino. Venice to San Martino: about 3 hrs.

Or exit A31 at Dueville and follow local roads to Fiera and San Martino. Venice to San Martino via Dueville: about 2½ hrs.

MAJOR ROAD PASSES INTO THE AREA

	Elevation
Passo Rolle	1980m
Passo Valles	2033m

Doronicum clusii

Village of San Martino di Castrozza

SAN MARTINO DI CASTROZZA

APPROACHES

If you are coming from the west plan to arrive at the Passo Rolle by early afternoon to enjoy the play of sunlight on the rock faces of the Pale. Once at the passo you first glimpse the imposing Cimon della Pala. Vistas all around are unobstructed before you wind your way down through woods to San Martino.

From the south you travel first through the lovely village of Fiera, then gaining altitude in the Val Cismon, the Pale di San Martino looms ever closer and more majestic as you approach San Martino.

SETTING

The peaks and spires of the Pale appear as a compact ridge separated from neighboring mountains—it extends for almost 12 kilometers, rising above virtually the entire length of the Val Cismon, from Fiera in the south to the Passo Rolle in the north. The most noted peak in the group is not the highest, but the most elegant—the Cimon della Pala (3186m). Just north of the Cimon

Val Cismon

is the highest in the group—the Cima della Vezzana (3191m).

Across the Val Cismon, to the west of this world of towering rock, are gentle mountains, meadows, and forests. From here, views of the Pale rising over San Martino are absolutely stupendous. The ski slopes are on this western side of the Val Cismon, as are many easy summer walks and hikes. Most of the mountain areas on both sides of the valley are included in the Parco Naturale Paneveggio-Pale di San Martino.

HISTORY

In the 11th century, San Martino was established by the Benedictine friars as a hospice for pilgrims making their way in the Val Cismon between Fiera and the Val di Fiemme. In the 14th century this area was important to the Hapsburgs because of the rich silver mines discovered in the vicinity of Fiera di Primiero; shortly thereafter it became part of their holdings. International attention was focused here in the mid-19th century when many famous British explorers and mountaineers came to scale the peaks. The Cimon, for example, was first climbed by the Englishman J. Whitwell in 1870.

San Martino was greatly affected by World War I. The Austrians, for strategic reasons, had to retreat and establish their main front to the west and north of San Martino. By the end of 1915, San Martino and Fiera found themselves behind the Italian lines. Many of the grand old hotels were destroyed during the War but afterward were quickly rebuilt.

ECONOMY

The economy of San Martino is essentially supported by tourism so the village is lively during the high seasons of summer and winter. At other times of the year it can appear to be closed-up. Fiera, 700 meters lower in elevation, has a warmer climate and a year-round economy, with agriculture as an important business.

GEOGRAPHIC FEATURES

Mountain Groups and Their Major Peaks:	Summit Height
Peaks of the Pale di San Martino	
Cimon della Pala	3186m
Cima della Vezzana	3191m
Cima Focobon	3054m
Sass Maor	2814m
Other Features:	
Valle dei Canali	

SAN MARTINO DI CASTROZZA

MAJOR VILLAGES

San Martino di Castrozza, small in size, with a population of 600, is the very model of an Italian alpine village. There is a small central piazza with a picturesque old church and 13th century campanile. An amazing array of boutiques, sport and craft shops line the main street with many others tucked along the adjacent streets. On one of these side streets is a wonderful café that serves some of the best home-made ice cream in the Dolomites. Wander from the village center on these streets and lanes and you abruptly find yourself among meadows and woods with mountain views.

A few kilometers south is the busy village of **Fiera di Primiero**, population 2,400. There are a number of historic buildings, including a 14th century Palace of the Mines and a 15th century church. There is the usual bustling piazza, plus side streets and shops to explore.

Clematis alpina

Exploring the Pale di San Martino

THINGS TO DO AND SEE

Museums, Churches, Buildings
San Martino: An historic church and 13th century campanile.
Fiera di Primiero: The Palace of the Mines, 14th and 15th century churches.

Natural Park
Parco Naturale Paneveggio-Pale di San Martino

Other Summer Activities
Indoor and outdoor swimming • Tennis • Minigolf • Cinema • Mountain climbing schools • Fishing • Horseback riding • Hang gliding • Camping • and more.

SAN MARTINO DI CASTROZZA

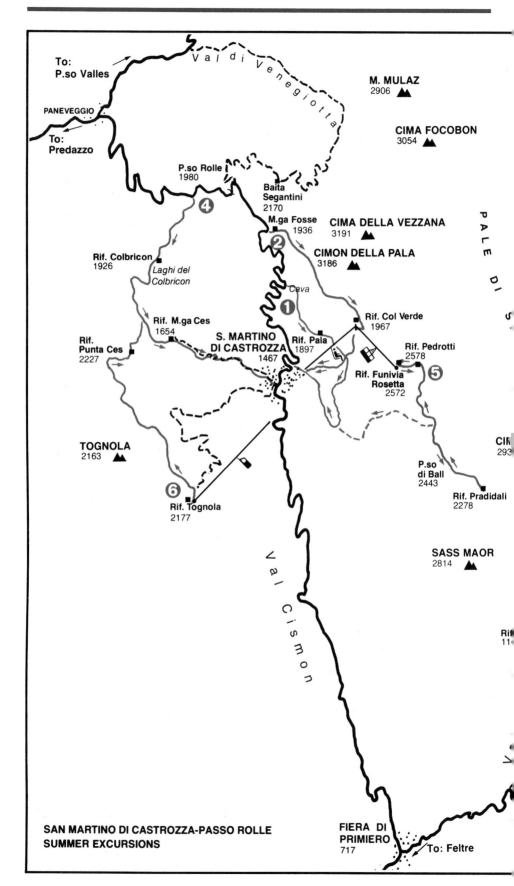

SAN MARTINO DI CASTROZZA

LEGEND

~~ **Roads**

~~ **Private, Restricted, and/or Unpaved Roads**

○ **Autostrada Exits**

↯ **Passes**

▲ **Mountains**

■ **Rifugio**

• **Top Lift Station**

🚡 **Cable Cars**

🚠 **Gondolas**

🚡 **Chairlift**

① **Route Number**

~~ **Trail**

-- **Alternate Trail**

← **Direction of Travel on Trail**

T I N O

DUSTA

Rif. Treviso
1630

C a n a l i

M.ga Canali

③

al ■

To: Agordo

P.so Cereda
1361

0   1   2 km.

Descending to San Martino di Castrozza

Using iron cables on the Pale

Cerastium uniflorum

SAN MARTINO DI CASTROZZA

OUTINGS AND EXCURSIONS

The following are only a few ideas for exploring this vast scenic area. It includes the entire Val Cismon from Fiera di Primiero through San Martino to Passo Rolle, and also the western approach to the Passo Rolle beginning at the Parco Naturale Paneveggio-Pale di San Martino.

Half-day Drives
San Martino-Valle dei Canali: A delightful forested valley with rushing streams and mountain views.

San Martino-Falcade: A scenic drive with views of the Pale. Falcade is a pleasant village with old farmhouses.

San Martino-Fiera-Gosaldo: A lovely valley drive with a large village and many small hamlets. Mountain views are particularly striking near Gosaldo.

View Panoramas
Passo Rolle
Passo Valles
Passo Rolle to Baita Segantini

Observation deck, Rosetta lift

Rambles
Around San Martino and Fiera to enjoy the atmosphere of these villages.

Walk on the side streets of San Martino and meander below the Pale.

Wander in the Valle dei Canali to enjoy forests, rivers and mountains.

Park your car at the entrance to Val di Venegiotta; stroll into the quiet pastoral valley beneath the towering Cimon della Pala.

Using Lifts
Rosetta lift: Fabulous panoramic view over San Martino and back into the heart of the mountain tundra of the Pale.

Tognola lift: Wonderful view of San Martino and the entire Pale di San Martino.

SAN MARTINO DI CASTROZZA

WALKS AND HIKES

There is a range of hiking grades in this area so it is important to know your own capabilities and to plan your itineraries carefully. The walks and hikes near the Pale are well marked but tend to be quite challenging as the trails go over rock and some require use of a Via Ferrata. Trails on the west side of the Val Cismon—the Tognola area—and some near the Passo Rolle are easier as they cross meadows and often meander through woods.

Maps: 1:50,000: Tabacco #4, Kompass Pale di San Martino #76; 1:25,000: Geo Pale di San Martino #10.

ROUTE ❶—CAVA TO RIFUGIO PALA TO SAN MARTINO
A pleasant walk through woods with views of the west side of the Val Cismon.

Distance: 3 to 4 km one way.
Time Required: 2 to 3 hrs one way.
Grade: Moderate.
Special Considerations: This is a one-way route so you must plan your transportation back to the beginning point.

Starting Point: This is somewhat difficult to find. Just before arriving in San Martino from Passo Rolle, you will see a small parking spot along the east side of the road. About 100 meters below this, between roadside markers 90.8 and 90.9, look for a signpost marked with trail #725.

You first walk through a forest on a well-marked trail and cross two stream beds (dry in late summer). Then you descend sharply and, at the bottom of a landslide, you may observe interesting geological layers above. Now you ascend to a clearing where you have views above of the Pale. Continue down to Rifugio Malga Pala. From the rifugio stay on trail #725 and after a short way you have a choice. Trail #725 gradually descends to intersect a lane from San Martino; or take a steeper, more direct way through the forest on trail #701 under the lift to the village.

ROUTE ❷—MALGA FOSSE TO RIFUGIO COL VERDE TO SAN MARTINO
A walk high above the valley with striking views of San Martino and the Pale.

Distance: About 5½ km one way.
Time Required: 2 to 3 hrs one way.
Grade: Intermediate.
Special Considerations:
1. This is a one-way itinerary so you must plan your return transportation.
2. Much of the way is a rocky path.

Starting Point: Malga Fosse is on the main road a few kilometers north of San Martino. Walk a bit south from the malga to trail #712.

This is quite an interesting short itinerary and gives the real flavor of the area. The first part is a rather steep ascent to a forcella; you then begin a short descent to the Rifugio Col Verde. For your return to San Martino, take trail #701.

Alternative: Rifugio Col Verde is the mid-point for the lift ride from San Martino to the Rosetta. You may choose to take the lift from here down to San Martino.

ROUTE ❸—VALLE DEI CANALI TO RIFUGIO TREVISO
A short ascent through woods in spectacular scenery to an ideally sited rifugio.

Distance: 3 to 4 km round trip.
Time Required: Round trip about 3 hrs.
Grade: Intermediate.

Starting Point: From Malga Canali walk along the road on trail #707.

This route, essentially, is all uphill for about 300 meters; however, it is short and the scenery is fabulous. Take your time and you will arrive at the Rifugio Treviso before you know it. The view from here into the south end of the Pale and down to the lovely green valley is an ample reward for your ascent.

SAN MARTINO DI CASTROZZA

ROUTE ④—PASSO ROLLE TO LAGHI DEL COLBRICON TO RIFUGIO MALGA CES TO SAN MARTINO

A gradual ascent to two small lakes with views of the Pale and distant Dolomite peaks; then a descent to San Martino.

Distance: About 7 km one way.
Time Required: About 3 hrs.
Grade: Intermediate.
Special Considerations: This is a one-way itinerary so you must plan accordingly.

Starting Point: On the main road, about 1 km west of the Passo Rolle, look for trail head #348 (near Malga Rolle), continue towards Laghi del Colbricon.

This popular trail ascends through pleasant woods to open country where you find two picturesque alpine lakes—one above the other. You may wish to stop at the cozy Rifugio Colbricon to have a snack and admire the views of the Pale and distant mountains. Your descent is rather steep at first on trail #14, but after a short time you re-enter the woods and arrive at the popular Rifugio Malga Ces. You may plan your arrival time to have either lunch or dinner at the malga, one of the most noted eating spots in the Dolomites. Many people drive here for meals so perhaps you can pre-arrange transportation back to San Martino. However, it is an easy walk along an unpaved road from Rifugio Malga Ces to San Martino.

Rifugio Pradidali, Pale di San Martino

ROUTE ⑤—ROSETTA LIFT: ROSETTA TO RIFUGIO PRADIDALI AND RETURN TO ROSETTA

A challenging classic hike in the rocky world of the Pale.

Distance: About 10 km.
Time Required: About 6 hrs.
Elevation: Starting point 2572m; Rifugio Pradidali 2278m.
Change in Elevation: Gain of about 500m; Loss of about 500m.
Grade: Difficult to Expert.
Special Considerations:
1. This is a long route and should be started early.
2. Weather can change, so obtain a forecast and be prepared.
3. Snow and ice may be encountered.
4. There is exposure in parts but with well-placed fixed cables for support.
5. Be sure of lift schedules and that rifugi are open.
6. Carry water and a snack.

Starting Point: Take the two stage lift to the top of the Rosetta and then trail #701 towards Rifugio Pedrotti.

The view from the rifugio at the top of the lift is thrilling, so pause here before you begin the route. Walk to Rifugio Pedrotti, a few hundred meters beyond over the level rock table land; from here take trail #702. Continue over the rocky plateau before beginning a switchback

SAN MARTINO DI CASTROZZA

descent of nearly 300 meters. The drama increases as more towers of the Pale appear ahead and above you. After the descent, you wander over a small grassy ledge and traverse a flank with some exposure; move slowly and take advantage of the fixed cable for support. The vistas are outstanding. You ascend to a rocky pass, Passo di Ball, where there is a view of your destination—Rifugio Pradidali. You must descend to the rifugio, a delightful spot for a rest and meal, before you return the same way to the Rosetta lift and back to San Martino.

Alternative: You may choose to return to San Martino on trail #702 from the trail junction on the Rosetta side of the Passo di Ball. This is quite thrilling, but very steep in places, with scree from recent rock slides. Inquire ahead of time about the condition of the trail should you wish to consider this return route.

San Martino di Castrozza and Pale from Tognola

ROUTE ⑥—TOGNOLA TO RIFUGIO PUNTA CES TO SAN MARTINO
A long and varied trail over open terrain and through woods, with continual views of the Pale and valley.

Distance: About 11 km.
Time Required: About 7 hrs.
Elevation: Starting point 2177m; Rifugio Punta Ces 2227m.
Change in elevation: Gain of about 350m; Loss of about 800m to Rifugio Malga Ces, 1000m to San Martino.
Grade: Intermediate to Difficult.
Special Considerations:
1. **Verify that lifts are operating and rifugi are open.**
2. **Carry water and a snack.**
3. **It is best to do this route in clear weather.**

Starting Point: Take the Tognola lift. From the top wander through a large open bowl towards a small malga that can be seen below to the northwest.

The views from the top are wonderful so enjoy them before starting your gentle descent to the malga. From the malga the way ahead on trail #9 undulates up and down, mostly in the clear, but also through lovely wooded stretches where wildflowers abound. Use your map as there are several options for a shorter return to San Martino should you wish not to negotiate the fairly steep ascent to Rifugio Punta Ces. However, the views are spectacular and the reward is well worth the trek to reach the rifugio. The descent from here on trail #10 is also steep. You end up at Rifugio Malga Ces where you can enjoy a snack before finishing the return to San Martino as in Route 4.

NORTHEAST

Lago di Misurina, Sorapiss in background

NORTHEAST

Cortina and the Sesto (Sexten) make up one vast and diversified travel area within the Northeast district. Here is some of the most stupendous mountain, lake and valley scenery in the Dolomites. Cortina is an important international resort offering every summer recreation opportunity. The Sesto is a large mountainous area surrounded by picturesque valleys with many charming Tyrolean villages. It contains an awesome collection of towering Dolomite peaks and spires. Both Cortina and the Sesto are noted for their hiking and mountaineering possibilities and can be toured interchangeably. Many hiking itineraries lead through World War I battle zones.

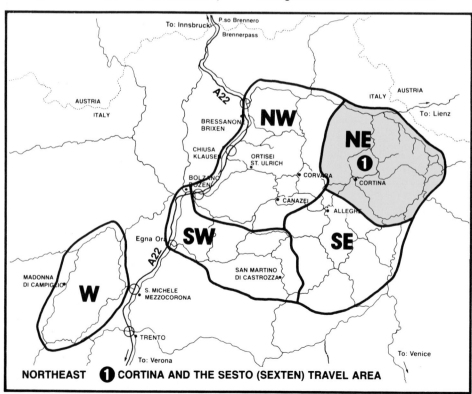

NORTHEAST **1** CORTINA AND THE SESTO (SEXTEN) TRAVEL AREA

Pastoral countryside around Cortina

IMPORTANT FEATURES
Regions: Veneto and Trentino-Alto Adige (Südtirol)
Provinces: Belluno and Bolzano (Bozen)
Valleys: Val d'Ampezzo, Val Boite, Val Pusteria (Pustertal), Val di Landro (Höhlensteintal), Val di Sesto (Sextental)
Villages: Cortina d'Ampezzo, San Vito di Cadore, Pieve di Cadore, Auronzo, Dobbiaco (Toblach), San Candido (Innichen), Sesto (Sexten)
Mountains: Tofane, Cristallo, Sorapiss, Antelao, Croda da Lago, Tre Cime di Lavaredo (Drei Zinnen), Tre Scarperi (Dreischuster Sp.), Cadini, Croda Rossa di Sesto (Sextener Rotwand), Cima Undici (Elferkofel), Croda dei Toni (Zwölferkofel), Popera
Lakes: Misurina, Braies, Landro, Dobbiaco

Tre Cime di Lavaredo

CORTINA AND THE SESTO (SEXTEN)

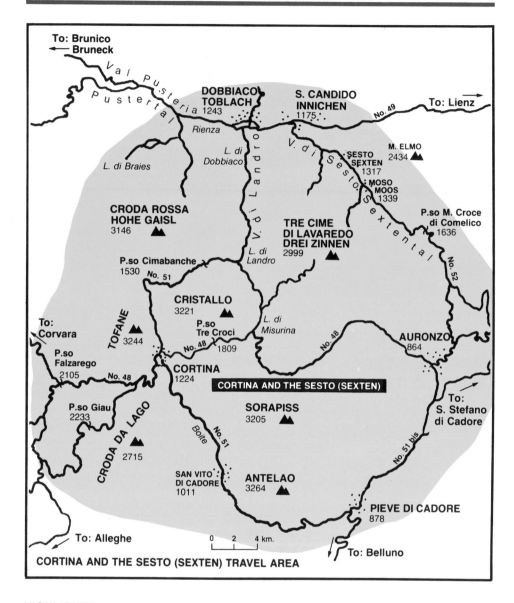

CORTINA AND THE SESTO (SEXTEN) TRAVEL AREA

Map labels:
To: Brunico / Bruneck
Val Pusteria / Pustertal
DOBBIACO TOBLACH 1243
S. CANDIDO INNICHEN 1175
No. 49
To: Lienz
Rienza
L. di Dobbiaco
L. di Braies
V. di Landro
V. di Sesto / Sextental
M. ELMO 2434
SESTO SEXTEN 1317
MOSO MOOS 1339
P.so M. Croce di Comelico 1636
CRODA ROSSA HOHE GAISL 3146
TRE CIME DI LAVAREDO DREI ZINNEN 2999
P.so Cimabanche 1530
No. 51
L. di Landro
No. 52
CRISTALLO 3221
To: Corvara
TOFANE 3244
P.so Tre Croci 1809
L. di Misurina
No. 48
AURONZO 864
P.so Falzarego 2105
No. 48
CORTINA 1224
No. 48
CORTINA AND THE SESTO (SEXTEN)
To: S. Stefano di Cadore
P.so Giau 2233
SORAPISS 3205
CRODA DA LAGO 2715
Boite
No. 51
No. 51 bis
SAN VITO DI CADORE 1011
ANTELAO 3264
PIEVE DI CADORE 878
To: Alleghe
0 2 4 km.
To: Belluno

HIGHLIGHTS

The Cortina-Sesto area is one of the most scenic and varied holiday spots in all the Alps. Amidst the grandeur of soaring and dramatic peaks, there are walks, hikes, museums, villages, hamlets, good hotels, restaurants and deluxe shopping to please everyone.

Cortina is magnificently situated in a sunny amphitheater, circled by soft green meadows and towering mountains. Sunrises and sunsets are splendid when the play of light reflects off the mountain walls. The village offers a variety of tourist facilities from deluxe hotels and comfortable bed and breakfasts (meuble), to roomy apartments. All are set within the village center or nestled in the surrounding pastoral countryside.

The Sesto is a wild and rugged mountain district of exceptional beauty. It is also a natural park, Parco Naturale Dolomiti di Sesto, and is just a 30-minute drive northeast of Cortina. This park is a mountain hiker's paradise with countless extraordinarily shaped peaks and remote valleys to explore. Some of the peaceful valleys that surround it have sparkling Tyrolean villages with quiet alberghi, pensioni and garni.

CORTINA AND THE SESTO (SEXTEN)

Cortina panorama, Sorapiss and Antelao in background

HOW TO ARRIVE

By Air:
International airports in Munich, Milan, Venice, or smaller airports in Verona and Innsbruck.

By Rail:
Nearest stations: Dobbiaco or Calalzo, then transfer by bus or car to your final destination.

By Bus:
Direct service from Munich and Milan to Cortina in the popular tourist months. Local service from important cities surrounding the Dolomites, including Venice.

By Car to Cortina:

From West, North:	Exit A22 at Bressanone. Take No. 49 to Dobbiaco, then south on No. 51 to Cortina. Bressanone exit to Cortina: about 1½ hrs.
	Or, if you are already in the Dolomites, use local roads over Passo Gardena, Passo Sella or Passo Pordoi to Passo Falzarego. Then continue to Cortina. Passo Sella to Cortina: about 1 hr.
From East: Southeast:	Take No. 51 from near Pieve di Cadore directly to Cortina. Pieve to Cortina: about 30 min.
	Or, use highway No. 52 from Santo Stefano di Cadore, turning west on No. 48 to Auronzo and continuing to Cortina. Santo Stefano to Cortina: about 1½ hrs.

By Car to the Sesto mountain district:

From West, North:	Exit A22 at Bressanone and drive to Dobbiaco as described above. Bressanone exit to Dobbiaco; about 1 hr. From Dobbiaco you can proceed south on No. 51 into the Val di Landro, or, continue to San Candido turning southeast on No. 52 into the Val di Sesto.
	Dobbiaco to the Sesto trailheads in the Val di Landro: about 15 min. Dobbiaco through San Candido to the villages of Sesto and Moso and the nearby trailheads in the Val di Sesto: about 30 min.
	Or, use local roads from Cortina to the trailheads near Lago di Misurina: Cortina to Lago di Misurina: about 30 min.
From East, South:	From Santo Stefano di Cadore take No. 52 to Sesto or Moso in the Val di Sesto. Santo Stefano to Moso: about 45 min.
	Or, branch west from No. 51 bis to No. 48 and drive through Auronzo, continuing to Lago di Misurina. There are trailheads before reaching the lake and near the lake. Junction of No. 51 bis and No. 48 to Lago di Misurina: about 45 min.

Village of Cortina d'Ampezzo

APPROACHES

To Cortina

Nearly any approach to Cortina is magnificent. If you are driving from the Val Pusteria in the north, turn south at Dobbiaco onto highway No. 51. After about 14 kilometers branch right at the Y and follow the road into Cortina. If you are not in a hurry, and particularly if you are traveling in the morning, take the left hand turn at the Y for the most scenic trip to Cortina, by way of Lago di Misurina and the Passo Tre Croci. If you are already in the Dolomites and coming to Cortina from the west, drive over Passo Falzarego. This is a beautiful way to approach Cortina any time of day.

From the east and southeast take No. 51 through the Val Boite. You can also go through Auronzo, but the former is more attractive. From the southwest you can either follow the road to Passo Falzarego or Passo Giau. The drive over Passo Giau is spectacular but has many hairpin turns.

To Sesto (Sexten)

The villages of Dobbiaco (Toblach) and San Candido (Innichen) are ideal bases for touring the Sesto district. The smaller villages of Sesto (Sexten) and Moso (Moos), in the Val di Sesto, are particularly good for hiking access into the eastern part of the district. From Moso you can drive southwest into the Val Fiscalina and then begin your hiking right at the base of the mountains. A good approach to the southern and western parts

of the district is to drive from Lago di Misurina to Rifugio Auronzo. This is also the easiest starting point for a walk to the famous Tre Cime di Lavaredo. There are also trailheads into the Sesto from the Val di Landro and the road connecting Auronzo and the Passo Tre Croci.

SETTING

Cortina

Cortina, nestled in lush green meadows, is encircled by extraordinarily beautiful mountains towering 2000 meters above the village. Beginning a visual tour west of the village you see the three famous pyramids of the Tofane. Northeast of the Tofane group is the block-like red rock of the Croda Rossa, then the markedly stratified Cristallo with adjoining Pomagagnon. Continuing the circle to the east and southeast of the village are the massive Sorapiss and the classically shaped Antelao.

South and southwest of Cortina you see a fascinating combination of mountain forms: a series of distinctly shaped towers, pinnacles and ridges rise from the base of an upwardly tilted plateau. First is the lonely Becco di Mezzodì, followed by the Croda da Lago, which looks like the spine of a giant dinosaur, then the table-like Lastoni di Formin, and finally the individual stone towers of the Cinque Torri standing like archaeological ruins.

CORTINA AND THE SESTO (SEXTEN)

Completing this 360° visual tour of Cortina and its environs is the Passo Falzarego, the junction point of three important valleys. Perched above the passo, and accessible by a cable car operating most of the year, is the Rifugio Lagazuoi. Here are some of the finest views in all the Dolomites.

The Sesto (Sexten)
The mountains of the Sesto rise abruptly from the rocky tundra plateaus, deep verdant valleys and highly eroded cliffs that surround them. There are innumerable jagged peaks with distinctive shape and character such as Tre Cime di Lavaredo (Drei Zinnen), Tre Scarperi (Dreischuster Sp.), and Croda dei Toni (Zwölferkofel).

Valleys on all sides border this mountain district. Smaller valleys—some green and forested, others rocky and inhospitable—penetrate deep into the mountain wilderness. On the northeast is the Val di Sesto, one of the most enchanting of all Dolomite valleys. It has a pastoral charm with white Tyrolean villages and breathtaking views

Peaks of the Sesto

into the mountains. Together with the Val Comelico, it forms the northeastern border of the Dolomites.

The forested Val d'Ansiei, from Auronzo to the Passo Tre Croci, forms the Sesto's southern border. Along the western side of the district are Lago di Misurina with postcard views of Tre Cime di Lavaredo and Sorapiss, and Lago di Landro with the magnificent north walls of Cristallo and Popena in the background. On the north, the district is bordered by the important commercial Val Pusteria which provides the major access by road and rail to this mountain paradise.

Croda da Lago

Caryophyllaceae

MAJOR ROAD PASSES INTO THE AREA	Elevations
Passo Falzarego	2105m
Passo Tre Croci	1809m
Passo Giau	2233m
Passo Cimabanche	1530m

CORTINA AND THE SESTO (SEXTEN)

Haystacks, Val di Sesto

HISTORY

Early History

The prehistory of this fascinating travel area is similar to that of the rest of the northern Dolomites. Archaeological finds verify the existence of ancient seasonal settlements. In 1985, the grave of a hunter dating from the Mesolithic Age was found near Cortina, not far from the southern base of the Lastoni di Formin at Mondeval de Sora (2150m). His 7000 year-old bones were completely intact and accompanied by deer antlers and stone artifacts.

About 500 B.C., the Celts moved into the area followed by the Romans who conquered in 15 B.C., then governed all the Alps. During their 500-year rule, the Romans constructed a military road through the Val Pusteria continuing past San Candido to near Lienz. Traces of stone road markers are extant near Brunico and San Candido. By the end of the Roman period the Ampezzano dialect of Ladin had evolved in Cortina; this dialect sounds quite different from the Ladin spoken in the valleys surrounding the Gruppo Sella.

After the fall of the Roman Empire in the 5th century, Cortina and the Sesto were subjected to differing cultural influences — Cortina more Italian, the Sesto more Tyrolean. These differences are readily apparent today in the architecture, food, and language of the areas.

Cortina after the Romans

Between the 6th and 8th centuries, the Lombards swept over northern Italy and left their mark on Cortina. Traces of Lombardian influence are still evident in the names of some of the oldest families in the valley. For example, a common Lombardian first name, Menegardo, is now the family name, Menardi.

The centuries-old system of land management, known as the Regole d'Ampezzo, is a tradition handed down from father to son since Celtic times. The earliest written documents are in Latin and date from 1225. Today, the Regole continues to control most of the farmland and forests around Cortina. (See Land Ownership). Historic coats of arms of the Regole decorate the outside of Cortina's Regole Museum.

The dukedoms of Cadore, Treviso, and Friuli (to the east and southeast) gradually assumed control over Cortina; however, in 1338, the Statuto Cadorino tempered these controls and guaranteed autonomy for the village. In the 15th century, the powerful Venetian Republic expanded and encompassed Cortina (1420) but reconfirmed the 1338 statuto. Early in the 16th century, conflicts between the great Hapsburg Emperor Maximilian I and the Venetian Republic resulted in Cortina being transferred to the Hapsburg Empire in 1511. The village was given considerable independence and maintained her cultural identity during the

Hapsburg period. For years Cortina was a favorite resort of the Hapsburg aristocracy.

Sesto after the Romans

The historical development of the Sesto following the Roman and Lombard eras differed from Cortina and was more closely linked to that of the northwestern Dolomite valleys. Around the 7th century, the Bavarians moved into and Germanized the Val Pusteria. In the following century, during the early Christian monastic movement, the Benedictine monks constructed a monastery (769) in San Candido. This lovely old Romanesque structure, now the Museo della Collegiata, is the oldest monastery in the Dolomites. Later, the Sesto came under the sphere of the Bishopric of Bressanone, followed by the Counts of Gorizia until about 1500 when it passed to the Hapsburgs.

Cortina and the Sesto from 16th Century to WWI

By the early 16th century, both Cortina and the Sesto belonged to the Hapsburgs. The situation remained stable until World War I, except for a brief time during the Napoleonic period. In 1809 French and Bavarian troops entered the Ampezzo valley and caused great destruction. After the fall of Napoleon, Cortina, Sesto, and all the former Hapsburg-held Dolomite regions again returned to the Austro-Hungarian Empire.

During World War I, the fighting was particularly bloody in this area because the border between Italy and the Austro-Hungarian Empire passed through the Sesto, continuing just south of Cortina and through the Dolomites to the southwest. When the war began in 1914, soldiers from Cortina and the Sesto fought for Austria. By mid-1915, after Italy entered the war, the Austrian-Italian main front was realigned in some places—the Sesto remained behind the Austrian line but Cortina was now within the Italian zone. This division was to have extraordinary effects on the local people. A young Cortina man, for example, was sent to the Russian front at the outbreak of the war to fight for Austria. When he returned in 1915, he found that his house with his wife and new-born child was now in the Italian zone. He was able to see them from the Austrian positions, just five kilometers from his home, but the family was not reunited for 2½ years. Along the front, from the Val di Sesto to Passo Falzarego, there are countless similar stories. By the end of 1917, the Austrians had regained Cortina. However, after the war Cortina and the Sesto, along with the rest of what had been the Austrian Dolomites, were ceded to Italy.

Passo Giau

Corso and historic campanile, Cortina

CORTINA AND THE SESTO (SEXTEN)

Alpine Guides of Cortina, 1901

ECONOMY

The local economy of Cortina centers around thriving summer and winter tourism—an industry that has continued to grow and expand since the 19th century. In the 1860s English, Austrian and German scientists and climbers came to explore and scale the many peaks, using local guides. The Viennese climber, Paul Grohmann, conquered the highest summits around Cortina between 1862 and 1865. His book *Wanderungen in der Dolomiten* (1877) publicized the Dolomites as did several books in English by F.F. Tuckett, John Ball and Amelia Edwards.

In 1871, a railroad through the Val Pusteria

was completed. It ran from the Valle Isarco to Lienz, with a station at Dobbiaco. Some of the early hotels were also built during this period including the Menardi, Silvano, des Alpes, and Hotel Cortina. When the Dolomite Road was completed in 1909, the role of Cortina as an international resort was established.

Cortina held its first international ski competition in 1937. World War II temporarily interrupted the growth of winter tourism. In 1956 Cortina hosted the Winter Olympics; since then the popularity of winter sports has resulted in a major boost to tourism.

The Sesto also draws mountain enthusiasts from around the world. Summer visitors walk, hike and climb, or attend the annual music festival honoring Gustav Mahler; in winter they enjoy cross-country skiing and many other sports.

For both Cortina and the Sesto agriculture continues to be a contributing factor to the economy. There are also a number of special handicrafts, including wood mosaics and artistic works in metal. Furniture and ski equipment are also made locally.

GEOLOGY

The mountains of Cortina and the Sesto lie within the eastern Dolomites; their geology and strata are somewhat different from the Dolomites west of the Cordevole river. Significant layers of the fossil-rich Dolomia Principale and Raibl Formation (more than 200 million years old) are found in many of these mountains such as the Tofane, Cristallo, Sorapiss, Croda

Rossa and Croda da Lago. An amazing collection of fossils from these formations, representing a lifetime of collecting by geologist Rinaldo Zardini (1902-1988), can be seen in the Regole museum in Cortina.

Campanulaceae

GEOGRAPHIC FEATURES

Mountain Groups and Their Major Peaks:
Cortina

Tofane	Summit Height
Tofana di Rozes	3225m
Tofana di Mezzo	3244m
Tofana di Dentro	3238m
Croda Rossa	3146m
Cristallo	3221m
Sorapiss	3205m
Antelao	3264m
Croda da Lago	2715m

Sesto (Sexten)

Tre Cime di Lavaredo (Drei Zinnen)	2999m
Tre Scarperi (Dreischuster Sp.)	3145m
Cadini	2839m
Paterno (Paternkofel)	2744m
Croda Rossa di Sesto (Sextener Rotwand)	2965m
Cima Undici (Elferkofel)	3092m
Croda dei Toni or Cima Dodici (Zwölferkofel)	3094m
Popera	3046m

Other Features in Cortina and the Sesto:
Val di Sesto (Sextental)
Val Fiscalina (Fischleintal)
Val di Landro (Höhlensteintal)
Val Boite
Lago di Misurina
Lago di Braies (Pragser Wildsee)
Lago di Dobbiaco (Toblachersee)
Lago di Landro (Dürrensee)
Rienza River
Boite River

CORTINA AND THE SESTO (SEXTEN)

MAJOR VILLAGES

Cortina, population 8,000, is a world-renowned international resort with a friendly and relaxed Italian atmosphere. Mornings and late afternoons are busy in the village center as shoppers explore the car-less main street, the *Corso*. Here there are antique stores, sport shops and elegant boutiques stocked with the latest Italian fashions. At the heart of the Corso is a grand old baroque church with a 75-meter high campanile that towers over the village. Restaurants and cafés line the Corso and its intersecting streets.

The small villages of **San Vito di Cadore** and **Borca** nearby in the Val Boite, are peaceful and well worth a visit for a change of pace from bustling Cortina.

Pieve di Cadore, population 4,200, is distinctly Italian, very busy, and prettily placed. Titian, the great Renaissance painter, was born here.

Dobbiaco (Toblach), population 2,700, in the Val Pusteria, is an attractive and thriving Tyrolean vacation base for touring the Sesto, Cortina and other areas nearby, such as Lago di Braies.

San Candido (Innichen), population 3,000, at the entrance of the Val di Sesto, is of ancient historic importance and well worth a visit.

Sesto (Sexten), population 1,800, is a quiet Tyrolean village in a scenic valley of the same name and is a good place from which to tour the Sesto. Within walking distance is **Moso (Moos)**, another small charming village. Each of these villages has a few large hotels; generally, however, there are small white stuccoed garni and pensioni adorned with stencils and frescoes. Window boxes are ablaze with colorful geraniums and petunias.

Espresso time, Cortina

APPROXIMATE DRIVING TIME TO MAJOR CENTERS

	From Cortina	Sesto
Milan	5 hrs	4½ hrs
Munich	4 hrs	3½ hrs
Salzburg	4 hrs	3½ hrs
Innsbruck	2½ hrs	2 hrs
Lake Garda	3½ hrs	3 hrs
Venice	2½ hrs	3 hrs
Verona	2½ hrs	3 hrs
Florence	5 hrs	5 ½ hrs
Rome	8 hrs	8½ hrs

PRINCIPAL LANGUAGES: Italian and Ladin in Cortina. German and Italian in the Sesto.

CORTINA AND THE SESTO (SEXTEN)

Fountain, Pieve di Cadore

THINGS TO DO AND SEE

Museums, Churches, Buildings

Cortina:
Museo de ra Regoles (ethnographical and paleontological museum in the Ciasa de ra Regoles).
Pinacoteca Rimoldi (picture gallery in the Ciasa de ra Regoles).
Parish church, 1775, and adjoining campanile.

Pieve di Cadore:
Titian's home (Born in Pieve, 1487, died in Venice, 1576).
Parish Church—inside is a painting by Titian.
Magnifica Comunità del Cadore, building in the village center.
Cadore Museum.

Dobbiaco (Toblach):
Parish Church (1782)

San Candido (Innichen):
Museo Etnografico
Museo della Collegiata (Romanesque church, 769)
Duomo di San Candido

Sesto (Sexten):
Rudolf Stolz Museum (local painter, 1874-1960)

Characteristic Old Houses/Villages
Cortina and environs
Dobbiaco (Toblach)
San Candido (Innichen)

Other Summer Activities
Indoor and outdoor swimming • Tennis • Minigolf • Cinema • Mountain climbing schools • Fishing • Ice skating • Horseback riding • Camping • Music Festivals • and more.

CORTINA AND THE SESTO (SEXTEN)

OUTINGS AND EXCURSIONS

This is an immense area with scenic excursions by car to hamlets and mountain lakes, pastoral rambles through villages and farmlands and unparalleled panoramas from the tops of lifts.

CORTINA

Half-day Drives
Cortina-Lago di Misurina-Rifugio Auronzo: A beautiful lake, mountain scenery, and a large attractively placed rifugio.

Cortina-Lago di Braies: A small mountain lake at the end of a verdant peaceful valley.

Cortina-San Vito di Cadore-Pieve di Cadore: Through a lovely valley with villages to an important town for sightseeing.

View Panoramas
Passo Tre Croci
Passo Giau
Passo Falzarego

Rambles
Around Cortina on both sides of the Boite River.

Village of San Vito di Cadore.

Around Lago di Braies and Lago di Misurina.

Drive to Malga Ra Stua just north of Cortina, then wander in this secluded pastoral setting.

CORTINA LIFTS
Tofane 3-stage lift: From Cortina. Take the 3-stage lift to the summit—one of the "musts" on every visitors' list. Breathtaking views of Cortina and the mountain amphitheater.

Lagazuoi lift: From Passo Falzarego. A panorama many call the best in the Dolomites. In addition to the mountains near Cortina, you see in the distance Civetta, Pelmo, Marmolada, Gruppo Sella, and the Pale di San Martino. The entire area around the upper lift station is an historic World War I battle zone.

Faloria lift: From Cortina. Lovely vistas of Cortina, the Tofane, and Cristallo.

Cinque Torri lift: From the road to Passo Falzarego. For close-up views of the surrounding mountains.

Cristallo lift: From Cap. Rio Gere. Views of Cortina and the Sesto Dolomites.

SESTO (SEXTEN)

Half-day Drives
Val di Sesto to enjoy the charm of villages and views into the heart of the Sesto mountains.

Val Pusteria to see Dobbiaco and San Candido.

Rambles
Around and between Sesto and Moso (Moos) in the Val di Sesto—one of the most scenic valleys in the Dolomites.

Wander through the small peaceful Val Fiscalina towards the mountains.

SESTO (SEXTEN) LIFTS
Val Fiscalina lift: From Moso towards Croda Rossa di Sesto. Lovely meadows surround the upper lift station and there are views into the Sesto mountains.

Monte Elmo lift: From village of Sesto. Panoramas of the Sesto mountains.

CORTINA AND THE SESTO (SEXTEN)

Panorama from Rifugio Lagazuoi, Pelmo and Civetta in distance

Lago di Landro, Cristallo in background

CORTINA AND THE SESTO (SEXTEN)

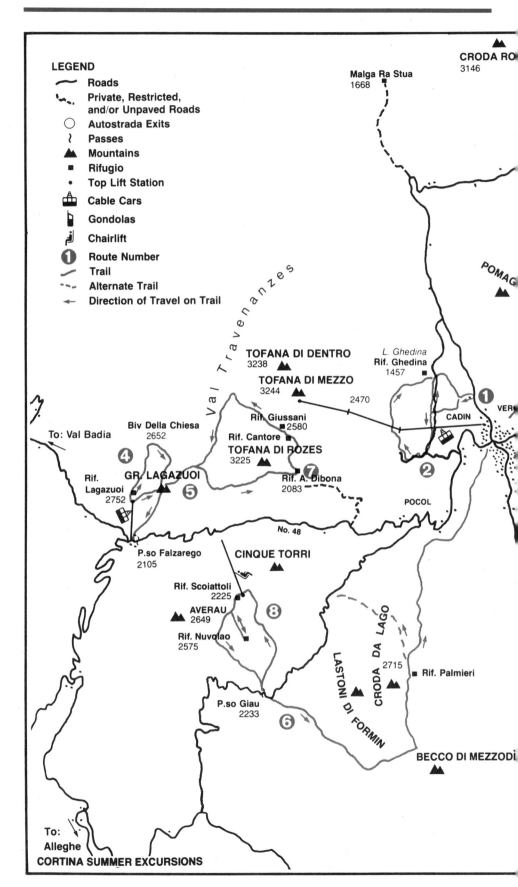

CORTINA AND THE SESTO (SEXTEN)

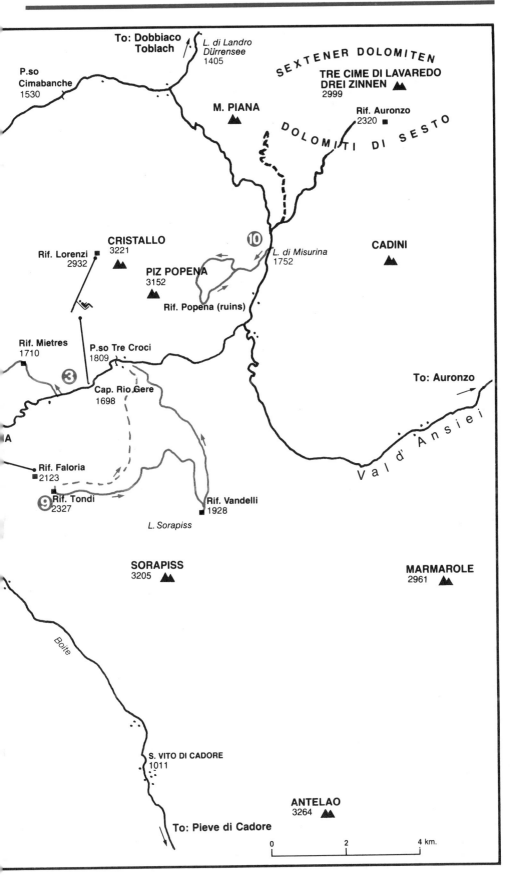

To: Dobbiaco
Toblach

L. di Landro
Dürrensee
1405

SEXTENER DOLOMITEN

TRE CIME DI LAVAREDO
DREI ZINNEN
2999

P.so
Cimabanche
1530

M. PIANA

Rif. Auronzo
2320

DOLOMITI DI SESTO

CRISTALLO
3221

Rif. Lorenzi
2932

PIZ POPENA
3152

⑩

L. di Misurina
1752

CADINI

Rif. Popena (ruins)

Rif. Mietres
1710

P.so Tre Croci
1809

③

To: Auronzo

Cap. Rio Gere
1698

A

Rif. Faloria
2123

Val d'Ansiei

⑨ Rif. Tondi
2327

Rif. Vandelli
1928

L. Sorapiss

SORAPISS
3205

MARMAROLE
2961

Boite

S. VITO DI CADORE
1011

ANTELAO
3264

To: Pieve di Cadore

0   2   4 km.

CORTINA AND THE SESTO (SEXTEN)

WALKS AND HIKES

There is an extraordinary variety of walks and hikes in this famous alpine area and through every imaginable type of terrain and setting. The following is just a sampling; routes are divided between Cortina and Sesto. The Sesto trailheads are accessible from the roads that surround this mountain district. It is specifically noted when particular routes are through portions of World War I battle zones. Some itineraries require the use of uphill lifts.

CORTINA

Cortina Maps:
1:50,000: Tabacco #1, Kompass Cortina #55, F&B Cortina #5.
1:25,000: Geo #1 Cortina, Tabacco #03.

ROUTE ❶ — CORTINA (CADEMAI) TO RIFUGIO GHEDINA LOOP

A gradual ascent through rural Cortina, then a level walk through woods to a small secluded lake and rifugio.

Distance: 4 to 5 km loop.   Time Required: 2 to 3 hrs.   Grade: Moderate.

Starting Point: Cademai neighborhood of Cortina. Look for road (and trail #415) west towards Cadin and Lago Ghedina.

After crossing the Boite River in the Cademai neighborhood of Cortina, take trail #415 beside villas and farmhouses, turning left to Cadelverzo. From here follow trail #450 uphill into a wooded area to the intersecting road. Turn right and walk along the road through woods until you reach the small secluded Lago Ghedina; the charming Rifugio Ghedina is on the shoreline. You may then circle back through open rural countryside.

Towards Ristorante Pietofana

ROUTE ❷ — COLFIERE TO RISTORANTE PIETOFANA TO LAGO GHEDINA LOOP

A walk through meadows and woods, ending at a picturesque small lake.

Distance: 7 to 8 km loop.   Time Required: About 4 hrs.   Grade: Moderate.

Starting Point: Drive past Colfiere—about 3 km west of the village center to road junction. Park your car and begin your walk following the branch of the road which goes uphill—this is also trail #407.

As you gradually ascend the road, the Tofane rises above and the Val Boite appears below on your left. At the Ristorante Pietofana branch right and walk through a small wooded saddle beneath the Tofane lift. You then enter a forest and have a fairly steep descent before reaching the enchanting Lago Ghedina. Loop back on the road—this is trail #414.

ROUTE ❸ — CAP. RIO GERE TO RIFUGIO MIETRES TO VEROCAI

An easy descent through woods to open meadows with views of Cortina and the Tofane.

Distance: About 4 km one way.
Time Required: About 2 hrs one way.
Grade: Moderate.
Special Considerations: This is a one way itinerary.

CORTINA AND THE SESTO (SEXTEN)

Starting Point: Between Cap. Rio Gere and Ristorante Malga Lareto take the unpaved road toward the working malga.

You walk along an unpaved road through a lush forest, to a working malga with livestock, and then through woods to the Rifugio Mietres. From here you descend towards Cortina — ending in the Verocai residential district of the village.

World War I ruins and trail near Bivacco della Chiesa

ROUTE ❹—USING LIFT FROM PASSO FALZAREGO: RIFUGIO LAGAZUOI TO BIVACCO DELLA CHIESA LOOP—A WORLD WAR I ITINERARY

An exciting hike among spires and pinnacles with varied mountain and valley vistas.

Distance: 4 to 5 km loop.
Time Required: About 3 hrs.
Elevation: Starting Point Rifugio Lagazuoi 2752m; Bivacco della Chiesa 2652m.
Change in Elevation: Gain of about 360m; Loss of about 800m.
Grade: Difficult
Special Considerations: There is some exposure on the initial part and the way can be cold and windy. It is possible to encounter snow or ice during certain months.

Starting Point: Park your car at the Passo Falzarego and take the lift to Rifugio Lagazuoi. After admiring the vast panorama from the deck of Rifugio Lagazuoi, start down a wide open slope adjacent to the rifugio. Follow several switchbacks and at the large sign indicating "Armentarola and Falzarego" bear left on trail #20 towards Armentarola.

The first stretch on trail #20 is over a wide and gentle, though rocky, grade to a steep gully below the Lagazuoi Grande ridge. You will pass through World War I ruins and enjoy distant views of the soft green Val Badia, Gruppo Sella and other peaks. Now you ascend on trail #20b up a steep scree gully with some exposure.

The trail wanders around and between pinnacles then up over a crest before reaching the tiny Bivacco della Chiesa. The way to this point is well marked, but the trail is narrow in spots and exposed. War ruins can be spotted in the nearby gullies. The bivacco (a small metal shed) is a resting point for those about to tackle the nearby Via Ferrata. You continue through a small tunnel, over another crest, and following trails #20b and #402, you have an easy walk down to the parking area at Passo Falzarego.

Overnight alternative: Rifugio Lagazuoi (phone 0436-867-303) is one of the most comfortable in the Dolomites — good food and excellent accommodation. You might consider spending the night here to enjoy the late afternoon sunset and early morning sunrise.

CORTINA AND THE SESTO (SEXTEN)

Towards Tofane and Rifugio Dibona

ROUTE ❺—USING LIFT FROM PASSO FALZAREGO: RIFUGIO LAGAZUOI TO RIFUGIO DIBONA—A WORLD WAR I ITINERARY
A spectacular walk beneath the towering walls of the Tofane.

Distance: About 6 km one way.
Time Required: About 3 hrs.
Elevation: Starting point 2752m; Rifugio Dibona 2083m.
Change in Elevation: Gain nil; Loss of about 700m.
Grade: Intermediate.
Special Considerations:
1. **Starting and ending points are separated, so make transportation arrangements.**
2. **Rifugio Dibona is at the end of a rather rough road. Taxis do make the trip if your own car cannot manage it.**

CORTINA AND THE SESTO (SEXTEN)

Starting Point: From Rifugio Lagazuoi, take trail #401 (Alta Via #1) down into the Val Travenanzes.

You immediately descend into the heart of a World War I battle zone and pass beside cut-away galleries constructed during the war. If you look above at the surrounding mountain walls you will see squared openings into this ingenious network of tunnels. Shortly thereafter, you come upon a large directional sign. Branch right on trail #402 towards Forcella Col dei Bos. In a few minutes branch left onto trail #404 at the Forcella Col dei Bos. The remains of trenches and bunkers are everywhere. You break into the open and ahead is the trail you follow beneath the Tofane walls. Unobstructed views to the south toward the Cinque Torri and Croda da Lago are marvelous. You gradually descend until Rifugio Dibona is in sight. The last stretch down is fairly steep, but hikers have made several optional paths from which you may choose.

Trail to Rifugio Palmieri

ROUTE ⑥—PASSO GIAU TO RIFUGIO PALMIERI TO CORTINA
A varied and interesting hike around the Croda da Lago.

Distance: About 14 km one way to Cortina.
Time required: About 7 hrs to Cortina.
Elevation: Starting point 2233m; Rifugio Palmieri 2046m; Cortina 1224m.
Change in elevation: Gain of about 300m; Loss of about 1250m.
Grade: Intermediate.
Special Considerations:
1. Verify that Rifugio Palmieri is open. Carry water and a snack.
2. You finish a long way from the starting point so plan accordingly.

Starting Point: Passo Giau. Take trail #436 (Alta Via 1) towards the east and Forcella Giau.

After reaching Forcella Giau continue on trail #436 beneath the vertical walls of the Lastoni di Formin. You hike over undulating soft terrain with massive boulders all around and wonderful views of Pelmo and Civetta on your right. You will also see the Marmolada and many deep verdant valleys. It was near this site that the prehistoric grave of a hunter was discovered in 1985. The way is rather flat for a while, then gains elevation as you near a small spectacular trail junction at a pass. To the left is the Cortina amphitheater while directly ahead is the imposing Antelao. Turn left on trail #434 for an easy, short descent to Rifugio Palmieri, located beside a small lake below the walls of the Croda da Lago. Take trail #431 from behind the rifugio down to Cortina.

Alternatives: You can return the same way to Passo Giau. Or, you can take trail #434 from behind Rifugio Palmieri to #437 to the road, but it is a rather steep long walk up the road back to Passo Giau.

CORTINA AND THE SESTO (SEXTEN)

View from the top of Tofana di Rozes

ROUTE ❼—AROUND THE TOFANA DI ROZES; RIFUGIO DIBONA TO RIFUGIO GIUSSANI TO VAL TRAVENANZES LOOP—A WORLD WAR I ITINERARY

A strenuous but magnificent mountain trek over rugged tundra between towering mountain walls.

Distance: About 11 km loop.
Time Required: 7 to 8 hrs.
Elevation: Starting point 2083m; Rifugio Giussani 2580m.
Change in Elevation: Gain of about 1000m; Loss of about 1000m.
Grade: Difficult to Expert.
Special Considerations:
1. **There are steep stretches up and down over scree but no serious exposure.**
2. **Fog, clouds, rain or snow can move in fast. Ice may be encountered on the trail so ask about conditions.**
3. **It is a good idea to carry water and food because there are long stretches without rifugi.**

Starting Point: From Rifugio Dibona take trail #403 northwest towards the open scree slope separating the Tofana di Rozes from the Tofana di Mezzo.

From Rifugio Dibona you switchback up a steep scree slope, albeit with good footing, into the heart of the Tofane group. After passing a narrow point at the top of the slope, you see on your left the deserted Rifugio Cantore surrounded by the remains of a World War I encampment. A few minutes later you arrive at the relatively new Rifugio Giussani. Start your descent from here, still on trail #403, over a gentle rock and talus slope separating the Tofana di Rozes from the other Tofane. You finally reach the long Val Travenanzes and intersect trail #404. Turn left and take this trail beneath the Rozes walls ascending to the Forcella Col dei Bos. From here continue on trail #404 to Rifugio Dibona (as described above in Route 5.)

Alternative 1: A less ambitious Intermediate grade program is to simply ascend to and stop at Rifugio Giussani. Explore the World War I ruins around the nearby Rifugio Cantore. Your return descent, the same way to Rifugio Dibona, requires only an hour.

Alternative 2: If you have a clear day you may decide to make your way to the top of the Tofana di Rozes. This trek is steep, over scree and talus slopes, and is only partially marked with blue circles. Route finding is difficult but the view from the top is worth the challenge. It requires two hours for the ascent from Rifugio Giussani. This is an Expert grade itinerary for the strong hiker experienced in climbing. Be sure you have dependable weather and the way is free of snow and ice.

CORTINA AND THE SESTO (SEXTEN)

Relaxing near Rifugio Nuvolau, Gruppo Sella in distance

ROUTE ❽—CINQUE TORRI LIFT: RIFUGIO NUVOLAU TO PASSO GIAU TO CINQUE TORRI LOOP

A justifiably popular walk on one of the most spectacular trails in the area.

Distance: 6 to 7 km loop including trip to Rifugio Nuvolau.
Time Required: 4 to 5 hrs.
Grade: Intermediate.
Special Considerations: Verify lift schedule.

Starting Point: At top of Cinque Torri lift, take the well-marked trail #439 towards Rifugio Averau and Nuvolau.

You begin on trail #439, a wide trail that takes you to the base of Averau. At the junction of trail #452, take #439 for a round-trip diversion up and back to Rifugio Nuvolau where the 360° view is remarkable. Returning to the junction, continue on trail #452 for a beautiful flank walk around Nuvolau towards Passo Giau. Before the passo, trail #443 intersects from the east side of Nuvolau; take this trail back to the Cinque Torri lift. This is an interesting undulating trail among rocks and meadows with views of Cortina, the Sorapiss, Tofane, and Croda da Lago.

Alternatives: You can end your hike at Passo Giau if you have arranged transportation for your return.

ROUTE ❾—FALORIA LIFT: HIKE TO RIFUGIO VANDELLI (SORAPISS) TO PASSO TRE CROCI

An arduous mountain hike on the flanks of the Sorapiss, with spectacular views of the mountains surrounding Cortina, the Tre Cime and other distant peaks.

Distance: 11 to 12 km one way to Passo Tre Croci.
Time Required: 7+ hrs to the passo.
Elevation: Starting point 2123m; High point 2378m; End point 1791m.
Change in Elevation: Gain of about 400m; Loss of about 800m.
Grade: Expert.
Special Considerations:
1. **There are steep and exposed portions.**
2. **This is an itinerary for a strong experienced mountain hiker.**
3. **In spots there is some scrambling and the need for using fixed cables.**
4. **Carry water and snacks.**
5. **Parts are not well-marked.**
6. **Plan for your return as you finish many kilometers from Cortina.**
7. **This itinerary is north-facing and can be cold with patches of snow and ice. It should not be attempted in bad weather or if there is a great deal of snow and ice.**

CORTINA AND THE SESTO (SEXTEN)

Towards Rifugio Vandelli, Sorapiss in distance

Starting Point: Walk up the wide ski slope at the back of the second lift station to Rifugio Tondi. The trail is not well marked until you reach the rifugio. Here you will find the marker for trail #213.

As you walk up this slope, you see expansive vistas of the surrounding mountains and Cortina. Beginning on trail #213 at Rifugio Tondi you walk along a crest with sweeping views below on both sides. After a short descent walk over scree and talus along the flanks of Sorapiss with views of Cristallo and nearby peaks. The footing is tricky in places and the trail is not well marked. If you are lucky, you may see many camosci along this stretch.

After some ups and downs, and traveling along exposed parts using iron cables, you reach the high point of the hike. Here there are stupendous panoramas of Cristallo, the Tre Cime, Lago di Misurina, and Cadini. You have left trail #213 now, and are on trail #223. After a slight bend in the trail, you join with and continue on trail #216 towards Sorapiss. Soon Rifugio Vandelli will be visible ahead, but before arriving you must negotiate a steep snaky descent through a mugo pine forest. Before reaching the rifugio, you see the small Lago di Sorapiss behind it. You have come through an amazing variety of terrain and environment and deserve a rest at the rifugio. The return along the flanks of a steep valley is interesting because you are heading directly towards Cristallo. The last part of the hike is rather long and flat through a lovely forest with glimpses through trees of Cristallo and Popena towering above.

Alternative 1: You may turn back after reaching the high point on trail #216 and follow trail #216 the other way towards Cristallo. You descend at first then ascend to a forcella and finally make a steep descent to meet trail #213 for the return to Passo Tre Croci. Grade: Expert.

Alternative 2: There is a well-marked lower trail #213, reached just before Rifugio Tondi that takes you over easy and pleasant terrain with lots of wild flowers and larch trees. It avoids exposure and any major problem of snow and ice. While the descent is a bit steep at first, you soon join a logging road. Views of Cristallo are very dramatic. Grade: Intermediate.

ROUTE ⑩—LAGO DI MISURINA TO RUINS OF RIFUGIO POPENA LOOP
A marvelous short hike, rich in scenic variety.

Distance: About 6 km loop.
Time Required: About 4½ hrs.
Elevation: Starting point 1752m; Rifugio ruins about 2214m.
Change in Elevation: Gain of about 700m; Loss of about 700m.
Grade: Intermediate to Difficult.

132

CORTINA AND THE SESTO (SEXTEN)

Special Considerations:
1. Carry some water and food with you as there are no rifugi.
2. After the rifugio ruins the way is steep for about 50 meters and at this point there could be snow and ice at certain times of the year.

Starting Point: At the midpoint along the western shore of Lago di Misurina is a large hotel. Walk up about 200 meters behind this hotel on the short ski slope until you meet the well-marked trail #224.

Your ascent on this well-marked trail is through woods with views of the Tre Cime, Lago di Misurina, and many nearby mountain groups. After about an hour you meet a trail joining from the left—this will be your "return" trail. Continue straight ahead on the right-hand trail to complete your ascent to the crest of the ridge. After meandering over the crest you descend into a secluded gentle valley below the Popena. Re-ascend to meet trail #222. Turn left—south—and walk with little elevation gain to the beautifully situated ruins of Rifugio Popena. You are likely to see camosci here. From the rifugio ruins there is a short steep scree portion. Look carefully because there are several switchbacks to choose from and with care you can make this part easier. After a descent of perhaps 50 meters follow trail #222 through shrub and over scree, until you meet trail #224 for your return to the lake shore.

Above Lago di Misurina, Tre Cime di Lavaredo in distance

Lago di Misurina

CORTINA AND THE SESTO (SEXTEN)

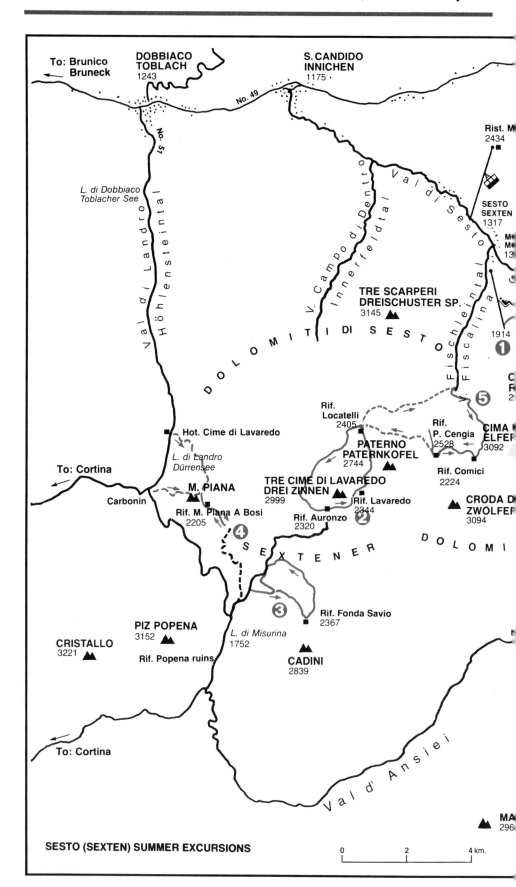

SESTO (SEXTEN) SUMMER EXCURSIONS

134

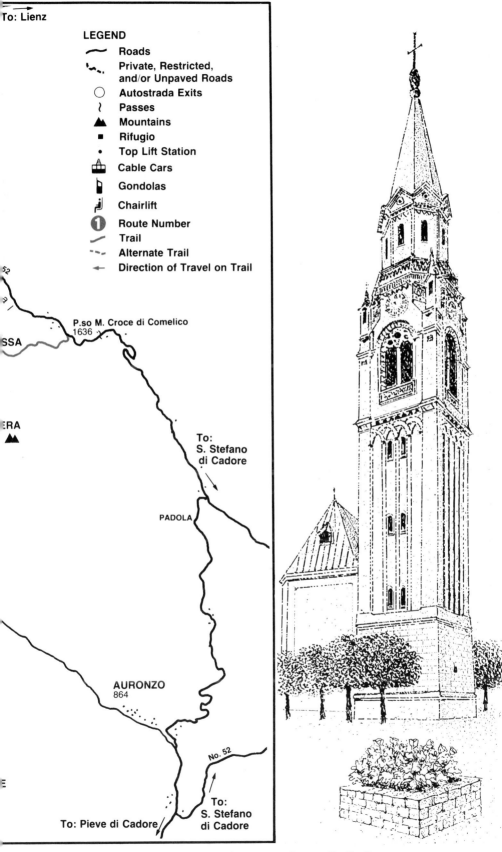

To: Lienz

LEGEND

⌒	Roads
`-..`	Private, Restricted, and/or Unpaved Roads
○	Autostrada Exits
⌇	Passes
▲	Mountains
■	Rifugio
•	Top Lift Station
⛟	Cable Cars
▯	Gondolas
⌿	Chairlift
❶	Route Number
⌒	Trail
`-.-`	Alternate Trail
←	Direction of Travel on Trail

52

P.so M. Croce di Comelico
1636

SSA

ERA
▲▲

To:
S. Stefano
di Cadore

PADOLA

AURONZO
864

No. 52

To: Pieve di Cadore

To:
S. Stefano
di Cadore

Campanile, Cortina

135

SESTO (SEXTEN)

Sesto Maps:
1:50,000: Tabacco #1, Kompass #58, F&B Sextener #10.
1:25,000: Geo #2, Tabacco #010, Wanderkarte Sextener.

ROUTE ❶ —USING MOSO LIFT: HIKE ALONG FLANKS OF CRODA ROSSA DI SESTO TO PASSO MONTE CROCE
A mostly level hike along the flanks of the Croda Rossa then a descent to the passo.

Distance: About 6 km one way to the passo.
Time Required: About 2½ hrs to the passo.
Grade: Moderate.
Special Considerations:
1. Verify lift schedule.
2. Make transportation plans for your return.

Trail towards Croda Rossa di Sesto

Starting Point: Take the lift in the Val Fiscalina. From the top walk up a bit and look for signs and markers for trail #15a.

The lift ride above the green narrow valley is beautiful. At the top there are lovely meadows and rifugi where many people spend hours relaxing and enjoying the views. As you begin your hike, you can see a portion of your route along the flanks of the Croda Rossa. After a short ascent, you begin to walk along the sides of the mountains with pleasant views of the Val di Sesto below and the Austrian Alps in the distance. The walls of the Croda Rossa rise to your right. The path is well marked and before you descend to the passo you will see bunkers and remains from World War II.

ROUTE ❷—RIFUGIO AURONZO TO RIFUGIO LOCATELLI LOOP—A WORLD WAR I ITINERARY
An inspiring loop around the Tre Cime di Lavaredo—one of the classic walks in the Dolomites.

Distance: About 8 km.
Time Required: About 4 hrs.
Grade: Intermediate.

Starting Point: From the parking area of Rifugio Auronzo take trail #101-#104 towards Rifugio Lavaredo.

You will be joined by many other walkers on this popular excursion. Look for mountain climbers on all the faces of the Tre Cime.

CORTINA AND THE SESTO (SEXTEN)

You begin on a wide, well-trodden path with distant views of the spires of the Cadini. Continue to Rifugio Lavaredo. At a broad pass stay on trail #101, but stop here to admire the sheer vertical walls of the Tre Cime. Ahead and to your right is Mt. Paterno (Paternkofel), the scene of heavy fighting during World War I. In this pyramid-shaped mountain, you can see openings into the wartime galleries. Here, Sepp Innerkofler, a famous local mountain guide, met his death in 1915. (See also World War I section.) Continue under the shadow of the Paterno and after a short ascent, you see Rifugio Locatelli. For your return from the rifugio, take trail #105 (Alta Via #4) which branches down into a flat rocky cirque, and continues around the western edge of the Tre Cime to your starting point.

Trail to Rifugio Fonda Savio

ROUTE ❸—RIFUGIO FONDA SAVIO LOOP
A steep ascent to Rifugio Fonda Savio in the heart of the spires and pinnacles of the Cadini followed by a thrilling return descent.

Distance: About a 5 to 6 km loop.
Time Required: 3 to 4 hrs.
Elevation: Starting point 1896m; Rifugio Fonda Savio 2367m.
Change in Elevation: Gain of about 500m; Loss of about 500m.
Grade: Difficult to Expert.
Special Considerations:
1. **The easiest return is to retrace your way on trail #115.**
2. **You must be sure-footed.**
3. **Trail #117 should not be attempted in poor weather or with snow and ice.**
4. **After leaving the rifugio on trail #117, there is an exposed and steep descent with fixed cables.**

Starting Point: As you drive on the main road, from Lago di Misurina to the Tre Cime, watch carefully for a large sign indicating trail #115 to Rifugio Fonda Savio. Turn off here, and if your car can negotiate a rough road, continue nearly a kilometer to the parking area. Begin here on trail #115. Otherwise, park just off the main road and walk on the rough road to the same starting point.

You immediately begin by switchbacking up over a rocky thinly-wooded slope with views ahead of the Cadini and behind of Popena. You complete the steepest part of the ascent and cross over a "lip" into a glacial cirque leaving the valley below and heading for the rifugio which is now in sight. Once at the rifugio you may wonder why it is situated in this seemingly uninteresting spot. However, when you begin your return and descend on trail #117 you will quickly understand. The way is steep and thrilling with marvelous views of the Tre Cime and countless other soaring peaks of the Sesto. As you walk towards the Tre Cime, you scramble over rocks, down a steep gully with the valley far below, then over a short section that could have some snow and ice before reaching a level stretch. After a short ascent to a forcella you meet and take trail #119 through wooded, grassy, and gentle terrain, looping around to your beginning point on the main road or trail #115.

CORTINA AND THE SESTO (SEXTEN)

World War I cavern on Monte Piana, Cristallo in background

ROUTE ④—MONTE PIANA—A WORLD WAR I ITINERARY

A visit to a strategic battle zone of World War I with varied hiking possibilities.

Historical and General Notes: This itinerary should not be missed for its historical interest and marvelous panoramic views. The table-topped Monte Piana was of crucial importance during World War I. Not only did the historic political border between Italy and the Austro-Hungarian Empire run across the top, but also the main battle line between the two powers ran over this strategic site. Fierce fighting continued here for more than two years at a cost of over 10,000 lives. The Austrians controlled the more northerly shady side, the Italians the more southerly sunny side. Opposing forces were sometimes only meters apart on the large flat summit.

Rifugio Angelo Bosi (Monte Piana) on the summit plateau is delightful and has a small museum displaying photos, armaments and other items from the war. It is a good idea to stop at the rifugio and ask advice on how best to tour the area. You can also purchase a pamphlet which describes the summit battle area and directs you over the zone. Recently, part of the summit was carefully restored by the noted World War I historian, Walther Schaumann. Wander all over the rather flat summit plateau but be careful when exploring the edges and the ruins on the flanks; it is precipitous and requires sure-footedness.

Distance: About 5 km depending on your choice of routes.
Time Required: 3 to 4 hrs.
Elevation: Starting point about 1850m; High point about 2320m.
Change in Elevation: Gain of about 500m: Loss of about 500m.
Grade: Intermediate.

CORTINA AND THE SESTO (SEXTEN)

Basic Itinerary: Take the main road just north of Lago di Misurina that branches towards the Tre Cime di Lavaredo. After a few hundred meters turn left on a small paved road and continue for about 1 kilometer until the pavement ends and the road continues unpaved and becomes steep. Park here and walk the road or adjacent trail to the top. The walking ascent on the unpaved road poses no problems, and you have views in all directions. You descend the same way.

Alternative 1: Hire a jeep and driver to take you up and back if you just want to wander over the battlefield and enjoy the views from the top. An Easy to Moderate grade walk.

Alternative 2: About 500 meters from Carbonin, on the road to Misurina, start on trail #6 up the southwest side of Monte Piana. Refer to your map to find the easy starting point. This is a steep but exciting ascent with marvelous views of Popena, Cristallo and near-by peaks. It adds an hour to the basic itinerary and raises the grade to Difficult. Take the easy way down the unpaved road but you must arrange for transportation to your starting point.

Alternative 3: Ascend trail variant #6 (Alta Via #3) up the northwest side of Monte Piana. Refer to your map and begin at a main trail junction off the road between Cortina and Dobbiaco just south of the Hotel Cime di Lavaredo. This demanding steep route can add 1½ hours to your itinerary and change this hike from Intermediate to Expert. Descend on the unpaved road but you must make plans for your return to the starting point.

ROUTE ❺—VAL FISCALINA TO RIFUGIO PIAN DI CENGIA—A WORLD WAR I ITINERARY

A spectacular excursion into the world of the Sesto Dolomites.

Distance: About 12 to 13 km.
Time Required: 7 to 8 hrs.
Elevation: Starting point 1454m; Rifugio Pian di Cengia 2528m; Viewpoint 2675m.
Change in Elevation: Gain of about 1200m; Loss of about 1200m.
Grade: Intermediate.
Special Considerations: Plan to start early in the day as this is a long route. Carry some food and water even though rifugi are well spaced.

Starting point: Drive to the end of the paved road in the Val Fiscalina and leave your car in the large parking lot. Take trail #103 from here towards Rifugio Comici.

At first you walk on the valley floor through woods with vistas above and ahead of the Cima Una, Cima Undici and Croda dei Toni. You now ascend into a world of steep towering peaks on the well-marked easy trail #103 to the popular Rifugio Comici. This is a fine place to watch the hikers traversing the famous Alpini Route and to observe the ever- changing sun and shadow pattern on the surrounding peaks. From the rifugio take trail #101 to the small charming Rifugio Pian di Cengia. Look for a well-worn, unmarked trail to the right of the rifugio which, in 30 minutes, leads you up to your viewpoint—one of the most spellbinding in this part of the Dolomites. (You may wish to ask the way, using this guide and a map as reference.) Descend to the rifugio and return the same way.

Alternative: Instead of visiting the viewpoint, continue past Rifugio Pian di Cengia on trail #101 to Rifugio Locatelli and loop back to your beginning point on trail #102. This is a classic loop in the Sesto with some of the best views of the Tre Cime.

Rifugio Locatelli, Croda Rossa in distance

SOUTHEAST

Picturesque village, Pelmo in distance

SOUTHEAST

The Southeast district features three giant mountains: Pelmo, Civetta, and the Marmolada with its immense glacier. Each is surrounded by scenic valleys, tranquil small villages, and countless charming hamlets.

The district is more remote and untouched than the other districts, and includes only one sizeable village, Agordo. There are two travel areas, **Cordevole and Fiorentina-Zoldo** and the **Marmolada.**

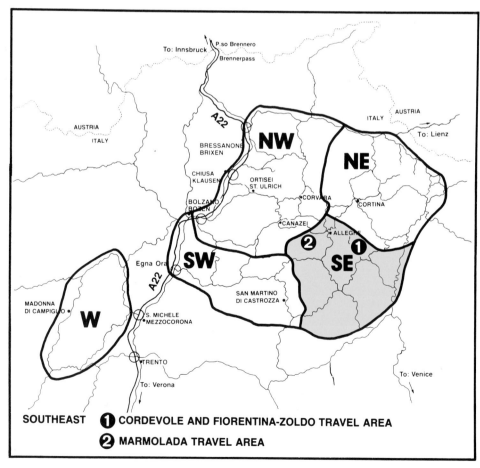

SOUTHEAST

Village of Alleghe, Lago di Alleghe

IMPORTANT FEATURES

Regions: Veneto and Trentino-Alto Adige (Südtirol)
Provinces: Trento and Belluno
Valleys: Cordevole, Fiorentina, Zoldo
Villages: Agordo, Alleghe, Rocca Pietore, Malga Ciapela
Mountains: Pelmo, Civetta, Agner, Marmolada
Lake: Alleghe

Hamlets in Val Cordevole

CORDEVOLE & FIORENTINA~ZOLDO

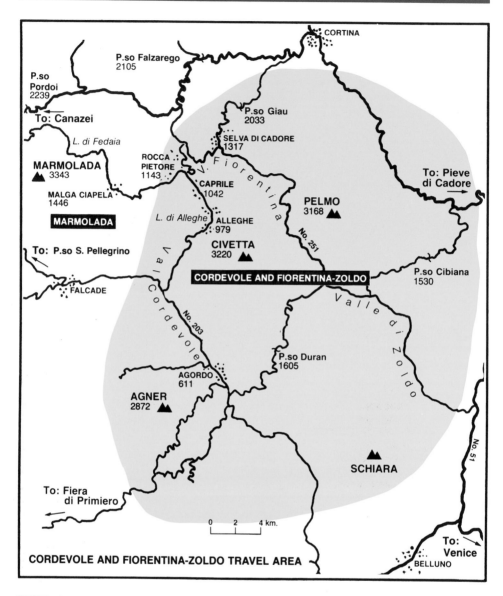

CORDEVOLE AND FIORENTINA-ZOLDO TRAVEL AREA

HIGHLIGHTS

This uncongested scenic area is ideal for touring by car or exploring by foot. Two solitary giant massifs, Pelmo and Civetta, both eastern (Orientali) Dolomites, rise nearly 2000 meters above the verdant Cordevole, Fiorentina and Zoldo valleys. Small, typically Italian villages along the road offer a modest selection of alberghi, pensioni, and garni. Tiny hamlets perch above the narrow valleys.

MAJOR ROAD PASSES INTO AREA	
	Elevation
Passo Falzarego	2105m
Passo San Pellegrino	1918m
Passo Valles	2033m
Passo Giau	2233m
Passo Duran	1605m

Towering Pelmo

142

CORDEVOLE & FIORENTINA~ZOLDO

Colle Santa Lucia, Pelmo in background

HOW TO ARRIVE

By Air:
International airports at Munich, Milan, Venice, or smaller airports in Verona and Innsbruck.

By Rail:
Nearest station: Belluno.

By Bus:
Service from Milan several times a week during the high season. Frequent service from Belluno. Service also from Bolzano during peak holiday periods.

By Car:

From North and West:	Exit A22 at Ora, take highway No. 48 to Canazei over Passo Pordoi to near Cernadoi, then south to Alleghe. Ora to Alleghe: 2½ hrs.
	Or exit A22 at Ora, take highway No. 48 to Moena and then drive east over Passo San Pellegrino to Alleghe. Ora to Alleghe: 2 hrs.
	Or exit A22 at Bressanone, drive by way of Corvara and Passo Falzarego to Alleghe. Bressanone exit to Alleghe: about 2 hrs.
From South:	Use No. 203 from Belluno through Agordo to Alleghe. Belluno to Alleghe: about 1 hr.
From East:	Pieve di Cadore, take No. 51 and after a few kilometers turn south on No. 347 at Venas to Forno di Zoldo. Pieve to Selva di Cadore: about 1¼ hrs.

GEOGRAPHIC FEATURES

Mountain Groups and Their Major Peaks: Summit Height

Pelmo	3168m
Civetta	3220m
Agner	2872m

Other Features: Valle Sarazana, Val Cordevole, Valle di San Lucano, Val del Biois, Lago di Alleghe

CORDEVOLE & FIORENTINA~ZOLDO

Late afternoon sun on Civetta

APPROACHES

Traveling from Cortina, take the road over Passo Falzarego. This route is particularly attractive in the afternoon when both Pelmo and Civetta catch the setting western sun. An alternate way, also from Cortina, is over the Passo Giau. This is spectacular, but the road is steep with many hairpin turns.

From the west, the easiest way is over Passo San Pellegrino. This is best, too, in the afternoon when the sun illuminates the north wall of Civetta.

From the south, roads go through Agordo. If convenient, take scenic No. 347 from Fiera di Primiero to see colorful hamlets and to drive along the base of Agner.

If you are coming from the east on highway No. 51, you have two attractive but winding choices. One from Longarone on No. 251, the other from Pieve di Cadore, turning south after a few kilometers on No. 347.

SETTING

The contrast between high mountains and deep wooded valleys is particularly dramatic in this area. Colors continually change hues during the day as the sun passes over the narrow valleys and peaceful villages. Civetta (3220m) and Pelmo (3168m) dominate the entire area and are constantly in view. Civetta's north face towers above the picturesque lake and village of Alleghe. This crescent-shaped vertical wall is nearly 1300 meters high and spans almost four kilometers. It is an absolutely spell-binding sight. Pelmo, in comparison, is an amazingly symmetrical monolith with an easily identifiable silhouette. It rises gloriously to its summit, 1900 meters above the valleys and villages that surround it. Another important mountain in this travel area, Agner (2872m), is famous for its north wall—the highest vertical face in the Dolomites.

The Cordevole and Fiorentina-Zoldo are two valley systems that parallel each other and run north to southeast through the area. The larger is the Cordevole, which begins in the north near Passo Falzarego winding its way in narrow wooded twists steeply down to Alleghe. From here it flattens out, separating Civetta from the ridges and valleys across to the west. It continues beyond the Pale di San Lucano to a sunny bowl where the village of Agordo nestles, eventually ending near Belluno. The sunny Fiorentina-Zoldo valley system branches off the larger Cordevole valley a few kilometers south of Passo Falzarego. It continues south all the way to Forno di Zoldo and, along with the Fernazza plateau, separates Pelmo from Civetta. A succession of charming villages line the road through this valley system.

Myriad smaller tributary valleys carve deep recesses into the giant mountain massifs. Small hamlets in green, postcard-like settings sit on meadowed benches above the valleys.

MAJOR VILLAGES	Population	Elevation
Agordo	4,300	611m
Alleghe	1,600	979m
Selva di Cadore	1,500	1317m

PRINCIPAL LANGUAGE: Italian

CORDEVOLE & FIORENTINA~ZOLDO

HISTORY

Because of its proximity to Venice, the early history of this area follows closely that of the Venetian Republic and the nearby Italian city states. The region has always been in the Italian sphere of influence—even before World War I.

For years, Civetta and Pelmo have attracted mountain climbers. Both were first scaled in the mid-19th Century, Civetta by the Englishman F.F. Tuckett, and Pelmo in 1857 by another Englishman, John Ball. Quite recently, people from these valleys who ventured to Germany and prospered in the ice cream business returned to build some attractive modern hotels and pensioni, restaurants and recreational facilities, including an impressive winter ski area.

MAJOR VILLAGES

Agordo, population 4,300, is quite low in elevation with views of some of the lesser known peaks. In the center of the village is a wide piazza with a large Italian baroque-style church. Radiating from the square are side streets with shops. There is an ample selection of hotels, restaurants, and cafés.

Alleghe, population 1,600, enjoys its own storybook setting on Lago di Alleghe, beneath the great wall of Civetta. A popular destination for travelers in summer and winter, the town has a variety of attractive small hotels, restaurants, and shops.

A short distance from Alleghe, in the Val Fiorentina, are several delightful villages well worth visiting. **Selva di Cadore** sits in the wide part of the valley. **Colle Santa Lucia** is one of the most photogenic.

THINGS TO DO AND SEE

Museums, Churches, Buildings
Church in Colle Santa Lucia—the cemetery behind the church commands a remarkable view of Pelmo.

Characteristic Old Houses/Hamlets
Colle Santa Lucia, San Tomaso, Laste

Other Summer Activities:
Swimming • Tennis • Cinema • Mountain climbing schools • Fishing • Ice skating • Horseback riding • Camping • and more.

OUTINGS AND EXCURSIONS

This is an excellent travel area to explore by car. Drives can be done in combination with walks and visits to villages and hamlets.

Half-day Drives
Colle Santa Lucia-Val Fiorentina-Valle di Zoldo: A series of charming hamlets in a small scenic valley beneath towering mountains.

Dont-Agordo: An uncrowded narrow mountain pass and a visit to the largest village in the area.

Valle di San Lucano: A narrow valley beneath the towering vertical wall of Agner.

San Tomaso and Laste: Two hamlets with narrow lanes, farms and spectacular views.

Cencenighe-Falcade: Two villages with interesting old houses. Small hamlets overlook these towns.

Agordo-Gosaldo loop, one way via Frassene, the other via Rivamonte: A winding drive among woods and hamlets.

View Panoramas
Belvedere just east of Colle Santa Lucia.

Rambles
Colle Santa Lucia, a colorful hamlet with pastoral countryside.
Around Alleghe to enjoy a lakeside village beneath Civetta.
Agordo, to visit this Italian village with shops, piazza, and church.
Zoppè di Cadore, a tiny village beneath Pelmo.

Using Lifts
For spectacular views of Pelmo, Civetta and other giant peaks, use the lifts from Alleghe, Pescul and Palafavera to reach the Fernazza plateau.

CORDEVOLE & FIORENTINA~ZOLDO

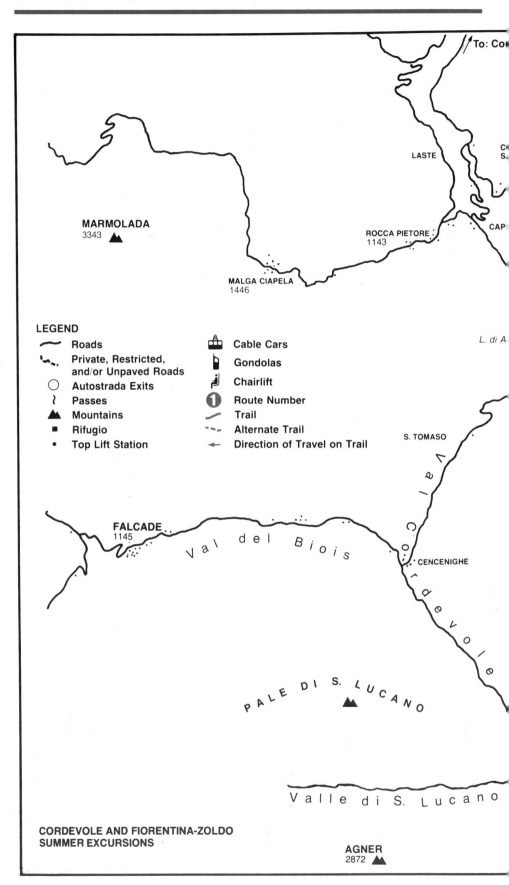

To: Co

LASTE

C
S.

MARMOLADA
3343 ▲▲

ROCCA PIETORE
1143

CAP

MALGA CIAPELA
1446

L. di A

LEGEND

⌒	Roads	🚋	Cable Cars
⌒	Private, Restricted, and/or Unpaved Roads	📱	Gondolas
○	Autostrada Exits	🪑	Chairlift
⌇	Passes	➊	Route Number
▲▲	Mountains	⌒	Trail
■	Rifugio	--⌐--	Alternate Trail
•	Top Lift Station	←	Direction of Travel on Trail

S. TOMASO

Val

FALCADE
1145

V a l   d e l   B i o i s

C
o
r
d
e
v
o
l
e

CENCENIGHE

P A L E   D I   S.   L U C A N O ▲▲

V a l l e   d i   S.   L u c a n o

CORDEVOLE AND FIORENTINA-ZOLDO
SUMMER EXCURSIONS

AGNER
2872 ▲▲

146

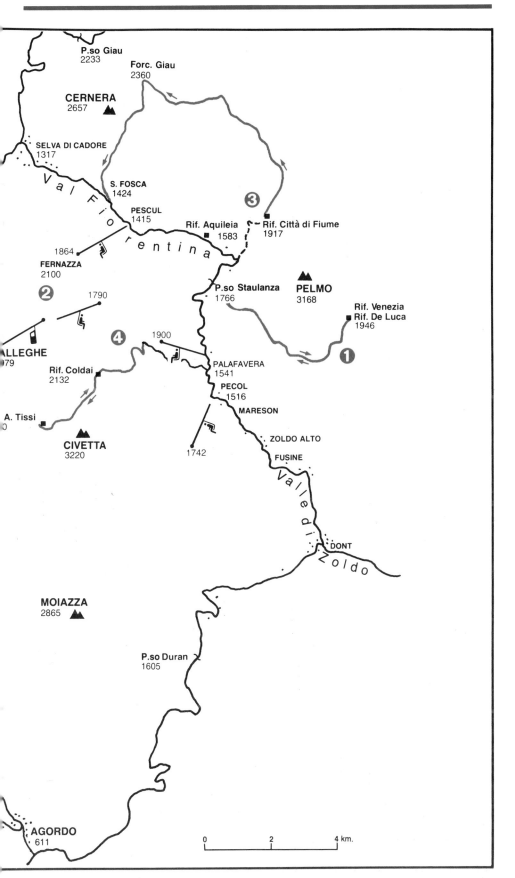

WALKS AND HIKES

Itineraries are generally on parts of Alte Vie—high-level hiking trails which cross the Dolomites. Footing varies: some trails on high rocky paths are more difficult; others over meadows are easy.

Maps: 1:50,000: Tabacco #1, #2, #4, Kompass Alpi Bellunesi #77; 1:25,000: Geo M. Pelmo, M. Civetta #3.

Rifugio Venezia, Sorapiss in background

ROUTE ❶—FORCELLA STAULANZA TO RIFUGIO VENEZIA
A rather level walk through woods at the base of Pelmo.

Distance: About 10 km round trip.
Time Required: About 5 hrs.
Elevation: Starting point 1766m; Rifugio Venezia 1946m.
Change in Elevation: Gain of about 265m; Loss of about 265m.
Grade: Intermediate.

Starting Point: The trailhead is across the road from Rifugio Staulanza. Look for trail #472 in the direction of Rifugio Venezia.

When you enter the forest Pelmo looms above while Civetta can be seen behind you. The pleasant trail is boggy, at times, but with soft footing and often a few stray cows to dodge. You circle around Pelmo, staying on #472 the entire way, with occasional open valley vistas to your right. A thrill awaits as you near the rifugio. At a bend in the trail there is a surprising view of Antelao rising above a nearby ridge. You ascend onto a small saddle. In the distance you see Rifugio Venezia; you are positioned to enjoy not only views of Pelmo but also the mountains framing the Val Boite up to Cortina. The return on the same trail is just as enjoyable. Pelmo is your companion on the right and Civetta again appears as you near your departure point.

CORDEVOLE & FIORENTINA~ZOLDO

ROUTE ❷—WALKS ON THE FERNAZZA PLATEAU
This soft undulating plateau, situated between Civetta and Pelmo and the Cordevole and Fiorentina-Zoldo valleys, is ideal for leisurely walking and exploring. You can wander comfortably in walking shoes, although hiking boots are still recommended. The plateau is easily accessible by foot, lift, and jeep roads from many different points. You have views of Pelmo, Civetta, the Marmolada, and Croda da Lago, with the Pale di San Martino to the southwest.

Distance: Itineraries can be 2 to 12 km.
Time Required: Walks can be any length but generally not more than 3 hours. However, if you hike up to the plateau from the Val Fiorentina or Valle di Zoldo, it will take you at least an hour. The walk back down requires less time.
Elevation: The plateau averages between 1900m and 2050m—the highest point is about 2100m. You have modest ups and downs on any excursion.
Grade: Easy to Moderate.
Special Considerations:
1. Trails are not always marked so carry your map. You will be able to orient yourself by noting the surrounding mountains and other key terrain features.
2. Study your alternatives for returning and plan accordingly.
3. Verify which lifts are running and if any rifugi are open.

Starting Points for reaching plateau: Lifts are from Alleghe, Pescul or Palafavera; there is a jeep road from near Passo Staulanza.

ROUTE ❸—RIFUGIO CITTÀ DI FIUME TO FORCELLA GIAU TO SANTA FOSCA
A beautiful hike over varied terrain with vistas of Pelmo and Civetta; and glimpses of Cortina, the Marmolada, and many other peaks.

Distance: About 10 km one way to Santa Fosca.
Time Required: About 6 to 7 hrs one way.
Elevation: Starting point 1917m; Forcella Giau 2360m; Santa Fosca 1424m.
Change in Elevation: Gain of about 300m; Loss of about 1300m.
Grade: Intermediate.
Special Considerations:
1. Carry drinks and food.
2. The way down from Forcella Giau is scenic and well-marked. The footing is good, however, it is very steep and hard on the knees.
3. Plan your return based on where you wish to join the main road.
4. It is best to do this trip on a day when visibility is good, as finding your way in fog could be difficult.

Starting point: Hire a jeep or taxi to take you up the rough road to Rifugio Città di Fiume. Alternatively you can begin at Rifugio Aquileia and walk to Rifugio Città di Fiume. This adds 3 kilometers, 350 meters of gain, and 1½ hours to your journey.

From behind Rifugio Città di Fiume take trail #467 (Alta Via #1) uphill towards Rifugio Palmieri. The walk begins gently through a young pine forest towards a *malga,* or farmer's hut, and the walls of the Rocchetta. The terrain is soft under foot and the views become expansive and remain so throughout the trip. You stay on the same trail. However, trail markings change from #467 to #458 to #436 as other trails join from the east. The rocky path along the Rocchetta and Becco di Mezzodì ends at Forcella d'Ambrizzola which is a junction for trail #434. This is an ideal point for photos of Croda da Lago, Cortina, Antelao and Sorapiss. Continue on trail #436 towards Forcella Giau and Passo Giau. It was near here that a prehistoric gravesite of a hunter was discovered in 1985. Views of the Marmolada, Civetta, and behind you, of Pelmo are fine along this entire stretch. After a gentle descent you pass through massive boulder fields below the walls of the Lastoni di Formin and then regain the same altitude as you travel up to the Forcella Giau. This is another wonderful viewpoint, especially of the Tofane.

From the forcella take trail #465 down. The initial descent is fairly level and well marked, but then becomes very steep as you proceed, first along a stream, then through a meadow and into trees. Panoramas of Civetta, the distant Pale di San Martino, as well as nearby valleys and villages, accompany you the entire way. The descent ends in the hamlet of Santa Fosca.

Rifugio Tissi, Civetta in background

ROUTE ④ —CASERE DI PIODA TO RIFUGIO TISSI
A dramatic hike below the great north wall of Civetta.

Distance: About 10 km round trip.
Time required: 6 to 7 hrs.
Elevation: Starting point 1816m; Rifugio Tissi 2280m.
Change in Elevation: Gain of about 450m; Loss of about 450m.
Grade: Intermediate to Difficult.
Special Considerations:
1. **Much of the trail is over rock and some scree. Do not attempt when a lot of snow or ice is present.**
2. **This is a high altitude hike so quick changes in weather can be expected.**
3. **Arrange for transportation to your departure point and from the same point upon your return.**

Starting Point: Hire a jeep to take you up the rough road from near Palafavera to the Casere di Pioda. Begin at this small malga where you will find obvious trail markings and signs for Alta Via #1, trail #556, along with directional signs for Rifugio Coldai and Rifugio Tissi. All the trails head towards Civetta.

This hike below the great north wall of Civetta is one of the most spectacular and popular hikes in the Dolomites. It can be crowded, particularly in the summer. The first stretch is a switchback trail up to a small saddle. From here you can see Rifugio Coldai, ideally positioned to take in a sweeping view of Pelmo. Now take trail #560 and after a short, gentle upward grade, and a few more switchbacks, you cross a second col and see a lovely lake in a glacial cirque. On clear days a splendid reflection of Civetta can be seen. Wander around the west side of the lake and a little above for some amazing views of Alleghe, 1300m below, and across to the Marmolada, Pale di San Martino and a host of other peaks.

Stay on trail #560 and after a few minutes you have a wonderful view of the great north wall of Civetta, the trail ahead, and in the distance, your destination—Rifugio Tissi. Descend to your right and follow the main signs of Alta Via #1 to the rifugio. (Another branch of the trail proceeds straight ahead but talus and scree make footing difficult.) After a few hundred meters, you must ascend another 300 meters to reach Rifugio Tissi, dramatically situated to hold you spellbound. You return the same way and will enjoy the afternoon light on the mountains.

MARMOLADA

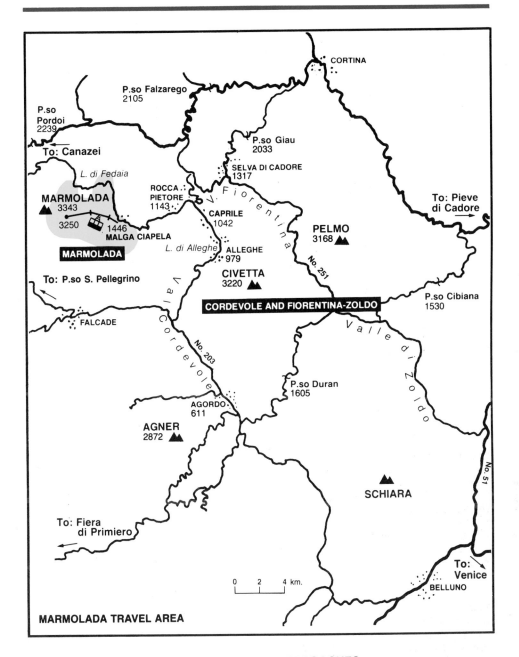

MARMOLADA TRAVEL AREA

Map labels:
- CORTINA
- P.so Falzarego 2105
- P.so Pordoi 2239
- To: Canazei
- L. di Fedaia
- P.so Giau 2033
- SELVA DI CADORE 1317
- To: Pieve di Cadore
- MARMOLADA 3343
- ROCCA PIETORE 1143
- 3250
- 1446
- MALGA CIAPELA
- CAPRILE 1042
- V. Fiorentina
- PELMO 3168
- **MARMOLADA**
- L. di Alleghe
- ALLEGHE 979
- To: P.so S. Pellegrino
- CIVETTA 3220
- **CORDEVOLE AND FIORENTINA-ZOLDO**
- P.so Cibiana 1530
- Valle di Zoldo
- FALCADE
- Val Cordevole
- No. 203
- P.so Duran 1605
- No. 251
- AGORDO 611
- AGNER 2872
- No. 51
- To: Fiera di Primiero
- SCHIARA
- 0 2 4 km.
- To: Venice
- BELLUNO

HIGHLIGHTS

The Marmolada is the highest mountain in the Dolomites—3343 meters—and has the largest glacier. Its glorious snow-covered summit can be admired from many distant valleys and vantage points. In the summer, a visit to the top of the Marmolada to see the incomparable panorama is a must. You will enjoy the thrilling cable car ride from Malga Ciapela to the restaurant at the summit and you may even be accompanied by summer skiers heading for the glacier. Some of the most dramatic views of the Marmolada are from Passo Falzarego, the Passo Sella—or, if hiking, from the popular Belvedere ridge in the Val di Fassa.

APPROACHES

The only lift system to the summit crest, a three-stage cable car, leaves from the small tourist complex of Malga Ciapela which is nestled in a narrow valley below the east side of the mountain. The principal access to this valley and Malga Ciapela is via Rocca Pietore, a small village north of Alleghe. Another way to Malga Ciapela is to drive over Passo Fedaia from Canazei in the Val di Fassa.

Sempervivum arachnoideum

151

MARMOLADA

The Marmolada, "Queen of the Dolomites"

SETTING

The Marmolada's massive snow covered northern flanks dominate the panorama of the central Dolomites. This huge mountain massif is surrounded, yet separated, from other giant peaks. There are two high points on the summit crest—the Punta Rocca (3309m), and Punta Penia (3343m). The mountain seems to be divided into two vastly different slopes. The northern slope, with the glacier, is more uniform in pitch, gradually inclining down to Lago di Fedaia. The south-facing side is a sheer vertical rock wall that drops some 1000 meters to a small scree valley below. This southern face is rather inaccessible, except to hikers and climbers, as it is separated from roads and other inhabited valleys by countless rocky valleys and smaller peaks.

NEAREST VILLAGES FOR EXCURSIONS TO THE SUMMIT OF THE MARMOLADA

Malga Ciapela, (1446m). The lifts to the Marmolada leave from here and there are also tourist accommodations.

Rocca Pietore, (1143m). A tiny village, near Alleghe, with tourist accommodations and transportation to Malga Ciapela.

HOW TO ARRIVE

Once you are in the Dolomites, the Marmolada is an easy day's excursion from most locations.

From North,
East, South: By car or bus to Malga Ciapela by way of Rocca Pietore near Alleghe.

From West: By car from Canazei over Passo Fedaia to Malga Ciapela.

PRINCIPAL LANGUAGE: Italian.

MARMOLADA

GEOLOGY

The Marmolada, scientifically speaking, does not consist of dolomite rock but of limestone with little magnesium carbonate. Nevertheless, the mountain's title, "Queen of the Dolomites," is justified by its central location, height, and the spectacular glacier that mantles its northern side.

HISTORY

Attempts to scale the Marmolada began as early as 1803 when a group of local climbers from Livinallongo tried to reach the summit. One of the first climbers and explorers of the Dolomites, the Englishman John Ball, first scaled the Punta Rocca in 1860. The great Viennese climber, Paul Grohmann, who conquered many peaks in the Dolomites, surmounted the Punta Penia in 1864.

Before World War I, the boundary between Italy and Austria crossed the Marmolada with about half falling to each country. Consequently, the Marmolada was the site of bitter fighting during the war. Between the spring of 1916 and autumn of 1917, the Austrian troops dug a network of caverns and galleries in the ice for defense and protection from the harsh winters. However, avalanches still took their toll—in 1916, 400 men died in a single avalanche. As recently as 1947, the frozen body of a uniformed Austrian soldier was accidently discovered in an ice cave on the mountain.

THINGS TO DO AND SEE

Summer glacier skiing.

Three-stage cable car ride from Malga Ciapela to the summit crest.

The World War I Museum of the Marmolada displays memorabilia and photographs. It is located at the second lift station.

OUTINGS AND EXCURSIONS

Take the three-stage cable car ride from Malga Ciapela to the top. Restaurants and viewing points are located at the two upper lift stations. You can wander along the summit crest from the upper lift station for incomparable panoramic views. Take along extra layers of clothing as it can be cold and windy.

WALKS AND HIKES

The hiking routes on the northern slopes over the crest to the south of the Marmolada are generally difficult, albeit thrilling, and extraordinary experiences. They require mountaineering ability and thus are beyond the scope of this book. However, there is a half-day Intermediate grade hike from Malga Ciapela (1446m). From here take trail #610 through the Valle Ombretta to Rifugio Fallier (2074m). In 3 hours you will reach the rifugio and beautiful views of the Marmolada's south face. This is an excellent spot to rest and watch the many climbers scaling the south walls. Return the same way and you will arrive back in Malga Ciapela within two hours.

Maps: 1:50,000: Tabacco #2; 1:25,000: Geo Marmolada/Gruppo di Sella #6, Wanderkarte Dolomiti di Fassa.

Gruppo della Marmolada

WEST

Chapel in the heart of the Brenta

WEST

The large West district encompasses part of the wild and beautiful Parco Naturale Adamello-Brenta, several attractive villages and many lakes. This district is west of, and separate from, the other Dolomite districts—and located northwest of the city of Trento. It is at least a one hour drive from major autostrade. **The Brenta** travel area features the magnificent blocks, towers, and ridges of the Dolomiti di Brenta and the three villages of Madonna di Campiglio, Pinzolo, and Molveno. Walking and hiking in and near the spectacular Brenta massif is an incomparable experience for any outdoor enthusiast.

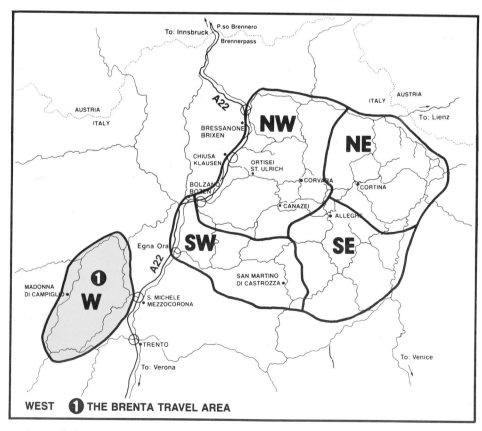

WEST ❶ THE BRENTA TRAVEL AREA

Traversing the Via delle Bocchette

IMPORTANT FEATURES
Region: Trentino-Alto Adige (Südtirol)
Province: Trento
Valleys: Val Rendena, Valle di Campiglio, Val Meledrio, Val di Non
Villages: Madonna di Campiglio, Pinzolo, Molveno
Mountains: Dolomiti di Brenta
Lakes: Lago di Molveno, Lago di Tovel

THE BRENTA

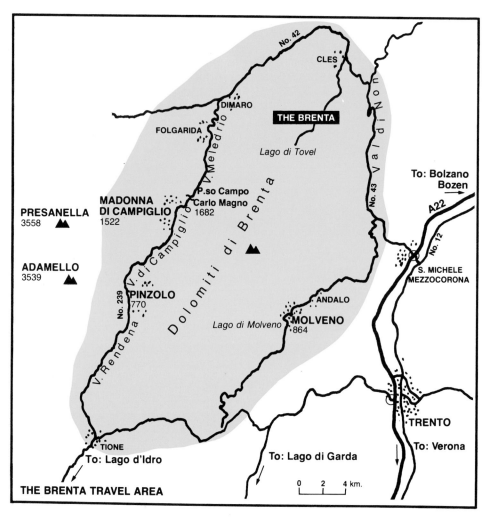

PRESANELLA 3558

ADAMELLO 3539

MADONNA DI CAMPIGLIO 1522

P.so Campo Carlo Magno 1682

PINZOLO 770

THE BRENTA

Lago di Tovel

Dolomiti di Brenta

DIMARO

FOLGARIDA

CLES

No. 42

V. Meledrio

V. di Campiglio

V. Rendena

No. 239

Lago di Molveno

MOLVENO 864

ANDALO

Val di Non

No. 43

To: Bolzano Bozen

A22

No. 12

S. MICHELE MEZZOCORONA

TRENTO

To: Verona

TIONE

To: Lago d'Idro

To: Lago di Garda

0   2   4 km.

THE BRENTA TRAVEL AREA

HIGHLIGHTS

The Dolomiti di Brenta are a magnificent block-like ridge of dolomitic towers and pinnacles that attracts hikers and mountain climbers from around the world. One of the most famous Vie Ferrate, the *Via delle Bocchette,* is located here. Even mountain climbers enthusiastically attest to the thrills of tackling this route. Twenty-seven rifugi are strategically located throughout the travel area and at the highest elevations to help you enjoy your mountain excursions.

Separated and west of the other Dolomites, the Brenta is part of the immense Parco Naturale Adamello-Brenta and some of its delights are lakes, waterfalls, forests, and wildflowers. Wildlife, protected in the Parco Naturale, thrive in this natural habitat. The area has well known tourist centers in Madonna di Campiglio, Pinzolo, and Molveno—which is set beside a lovely lake. A complete range of comfortable accommodation is available in each village.

Molveno

THE BRENTA

HOW TO ARRIVE

By Air:
International airports at Munich, Milan, Venice, or smaller airports in Verona and Innsbruck.

By Rail:
Nearest stations: Trento, Mezzocorona. Then transfer by bus or car.

By Bus:
Take major bus lines to Trento. There is frequent connecting service to Madonna di Campiglio and other major villages.

By Car:

From East North, South:	Exit A22 at San Michele (north of Trento), then follow No. 43 past Cles where it joins No. 42. Follow No. 42 to Dimaro where you turn south towards Madonna di Campiglio. A22 exit to Madonna: about 1½ hrs.
From West (Milan):	Exit A4 at Brescia Centro and follow local roads to Lago d'Idro then Tione, and finally Madonna di Campiglio. A4 exit to Madonna: about 2 hrs.
To Molveno from all directions:	Exit A22 at San Michele and follow signs to Molveno. A22 exit to Molveno: about 1 hr.

MAJOR ROAD PASSES INTO THE AREA
Passo Campo Carlo Magno, elevation 1682m.

Madonna di Campiglio, Dolomiti di Brenta in background

THE BRENTA

APPROACHES

From the north and east exit A22 at San Michele (Mezzocorona). If either Madonna di Campiglio or Pinzolo is your destination, go north towards Cles and take No. 42 to Dimaro, then south to Madonna. After Dimaro the road becomes tree-lined and narrow and your first glimpse of the Brenta ridge will be near Passo Campo Carlo Magno. If Molveno is your destination, you also exit at San Michele, branching south on a side road a few kilometers after Mezzolombardo, for a short sunny drive to the village.

If you are driving on local roads south and west of the area, you approach the Brenta by winding your way through wooded valleys and green farmlands dotted with small villages. As you near either Pinzolo or Molveno the scenery changes abruptly into a dramatic mountain environment.

The spectacular Vallesinella waterfalls

THE BRENTA

Sunlight on peaks of the Brenta

SETTING

The Brenta, a compact mountainous ridge about 35 kilometers long and 12 kilometers wide is, broadly speaking, sandwiched between the Val di Non on the east and the snow-clad peaks of Adamello and Presanella on the west. The central part of the ridge between Passo del Grostè and Cima Tosa is the most popular for hiking. The sunny valleys of Meledrio, Campiglio and Rendena run north to south along the base of the ridge on the western side. Gentle forested slopes rise from the valley floor where deer, roe deer, chamois, marmot, and even the brown bear live in their protected habitats. Here also, wildflowers appear abundantly in late spring and summer.

Terrain on the opposite side of the valleys, at the base of the Adamello and Presanella massifs, is gentler still.

Below the Dolomiti di Brenta on the east is the beautiful warm, sunny Val di Non. Located in this valley is the large Lago di Molveno, a popular recreation area, picturesquely situated below the Brenta massif. The resort village of Molveno nestles beside the north end of the lake. North of Molveno, and reachable by small roads leading south from near Cles into the Parco Naturale, is Lago di Tovel.

GEOGRAPHIC FEATURES

Mountain Groups and Their Major Peaks:

	Summit Heights
Cima Tosa	3173m
Cima Brenta	3150m

Other Features:
Lago di Molveno, Lago di Tovel

THE BRENTA

HISTORY

Until the 12th century, secluded shelters in the Brenta gave the only comfort to travelers or herdsmen taking cattle up to the alpine passes. The earliest shelter, or hospice, was built by a monk named Raimondo in 1100. For centuries the Brenta was under control of the Episcopal Principality of Trento and later the Hapsburg Empire. In 1862, Giambattista Righi bought most of the valley of Campiglio, turning it into a summer resort. It soon became a favorite retreat for the Hapsburg royalty and other aristocratic families. The Brenta escaped fighting during World War I since the front line passed to the west and south. The area was ceded to Italy after World War I.

Mountaineering has enjoyed a long tradition in this part of the Dolomites. For many years it was thought impossible to traverse the Brenta from east to west. However, in 1864, John Ball, the noted English climber who pioneered much of the Dolomites, discovered a pass, Bocca di Brenta, leading from Madonna to Molveno. This route opened the ridge to many hiking, climbing, and exploring possibilities. Ball and W.E. Foster reached the highest point of the Brenta, Cima Tosa, in 1865. To their dismay they learned that this peak had been scaled three weeks earlier by an Italian party. The second noted peak in the Brenta, Cima Brenta, was climbed in 1871 by the Englishmen Freshfield and Tuckett.

Over the last 100 years, the Rendena and Campiglio valleys have dramatically changed from places of relative isolation to international summer and winter holiday destinations—tourism is now the most important business. In summer, visitors flock to this mountain area for its variety of hiking and challenging Vie Ferrate. Each December Madonna di Campiglio hosts World Cup slalom ski events while Pinzolo stages a famous 24-hour cross-country ski marathon.

GEOLOGY

The Brenta Dolomites, the only dolomite group west of the Adige river, are similar to the eastern Dolomites—very little or no Sciliar Dolomite occurs here. The massif is made up largely of two different rock formations: the Dolomia Principale below and the overlying 300 meter thick Rhaetic black shale and limestone. The latter formation is unique to the Brenta.

A striking difference in geology occurs in this area. The granite rocks of the far younger Adamello and Presanella massifs (formed about 30 million years ago) are across the valley from the older well-stratified Dolomites of the Brenta group. This phenomenon is a result of the so-called Giudicarie Fault, a major Alpine fracture which runs through the valley from Dimaro in the north, continuing well past Pinzolo in the south.

MAJOR VILLAGES

Madonna di Campiglio, population 1,000, is an impressive tourist center. It is an up-to-date contemporary resort with an array of shops, hotels, discos, and restaurants to suit all tastes. This small village is completely surrounded by lush spruce and pine forests and many of the lifts are within a few minutes walk of the shopping district.

About 12 kilometers south, and much lower in elevation, is the village of **Pinzolo,** population 2,300. It is in a sunny location and is decidedly Italian in architecture and flavor. It enjoys a year-round economy as well as a flourishing tourist business.

Molveno, population 1,000, is a popular year-round vacation center near a number of other towns. Located at the eastern base of the Brenta, it is relatively low in elevation and is situated beside a sunny lake of the same name.

THINGS TO DO AND SEE

Museums, Churches, Buildings
Madonna di Campiglio: the Salone Hofer.
Pinzolo: the churches of San Vigilio and Santo Stefano.

Nature Parks and Lakes
Parco Naturale Adamello-Brenta
Lago di Tovel
Lago di Molveno

Other Summer Activities
Swimming • Golf • Tennis • Cinema • Mountain climbing schools • Fishing • Horseback riding • and more.

THE BRENTA

Rifugio Tuckett, the Brenta

OUTINGS AND EXCURSIONS

The following are suggestions for touring the Brenta. They can be combined in various ways to suit your goals for any specific day.

Half-day Drives
Madonna di Campiglio-Lago di Molveno and return: Forest, villages, open pastureland, and a lovely lake with views of both sides of the Brenta.

Madonna di Campiglio — Lago di Tovel and return.

View Panoramas
Passo Campo Carlo Magno.
Madonna di Campiglio: Drive to viewpoint 1 km south of village.
East side of Lago di Molveno.

Rambles
East side of Madonna di Campiglio to enjoy the village and forest.

Madonna di Campiglio to Lago Nambino to see a small mountain lake and dramatic vistas of the valley and Brenta.

Along Lago di Molveno from village; lake, and Brenta views.

Around Lago di Tovel to see this interesting lake with mountain backdrop.

Using Lifts
Cinque Laghi lift: From the center of Madonna to Rifugio Pancugolo to see Madonna di Campiglio and the Brenta ridge across the valley.

Spinale lift: From Madonna di Campiglio. Views of the village and a close-up of the Brenta ridge.

Grostè lift: Located 1 km north of Madonna di Campiglio. Lift rises towards the central part of the Brenta ridge with panoramas of Adamello and Presanella.

Pradalago lift: From Madonna di Campiglio. Outstanding views of the village and east to the Brenta ridge.

Pinzolo lift: From Pinzolo towards the Brenta. Fabulous scenes of the Brenta from the southwest, and west towards Adamello and Presanella.

Molveno lift: From Molveno northwest to Rifugio Montanara. Views of Lago di Molveno, village, and mountains.

Andalo lift: From Andalo southeast. Views of Lago di Molveno and sweeping panoramas of the east side of the Brenta.

THE BRENTA

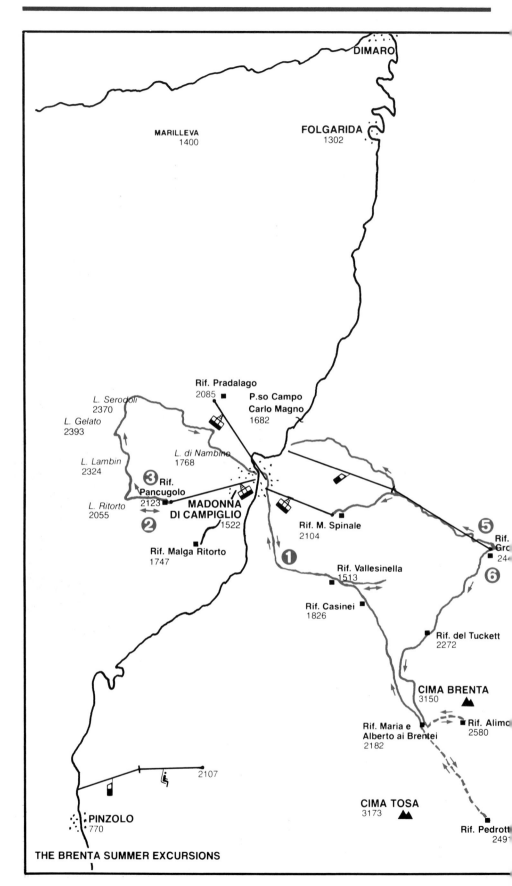

DIMARO

MARILLEVA
1400

FOLGARIDA
1302

Rif. Pradalago
2085

P.so Campo
Carlo Magno
1682

L. Serodoli
2370

L. Gelato
2393

L. di Nambino
1768

L. Lambin
2324

③ Rif.
Pancugolo
2123

L. Ritorto
2055

**MADONNA
DI CAMPIGLIO**
1522

②

Rif. M. Spinale
2104

⑤

Rif.
Gr
24

Rif. Malga Ritorto
1747

①

Rif. Vallesinella
1513

⑥

Rif. Casinei
1826

Rif. del Tuckett
2272

CIMA BRENTA
3150

Rif. Maria e
Alberto ai Brentei
2182

Rif. Alimo
2580

2107

CIMA TOSA
3173

PINZOLO
770

Rif. Pedrott
249

THE BRENTA SUMMER EXCURSIONS

THE BRENTA

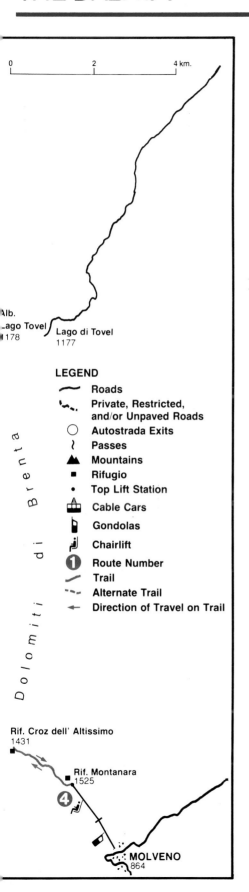

0   2   4 km.

Alb.
Lago Tovel   Lago di Tovel
178   1177

LEGEND

〜 Roads

🝰 Private, Restricted,
    and/or Unpaved Roads

◯ Autostrada Exits

🝰 Passes

▲ Mountains

▪ Rifugio

• Top Lift Station

🚡 Cable Cars

📱 Gondolas

🪑 Chairlift

❶ Route Number

╱ Trail

--- Alternate Trail

← Direction of Travel on Trail

Dolomiti   di   Brenta

Rif. Croz dell' Altissimo
1431

Rif. Montanara
1525

❹

MOLVENO
864

Campanile Basso

THE BRENTA

WALKS AND HIKES

The walks and hikes in the Brenta are generally either easy because there are many meadows and forests or quite challenging due to the abruptness of the peaks and pinnacles. However, you can change an itinerary during a hike and always return the same way to avoid a difficult or exposed stretch.

Maps: 1:50,000: Tabacco #10 1:30,000; Kompass #073 Dolomiti di Brenta
1:35,000: Parco Naturale Gruppo di Brenta

ROUTE ❶—MADONNA DI CAMPIGLIO TO RIFUGIO VALLESINELLA AND WATERFALLS

A gradual ascent through meadow and woods to the rifugio and waterfalls.

Distance: About 4½ km one way; 9 km round trip.
Time Required: About 2½ hrs to ascend; 1½ hrs to return.
Change in Elevation: Gain of about 200m; Loss of about 200m.
Grade: Moderate.
Special Considerations: It is possible to drive or take a taxi to Rifugio Vallesinella.

Starting Point: Begin on the east side of Madonna and take road—trail #375—towards Rifugio Vallesinella.

You start from the village, always walking on a road. In about 1½ hrs, you reach your first destination, the attractive Rifugio Vallesinella. Continue on the road, then on trail #375, to the waterfalls which is about one kilometer beyond the rifugio. Return the same way.

Trails near Lago Ritorto

ROUTE ❷—CINQUE LAGHI LIFT: RIFUGIO PANCUGOLO TO LAGO RITORTO

A gentle hike to a high mountain lake with sweeping mountain views.

Distance: 3 km round trip.
Time Required: About 1½ hrs.
Grade: Moderate.
Special Considerations:
1. There is some exposure but the trail has fixed iron cables for hand support.
2. Ask directions to be sure you start on the right trail.

Starting Point: Take the Cinque Laghi lift. Look for the main trail #232 behind Rifugio Pancugolo.

You walk along an easy, somewhat exposed, trail before arriving at the lake. Once there, you will want to relax at the small beach with incoming streams and wander among the wildflowers. Return the same way.

THE BRENTA

On the "many lakes" hike

ROUTE ❸–CINQUE LAGHI LIFT AND MANY LAKES TRIP: RITORTO TO LAMBIN TO SERODOLI TO NAMBINO.

An outstanding route among rock walls and lakes with wonderful scenes of the valley and Brenta.

Distance: About 10 km from top of lift station to Madonna.
Time Required: About 8 hrs from top of lift to Madonna.
Elevation: Starting point 2123m at top of lift; Lago Serodoli 2370m; Madonna 1522m.
Grade: Difficult.
Special Considerations:
1. This is a strenuous hike with lots of ups and downs; much of the way is over rock so some scrambling is required.
2. There is a possibility of encountering snow and ice.
3. Visibility can be a problem with fog or precipitation.
4. Verify lift schedules.
5. Carry food and water.
6. Most trail numbers are painted on rocks along the way.

Starting Point: From top of lift follow trail #232 to Lago Ritorto. (See Route 2).

From Lago Ritorto continue on trail #232 to Lago Lambin. Rugged cliffs loom above you with valley views below. Stay on #232 to Lago Serodoli, a good spot for lunch. Time permitting, you may take a side trip from Lago Serodoli to Lago Gelato and Passo di Nambrone to explore some fascinating rocky cirque terrain. This will add 1 to 2 hrs to your itinerary. From Lago Serodoli, you have a choice of trails to Lago Nambino but #226 to #266 is suggested. From Lago Nambino, follow the main trail #263 which connects with the road to Madonna.

Alternate: At Lago Serodoli you have an option if the Pradalago lift is operating. You can take trail #226, descending a bit to the lift station, and return by lift to Madonna.

ROUTE ❹—MOLVENO LIFT TO RIFUGIO MONTANARA: HIKE TO RIFUGIO CROZ DELL'ALTISSIMO

A level hike along mountain flanks with views into the Brenta and down to Lago di Molveno.

Distance: 2 km one way; 4 km round trip.
Time Required: About 2 hrs round trip.
Grade: Moderate.

Starting Point: Take lift from Molveno to Rifugio Montanara and then trail #340.

You start in woods along a mountain flank above the valley. The trail is wide and easy with open stretches, and the scenery is delightful the entire trip.

THE BRENTA

Dolomiti di Brenta from Spinale

ROUTE ⑤ - GROSTÈ LIFT TO RIFUGIO GROSTÈ; HIKE TO GROSTÈ PASS TO SPINALE SUMMIT TO MADONNA DI CAMPIGLIO
A gentle descent over high mountain meadows with sweeping views of the Brenta, Adamello, and Presanella.

Distance: About 7 km from top of lift to Madonna.
Time Required: About 3½ hrs for the descent to Madonna.
Elevation: Starting point Rifugio Grostè 2438m; Madonna 1522m.
Change in Elevation: Loss of about 900m.
Grade: Moderate.
Special Considerations: Check lift and rifugi schedules.

Starting Point: From the top of the Grostè lift station, take trail #315 (a service road).

Walk up a short way from Rifugio Grostè to the Passo del Grostè. Here you have mountain panoramas to the east, directly into the Brenta, and across to Adamello and Presanella. Return to the rifugio and take the service road— trail #315 —down towards Madonna. When you see trail #352 you can decide if you wish to take a side trip up to the Spinale summit. This requires an ascent on trail #352 to trail #331 and onto the summit where the views are well worth the added climb. If you choose this route be sure the lift is running from the summit for your return to Madonna. Should you elect not to ascend to the Spinale summit continue your descent on trail #315 leading to the lower Grostè lift station. Near the end of this descent you can take trail #384 to trail #386 if you prefer to finish near the center of Madonna.

ROUTE ⑥ —GROSTÈ LIFT; GROSTÈ PASS TO RIFUGIO BRENTEI TO RIFUGIO VALLESINELLA
A classic high mountain traverse with dramatic closeup views of the Brenta. Many alternatives are possible.

Distance: About 14 km from the lift to Rifugio Vallesinella.
Time Required: About 10 hrs for the hike to Rifugio Brentei and the descent to Rifugio Vallesinella.
Elevation: Rifugio Grostè 2438m; Rifugio Brentei 2182m; Madonna 1522m.
Change in elevation: Gain of about 300m; Loss of about 1100m.
Grade: Difficult.

THE BRENTA

Special Considerations:
1. **This is a very long hike so bring food and water.**
2. **The trail passes through many rocky stretches.**
3. **There may be snow and ice.**

Starting Point: From Rifugio Grostè at the top lift station take trail #316 south to Rifugio del Tuckett.

The route to Rifugio del Tuckett passes among boulder fields and traverses the flanks of the Brenta with exciting glimpses of stratified block-like peaks. When you arrive at the rifugio be sure to look up at the broad glacier field. You can also see the trail ahead and, if you wish at this point, you can change your plan and return to Madonna on trail #317. Otherwise, the route continues on trail #328 to trail #318 to Rifugio Brentei. The trail goes partly along a ledge where there is some exposure but there is a fixed cable for support. Once at Rifugio Brentei there are many choices but some are only possible if you plan to spend the night. To return from Rifugio Brentei you must retrace your way on trail #318 for about two kilometers and continue to Rifugio Casinei. Here, take trail #317 descending over many switchbacks through woods and over streams to Rifugio Vallesinella. You can call a taxi from the rifugio if you wish. The final walk back to Madonna can take another 1½ hours.

Dramatic setting of Rifugio Alimonta

Alternatives: Make reservations ahead of time for a night at the Rifugio Brentei so you can plan one of the following alternatives or any other you may wish to organize. Telephone number: 0465-41244.

Alternative 1: Rifugio Brentei to Rifugio Pedrotti—an exciting 5-hour trip up and back. You hike through the Val Brenta Alta on trail #318 to Rifugio Pedrotti. The first part is through a broad valley then over a snow field where you may need your ice axe. You next navigate a ledge with cable support and finally arrive at a pass—Bocca di Brenta. Here you can see the ladders and ledges of the Via delle Bocchette. A short and easy, but exposed path leads to the Rifugio Pedrotti. You return the same way. This grade Expert excursion should not be attempted in bad weather or when snow or ice are present. Even on clear days, an ice axe may be required.

Alternative 2: Rifugio Brentei to Rifugio Alimonta—2 hrs up and back. From Rifugio Brentei traverse shelves and ledges to Rifugio Alimonta. From here, you can proceed over a glacier, using an ice axe, and finish at a small pass where you peer up in awe at 200 vertical meters of metal ladders, a portion of the Via delle Bocchette. You must retrace your way to the Rifugio Brentei. This is an alternative with an Expert rating and should not be attempted in bad weather.

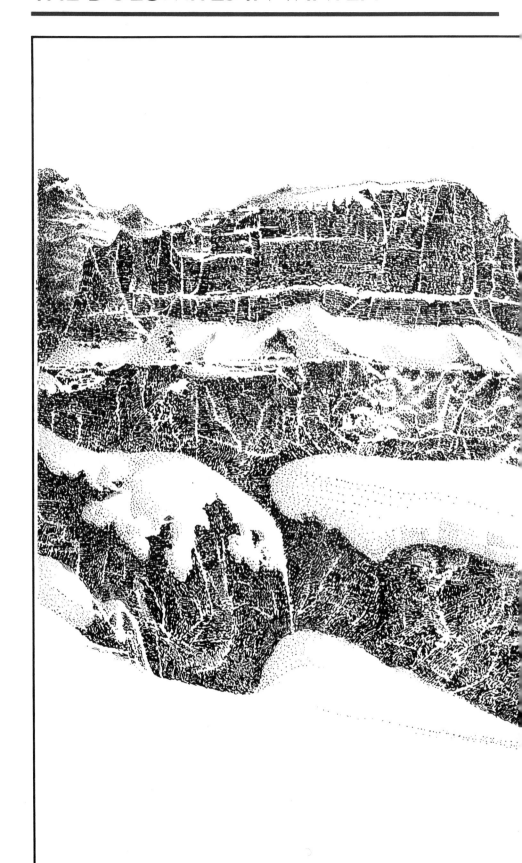

THE DOLOMITES IN WINTER

WINTER

Lunchtime on Alpe di Siusi

WINTER

Winter brings a fresh look of grandeur to the Dolomites. Picture-book villages nestle among white-carpeted meadows. Peaks tower above with their fresh mantles of snow. Sport and recreation possibilities include alpine (downhill), cross-country, or back-country skiing, ice skating, curling, sledding, along with old-fashioned touring by horsedrawn sleigh. Hundreds of kilometers of cleared footpaths are maintained daily for those who simply wish to stroll or hike in the crisp, refreshing winter air. You will find a complete variety of tourist accommodations in the many villages and hamlets. Nearly every large village has its own dining spots and après-ski activities—even indoor swimming and tennis are available.

The five geographic districts used in the Summer section of this book: Northwest, Southwest, Northeast, Southeast and West—are used in this Winter section. These districts are subdivided into fourteen winter regions. Skiing activities for each region are categorized into alpine and cross-country. When there are several alpine ski areas in a region they are each described separately.

A winter map-diagram locating the alpine ski areas is included for each region. Major lifts serving the greatest numbers of *piste,* ski runs, are shown on the map-diagrams. Also shown, in chart form, is the approximate number and type of lift for the different ski areas. Symbols indicate the cable car or *funivia,* gondola or *ovovia,* chairlift or *seggiovia,* and surface lift or *skilift.* (Surface lifts are T-bars or pomalifts, and are easy to use. They are quite often installed in the higher locations to connect the piste.)

DISTRICTS AND WINTER REGIONS

Northwest
Val Gardena (Gröden)
Val di Fassa
Alta Badia
Arabba
Plan de Corones (Kronplatz)
Bressanone (Brixen)

Southwest
San Martino di Castrozza-Passo Rolle
Val di Fiemme-Obereggen
Moena-Falcade

Northeast
Cortina
Alta Pusteria (Hochpustertal) -
 Val di Sesto (Sexten)

Southeast
Civetta-Pelmo
Marmolada

West
Madonna di Campiglio

WINTER

These map-diagrams should complement the ski maps you can purchase. Similar diagrams, pamphlets and materials are also available from the local tourist offices. You will occasionally find minor variations between elevations and names for geographic features among these various source materials.

ALPINE SKIING

The alpine skier has enormous opportunities, perhaps unsurpassed in any other area in the Alps, to ski from valley to valley and village to village. Amazing distances can be covered in the same day without ever repeating the same pista.

Piste are on varied terrain, many with exceptional views. Average "verticals" in the ski areas range between 700 and 1000 meters—in many cases considerably more. There are in excess of 600 lifts and 1200 kilometers of piste and most can be enjoyed on the same Dolomite area ski-pass, *Dolomiti Superski*. For the most part, slopes are immaculately groomed each night so deep moguls never become a problem. Even the advanced and expert skier will enjoy cruising the intermediate and beginner areas because of the moun-

tain vistas, variety of colorful places to stop, and friendly people. There are mountain restaurants of every description from cozy rustic *baite* (huts) and *rifugi* (mountain inns), to roomy modern cafeterias. Ski schools are available in each region and the quality of instruction is excellent. Nurseries for tots, and ski rental and repair shops are always nearby so there is little reason to lose any ski time. Frequent bus service connects ski areas within the regions and there are also taxis for hire.

CROSS-COUNTRY SKIING

The Dolomites offer cross-country skiing, *sci di fondo*, on hundreds of kilometers of tracks. These tracks travel through all types of scenery and terrain, such as narrow valleys bordered by steep canyon walls, broad valleys bordered by giant Dolomite peaks, or vast open alps with panoramic views. Long routes on well-maintained tracks challenge the cross-country racer and skater while slopes for the telemark enthusiast are everywhere. Generally, the cross-country areas are well-marked and posted; tracks are shown on the same maps with alpine skiing. Instruction is available in all major villages.

MAP DIAGRAM LEGEND

⌢ Roads	≀ Passes	♔ Cable Cars
		▯ Gondolas
⸴⸴⸴ Private, Restricted, and/or Unpaved Roads	▲▲ Mountains	▯ Chairlift
	■ Rifugio	▮ Ski Area
○ Autostrada Exits	• Top Lift Station	⛷ Cross Country Skiing
		⛷ Skilifts

Cross-country skiing in the Val di Landro, Cristallo in background

DOLOMITI SUPERSKI

The Dolomiti Superski is a completely computerized, multi-region ski-pass program that offers the largest selection of lifts on one pass anywhere in the world. Founded in 1974, it continues to expand each year as new ski areas, lifts and piste are added. Most people choose to buy the Dolomiti Superski pass because it enables them to ski freely from region to region. However, passes for a single region, usable for any specified number of days, can also be purchased.

SELLA RONDA DIAGRAM

VAL GARDENA (GRÖDEN)

ALTA BADIA

SELVA
WOLKENSTEIN
1563

No. 242

COLFOSCO
KOLFUSCHG
1645

CORVARA
1568

P.so Gardena
Grödner Joch
2121

GRUPPO SELLA

P.so Campolongo
1875

P.so Sella
Sellajoch
2244

PIZ BOE
3152

P.so Pordoi
2239

No. 48

ARABBA
1602

ARABBA

CANAZEI
1465

VAL DI FASSA

0 1 2 km.

SKI CIRCUITS

Touring by ski from one ski area to the next is a special experience in the Dolomites. You have little need to walk or use local transportation when making connections. With your Dolomiti Superski pass or area pass you proceed through most of the lift gates without delay.

One exciting ski circuit is the popular *Sella Ronda* which circles around the colossal Gruppo Sella massif traveling through parts of the Val Gardena (Gröden), Alta Badia, Arabba, and Val di Fassa. You can start the tour from any large village at the base of the mountain and route yourself clockwise or counterclockwise through an everchanging variety of scenery. Lifts on the circuit are efficiently linked so there is a minimum amount of poling. It can take 5 or 6 hours to complete the 26-kilometer tour over mostly intermediate slopes. Part of your travel time may involve waiting in lines at the major uphill lifts. However, this exhilarating experience more than justifies the delays. Be aware that if storms occur certain lifts may

close, but you will be informed of any difficulties as you proceed through the tour and alternatives will be suggested. You can purchase excellent maps that give you directions on how to complete this skiing adventure.

The Dolomiti Superski office or the Azienda di Soggiorno, in the major regions, will be happy to suggest other ski circuits. They can give you names of local guides and provide you with specific information such as lifts to use, direction of travel, vertical meters of piste you will ski, and the time required for the tour.

Rifugio Forcelles above Colfosco, Alta Badia

BACK-COUNTRY SKIING

There are two types of back-country skiing, *sci alpinismo* and *fuori pista*. Both call for professional guides because avalanche and snow conditions vary every day. Also, all ski regions desire to protect the environment, and local guides know where it is possible to tour. The sci-alpinismo adventure is for strong, experienced skiers, as lifts are not used and the outing often requires a considerable ascent. Off-piste, fuori pista, is the other type of back-country tour. In this case, normal lifts are used and the guides will lead you from the upper lift stations into wilderness terrain. For both types of excursions, you can use either mountaineering ski equipment (although regular alpine skis will suffice on fuori pista trips) or appropriate three-pin skis. The Val Gardena, Cortina, and Madonna di Campiglio are just a few of the winter regions where these exciting adventures are possible.

OFF-PISTE SKIING ON THE GRUPPO SELLA

The colossal table-shaped Gruppo Sella, famous for off-piste skiing, stands at the east end of Val Gardena and the north end of Val di Fassa; it borders the west end of Alta Badia and rises above the village of Arabba. Lift access to the summit plateau is at the Passo Pordoi, above Canazei, and there are piste from the top down to three of the bordering regions. One of the most dramatic is the Val Mezdì, curving its way

steeply down between giant canyon walls, ultimately arriving at the popular pista between the Passo Gardena and Corvara. A guide is highly recommended because skiing on the Sella is challenging, can be dangerous, and conditions change from day to day.

APPROXIMATE DRIVING TIMES BETWEEN MAJOR CENTERS AND THE NEAREST POINT IN THE DOLOMITES (Assumes normal traffic and weather conditions)	
	Hours
Milan	3½
Munich	3
Salzburg	3
Innsbruck	1½
Lake Garda	2
Venice	2½
Verona	2
Florence	4
Rome	7
Vienna	5½
Zurich	5½
Frankfurt	6
Amsterdam	9

Once arriving there can be an additional 2 hours of driving depending on your destination.

About to descend Val Mezdì, Gruppo Sella

TIPS FOR SKIERS

1. Detailed maps and publications of alpine skiing in the Dolomites are readily available and are kept current. They are indispensable aids in planning your ski adventures. You can write, telex or phone any village tourist office (Azienda di Soggiorno) for copies. Many major newspapers and manufacturers also sponsor annual guides to European ski areas. These do not cover all of the Dolomites but do describe some of the larger ski areas.

2. Lift facilities are always being modified and upgraded so that lift numbers and names may change. You are encouraged to contact the local ski schools, guides, local offices of Dolomiti Superski, or tourist offices to obtain the most recent information.

3. Before you arrive you may wish to know costs of ski passes, sizes of ski school classes, languages spoken and schedules for local ski bus systems. Contact the village tourist offices for this information.

4. Skiers must use all normal safety precautions regarding avalanche conditions. Do not ski off-piste except with a guide. It is best to ask local ski guides and ski schools for the most current information.

Farmhouses near Passo Sella

METRIC CONVERSION TABLE

Meters (m.)	Feet (ft.)	
1	3.28	1 Centimeter (cm.) = 0.3937 Inches (in.)
500	1640	1 Inch (in.) = 2.54 Centimeters (cm.)
1000	3280	1 Kilometer (km.) = 0.62 Miles (mi.)
1500	4921	1 Mile (mi.) = 1.61 Kilometers (km.)
2000	6562	
2500	8202	1 Kilogram (kg.) = 2.2 Pounds (lb.)
3000	9842	1 Pound (lb.) = 0.45 Kilogram (kg.)

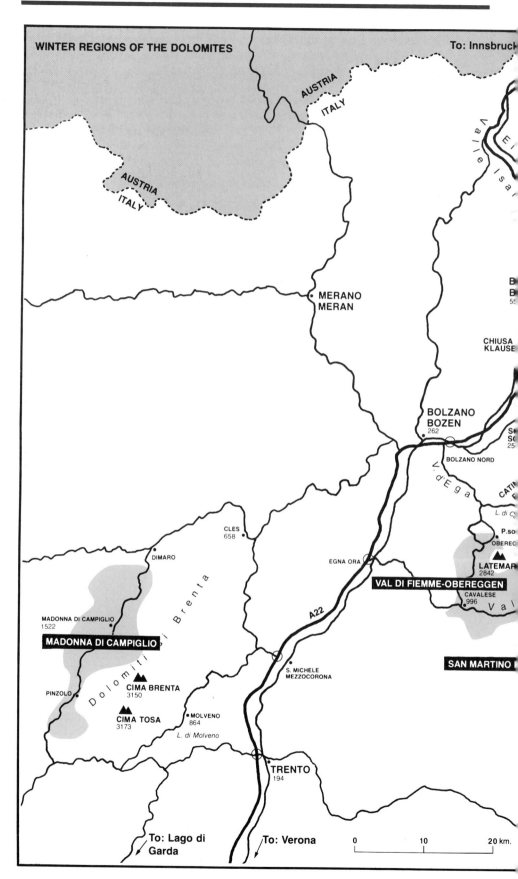

WINTER REGIONS OF THE DOLOMITES

To: Innsbruck

AUSTRIA
ITALY

AUSTRIA
ITALY

MERANO
MERAN

CHIUSA
KLAUSE

BOLZANO
BOZEN
262

BOLZANO NORD

CLES
658

DIMARO

P.so
OBEREG

LATEMAR
2842

VAL DI FIEMME-OBEREGGEN

CAVALESE
996

MADONNA DI CAMPIGLIO
1522

MADONNA DI CAMPIGLIO

A22

S. MICHELE
MEZZOCORONA

SAN MARTINO

PINZOLO

CIMA BRENTA
3150

CIMA TOSA
3173

MOLVENO
864

L. di Molveno

Dolomiti di Brenta

V. d'Ega

TRENTO
194

To: Lago di
Garda

To: Verona

0   10   20 km.

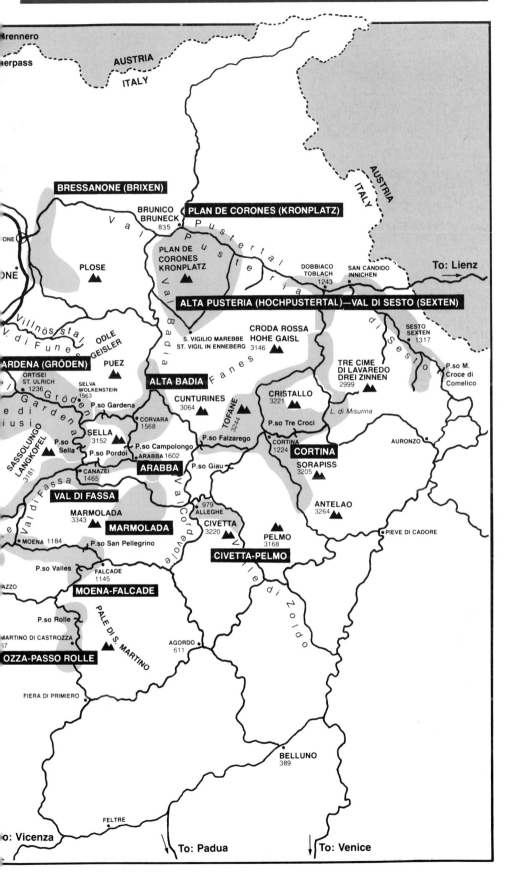

NORTHWEST

Early morning light on Sassolungo

NORTHWEST

The Northwest district offers the largest variety of winter sports and is the easiest to reach. The autostrada, A22, forms its western boundary with convenient exits at Bressanone (Brixen), Chiusa (Klausen), and Bolzano (Bozen). There are six varied winter regions within the district. The **Val Gardena (Gröden)** is an immense region with four alpine ski areas, a tremendous selection of cross-country tracks, and quite extensive opportunities for back-country skiing. It has several attractive Tyrolean villages. The **Val di Fassa** has more limited alpine skiing than the Val Gardena, but is noted for its very popular cross-country ski course connecting the Italianate villages in the valley. The **Alta Badia** offers delightful skiing for beginners and intermediates, and some cross-country tracks. It is very open and sunny and the Tyrolean villages here are small and peaceful. **Arabba,** a small village connected to the Alta Badia, is noted for alpine skiing with a wide range of piste for all abilities. **Plan de Corones (Kronplatz),** in the northernmost part of the district, has skiing on one large, rounded mountain served by lifts from the three Tyrolean villages at its base. Both cross-country and back-country skiing are also available. **Bressanone (Brixen)** is closest to the autostrada, and its main ski area is above this large medieval town.

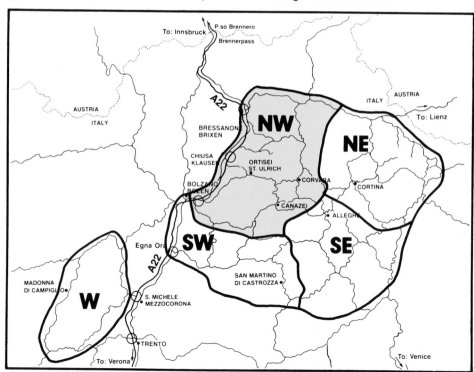

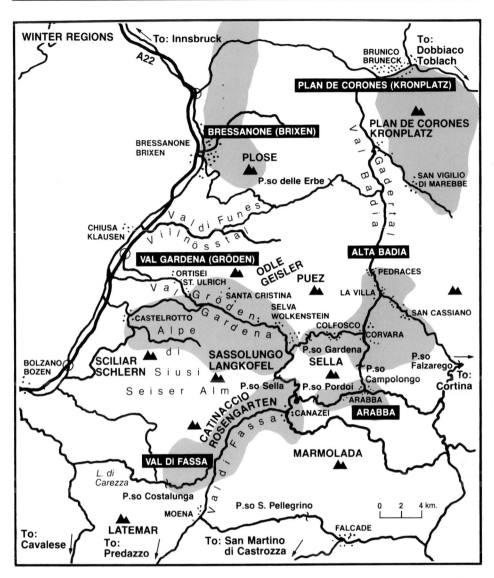

WINTER REGIONS

To: Innsbruck

A22

To: Dobbiaco Toblach

BRUNICO BRUNECK

PLAN DE CORONES (KRONPLATZ)

PLAN DE CORONES KRONPLATZ

BRESSANONE BRIXEN

BRESSANONE (BRIXEN)

SAN VIGILIO DI MAREBBE

PLOSE

P.so delle Erbe

Val di Funes

Villnösstal

CHIUSA KLAUSEN

Val di Funes

VAL GARDENA (GRÖDEN)

ODLE GEISLER

ALTA BADIA

ORTISEI ST. ULRICH

PUEZ

PEDRACES

Val Gardena

SANTA CRISTINA

LA VILLA

SAN CASSIANO

SELVA WOLKENSTEIN

COLFOSCO

CASTELROTTO

Alpe

CORVARA

di

SASSOLUNGO LANGKOFEL

P.so Gardena

BOLZANO BOZEN

SCILIAR SCHLERN Siusi

Seiser Alm

SELLA

P.so Campolongo

P.so Falzarego

To: Cortina

P.so Sella

P.so Pordoi

P.so Gardena

ARABBA

ARABBA

CATINACCIO ROSENGARTEN

CANAZEI

Val di Fassa

VAL DI FASSA

MARMOLADA

L. di Carezza

P.so Costalunga

MOENA

P.so S. Pellegrino

0 2 4 km.

FALCADE

To: Cavalese

To: Predazzo

To: San Martino di Castrozza

LATEMAR

Ski break on Plan de Corones, above San Vigilio di Marebbe

VAL GARDENA (GRÖDEN)

Ciampinoi ski slopes above Selva

HIGHLIGHTS

The Val Gardena, with its wide open, sunny expanses and magnificent towering peaks, is one of the most popular and diversified regions in the Dolomites for a winter holiday. Snows can begin as early as November and often by December the higher mountains and meadows are covered. The Tyrolean villages look like Christmas card scenes. Accommodation is plentiful, ranging from top hotels and apartments to modest inns and rooms in private homes. If you are driving, it is well to note that the two major passes, Passo Gardena from the east and Passo Sella from the south, can be closed at times. Generally, a car is not essential in the winter. Lifts are either within walking distance of the villages or easily accessible via the well-run local bus system or taxis. The latter are convenient for visiting more remote villages and ski areas in neighboring regions.

MAJOR VILLAGES

Ortisei (St. Ulrich) is the largest year-round village in the Val Gardena. It is less crowded than its neighbors up the valley but not as central for alpine skiing, requiring a few hundred meters walk to reach the major uphill lifts. There are shops of all kinds, a main piazza, and winding side streets to wander. It is a woodcarving center and there are unlimited possibilities to admire the craft. You can buy an inexpensive memento or a one-of-a-kind masterpiece.

Santa Cristina (St. Christina), between Selva and Ortisei, is on an uphill grade along the main valley thoroughfare. It is smaller than its neighbors but has a few fashionable shops and ample hotels and tourist accommodations. Lifts are a few hundred meters above and below the main village street.

MAJOR VILLAGES	Population	Elevation
Ortisei (St. Ulrich)	5,000	1236m
Santa Cristina (St. Christina)	1,500	1428m
Selva (Wolkenstein)	2,300	1563m
Castelrotto (Kastelruth)/Siusi (Seis)	2,800	900m-1100m

PRINCIPAL LANGUAGES: German, Italian, and Ladin.

VAL GARDENA (GRÖDEN)

Selva (Wolkenstein), at the east end of the valley, is the most accessible center to the greatest majority of lifts—some leaving right from the village. It has many shops, cafés, a fabulous bakery, and hotels along the main street. Above the center there are charming smaller hotels, a pretty village church, some wonderful cafés, and, of course, more shops in which to browse.

Castelrotto (Kastelruth), Siusi (Seis), and **Fiè (Völs)** are quieter villages with considerable charm. About a 30-minute drive from Ortisei, these villages are not near the major lift systems of the Val Gardena, but they have easy road access to all the winter activities on the sunny Alpe di Siusi.

Village of Selva

VAL GARDENA (GRÖDEN)

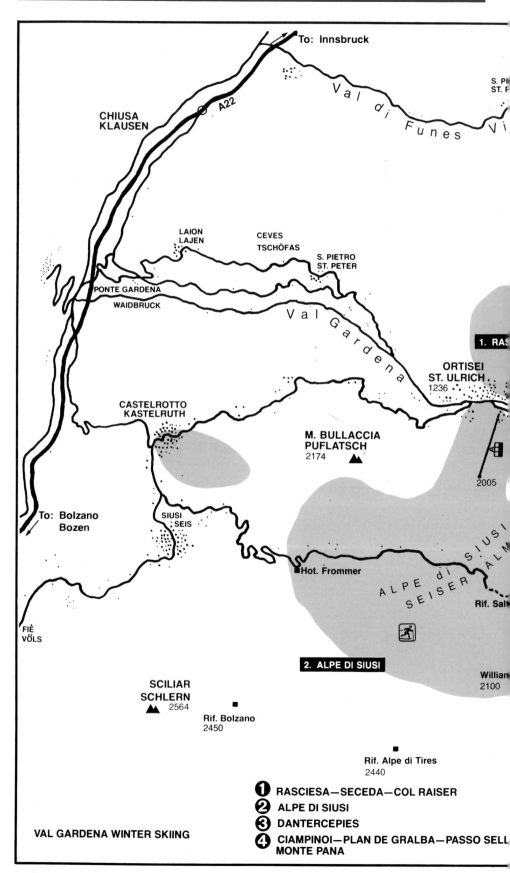

To: Innsbruck

CHIUSA
KLAUSEN

A22

Val di Funes

S. PI
ST. F

LAION
LAJEN

CEVES
TSCHÖFAS

S. PIETRO
ST. PETER

PONTE GARDENA

WAIDBRUCK

Val Gardena

1. RAS

ORTISEI
ST. ULRICH
1236

CASTELROTTO
KASTELRUTH

M. BULLACCIA
PUFLATSCH
2174 ▲▲

2005

To: Bolzano
Bozen

SIUSI
SEIS

ALPE di SIUSI

SEISER ALM

Hot. Frommer

Rif. Sal

FIÈ
VÖLS

2. ALPE DI SIUSI

Willian
2100

SCILIAR
SCHLERN
▲▲ 2564

Rif. Bolzano
2450

Rif. Alpe di Tires
2440

❶ RASCIESA—SECEDA—COL RAISER
❷ ALPE DI SIUSI
❸ DANTERCEPIES
❹ CIAMPINOI—PLAN DE GRALBA—PASSO SELL
MONTE PANA

VAL GARDENA WINTER SKIING

VAL GARDENA (GRÖDEN)

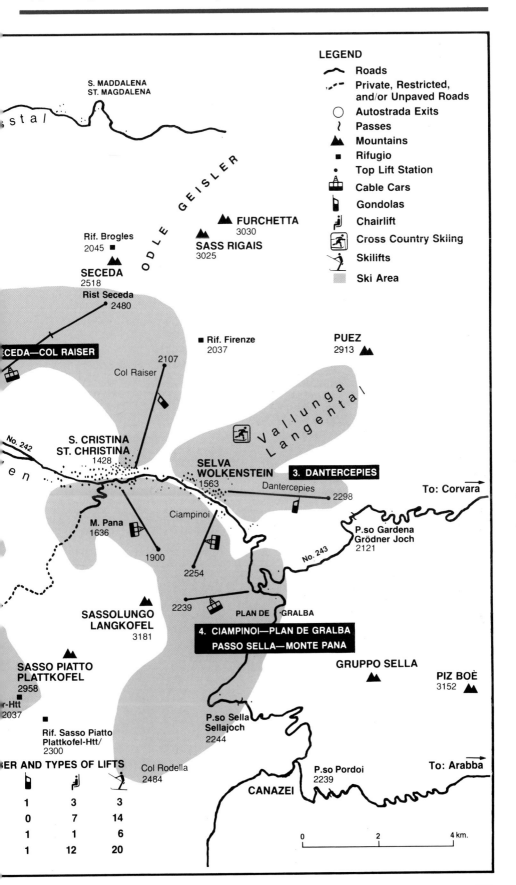

LEGEND

- ∿ Roads
- ⌐⌐ Private, Restricted, and/or Unpaved Roads
- ○ Autostrada Exits
- Passes
- ▲▲ Mountains
- ■ Rifugio
- • Top Lift Station
- Cable Cars
- Gondolas
- Chairlift
- Cross Country Skiing
- Skilifts
- Ski Area

s t a l

S. MADDALENA
ST. MAGDALENA

O D L E   G E I S L E R

Rif. Brogles
2045 ■

FURCHETTA
3030

SASS RIGAIS
3025

SECEDA
2518

Rist Seceda
• 2480

■ Rif. Firenze
2037

PUEZ
2913 ▲▲

CEDA—COL RAISER

2107
Col Raiser

V a l l u n g a
L a n g e n t a l

No. 242

**S. CRISTINA
ST. CHRISTINA**
1428

**SELVA
WOLKENSTEIN**
1563

3. DANTERCEPIES

Dantercepies
2298

To: Corvara

Ciampinoi

M. Pana
1636

P.so Gardena
Grödner Joch
2121

1900

No. 243

2254

2239

PLAN DE · GRALBA

**SASSOLUNGO
LANGKOFEL**
3181

**4. CIAMPINOI—PLAN DE GRALBA
PASSO SELLA—MONTE PANA**

GRUPPO SELLA

PIZ BOÈ
3152 ▲▲

**SASSO PIATTO
PLATTKOFEL**
2958

r-Htt
2037

Rif. Sasso Piatto
Plattkofel-Htt/
2300

P.so Sella
Sellajoch
2244

ER AND TYPES OF LIFTS

Col Rodella
2484

P.so Pordoi
2239

To: Arabba

CANAZEI

1	3	3
0	7	14
1	1	6
1	12	20

0   2   4 km.

VAL GARDENA (GRODEN)

ALPINE SKIING

The Val Gardena has one of the most complete lift networks in the Dolomites and hosts World Cup events annually. Four main ski areas offer a variety of skiing, from beginner to advanced, and there are also many possibilities for skiing into other regions, valleys and villages. Local bus service is all you need to take you from the villages to the ski areas. Selva, in particular, is closest to the lifts.

This region is so popular that there can be lines at the larger uphill lifts. However, once in the higher parts, there are enough surface and chairlifts, as well as piste, to disperse people well. There is an ever-increasing capability for snow-making and this, combined with a wide range of slope directions, makes it possible to seek the optimum combination of weather and snow conditions.

The Val Gardena is on the *Sella Ronda* circuit. This itinerary, using lifts, takes you around one of the most striking mountain massifs in the Dolomites—skiing through four regions. You can begin from the Val Gardena, Val di Fassa, Alta Badia or Arabba regions and route yourself clockwise or counterclockwise.

SKI AREAS

❶ Rasciesa-Seceda-Col Raiser: North above Ortisei and Santa Cristina. Access by major lifts from both of these villages.

The treeless, sunny, open bowl skiing here is delightful. With sufficient snow you can ski from the top all the way to Ortisei, Santa Cristina, or even Selva, with stops at different mountain restaurants along the way. You can also connect to the Col Raiser lift coming from Santa Cristina. Views are dramatic on the top with beautiful panoramas of the Val Gardena, Sassolungo, Gruppo Sella, Catinaccio and Odle. On a clear day the Tofane above Cortina and Pelmo loom in the distance.

While the area is primarily for intermediate skiers, even the most advanced skier will enjoy cruising the wide long bowl. Once above, the crowds are well dispersed but the slopes face south so they can be icy in the mornings. In early spring there is less snow. However, the increasing use of snow-making machines mitigates this problem. It would be wise to avoid the area in fog or low visibility due to a possible "white-out" condition.

❷ Alpe di Siusi: South and above Ortisei and Santa Cristina with access by a major lift from Ortisei. Access by private car or taxi is possible via Castelrotto and Santa Cristina.

Although this is an area renowned for its cross-country skiing, there are also many slopes for the beginner and intermediate alpine skier. Actually, skiers of all abilities will enjoy the area as it is alive with activities ranging from people walking on cleared footpaths to families piled in horse-drawn sleighs. There are wonderful mountain restaurants and new hotels dot the landscape.

Open bowl skiing on Seceda

VAL GARDENA (GRÖDEN)

The Sassolungo, Sciliar and Odle mountains are seen from all parts. Skiing is possible quite early to very late in the season as little snow cover is required. The area is less crowded than the others but lifts are separated so some poling is required between piste. There are plans to update the lift system throughout the entire area.

Winter activity on Alpe di Siusi, Sassolungo in background

VAL GARDENA (GRODEN)

❸ **Dantercepies:** West and above Selva. The major gondola is easily accessible from the village by using surface lifts or one small chairlift. This is a fairly steep, tree-lined area with three long and exciting piste for intermediate and advanced skiers.

It is easy to connect from this popular area to the Alta Badia region and other ski areas east of the Passo Gardena as well as those surrounding Selva and the Gruppo Sella. Dantercepies is on the Sella Ronda circuit so the slopes can get crowded. There is an excellent place for instruction and practice on the lower part served by the well-maintained and well-managed Risaccia lift. Here, it is entertaining to watch the weekly children's and amateur slalom events.

❹ **Ciampinoi-Plan de Gralba-Passo Sella-Monte Pana:** South and a bit east of Santa Cristina and above Selva on its south. Major lifts from each of these villages serve the area.

Ciampinoi, Plan de Gralba and the Passo Sella are connected by an extensive and efficient lift network which offers everything from World Cup downhill piste to beginner skiing in open bowls. From Ciampinoi into Selva or Santa Cristina there are beautifully maintained and wonderful piste for cruising. There are beginning level piste above Plan and from the Passo Sella into Plan and Selva. Slopes above Selva and Santa Cristina are tree-covered, those above Plan and near the Passo Sella are more open. The area is very busy due to its easy access and variety; part of it is on the Sella Ronda circuit. While the major uphill lifts can be crowded, there are additional lifts in the

Training on Dantercepies

higher parts that fan out through the open bowl dispersing skiers.

The Monte Pana area, reachable by car or lift from Santa Cristina, is an excellent area to learn to ski and is ideal for families. Piste are right below the Sassolungo and there are some delightful restaurants. There are future plans to connect Monte Pana by lift to the neighboring Ciampinoi-Plan de Gralba complex.

Plan de Gralba, Gruppo Sella in background

VAL GARDENA(GRÖDEN)

Ski tracks in Vallunga

CROSS-COUNTRY SKIING

The Val Gardena is one of the principal areas in the Dolomites for cross-country skiing with more than 100 kilometers of tracks. The flat immense Alpe di Siusi and the adjoining Monte Pana, are famous throughout Europe for cross-country skiing. This 55-square kilometer area holds a vast system of tracks and the many rifugi along the way are popular rest stops. In the valley below you can ski along the river between Santa Cristina and Ortisei on tracks that parallel the road. The cliff-sided Vallunga, just northeast of Selva, is yet another beautiful area for a cross-country excursion.

Horsedrawn sleigh

GENERAL PISTE INFORMATION

Longest: 9 km, Seceda to Ortisei.

Most vertical: 2518m-1236m, Seceda to Ortisei.

Ranking
  Beginner: Extensive
  Intermediate: Extensive
  Advanced: Some

Slope Exposures: All

Region is on the Dolomiti Superski pass.

VAL DI FASSA

Val di Fassa, Sassolungo in background

HIGHLIGHTS

The sheer walls of the snow-clad Catinaccio (Rosengarten) massif are a backdrop for all the winter excitement of the Val di Fassa. The center of activities is at the north end of this valley, in a bowl below the Passo Sella and Passo Pordoi. Here the lively village of Canazei and its quaint neighbor Campitello are located—they are convenient to the major lifts of this region as well as other neighboring regions. A famous cross-country ski race, the Marcialonga, is staged here annually at the end of January.

Accommodation is plentiful and varied in all of the villages. While public transportation is excellent in the region, a car is a definite advantage—especially if you stay in one of the smaller villages south of Canazei. Roads from the south through Predazzo and Moena are usually open; however, other approaches by way of Passo Sella (Sellajoch), Passo Pordoi, and Passo Costalunga (Karerpass) may occasionally be closed in the winter.

VILLAGES

Canazei, the largest village in the region, has a busy piazza where the main hotels and après-ski activities are centered. The winding side streets have additional shops and cafés; rustic old buildings are everywhere. The most important lift is a short walk from town but there is also a convenient local bus.

Campitello, just west of Canazei, is smaller and quieter but with plentiful tourist accommodations. A large cable car near the village takes you to the network of lifts and piste at the Passo Sella where it is also easy to join with the skiing in the neighboring Val Gardena.

Vigo di Fassa, central in the Val di Fassa, nestles on gentle sunny slopes below the Catinaccio. There are attractive small hotels conveniently located to the village and lifts. A car is helpful as the other villages and major ski areas are some distance away.

MAJOR VILLAGES

	Population	Elevation
Canazei	1,700	1465m
Campitello	700	1442m
Vigo di Fassa	950	1382m

PRINCIPAL LANGUAGES: Italian, German, and Ladin.

VAL DI FASSA

Village to village skiing in Val di Fassa

VAL DI FASSA

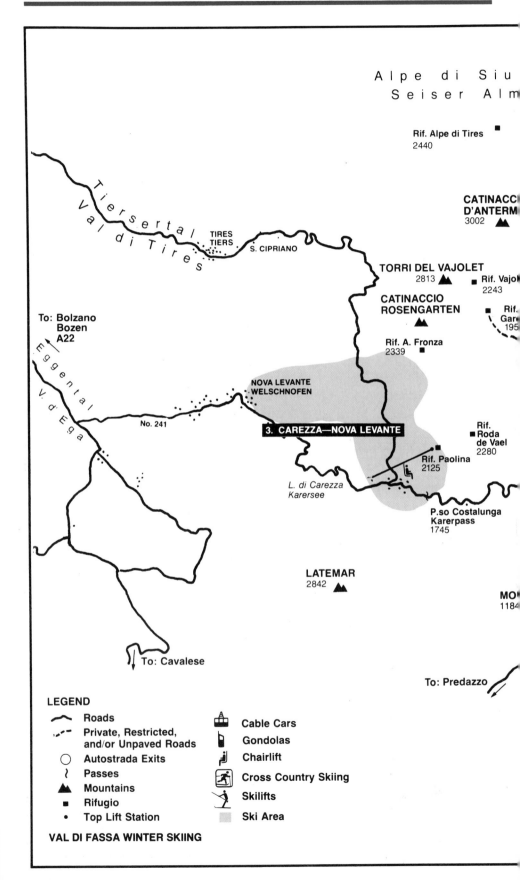

Alpe di Siu
Seiser Alm

Rif. Alpe di Tires
2440

CATINACC
D'ANTERM
3002

T i e r s e r t a l
V a l d i T i r e s

TIRES
TIERS
S. CIPRIANO

TORRI DEL VAJOLET
2813
Rif. Vajo
2243

CATINACCIO
ROSENGARTEN

Rif.
Gar
195

To: Bolzano
Bozen
A22

Rif. A. Fronza
2339

E g g e n t a l
V. d' E g a

NOVA LEVANTE
WELSCHNOFEN

No. 241

3. CAREZZA—NOVA LEVANTE

Rif.
Roda
de Vael
2280

Rif. Paolina
2125

L. di Carezza
Karersee

P.so Costalunga
Karerpass
1745

LATEMAR
2842

MO
1184

To: Cavalese

To: Predazzo

LEGEND

～	Roads	🚡	Cable Cars
･-･	Private, Restricted, and/or Unpaved Roads	🚠	Gondolas
○	Autostrada Exits	💺	Chairlift
⌇	Passes	🎿	Cross Country Skiing
▲	Mountains	🎿	Skilifts
■	Rifugio		Ski Area
•	Top Lift Station		

VAL DI FASSA WINTER SKIING

190

VAL DI FASSA

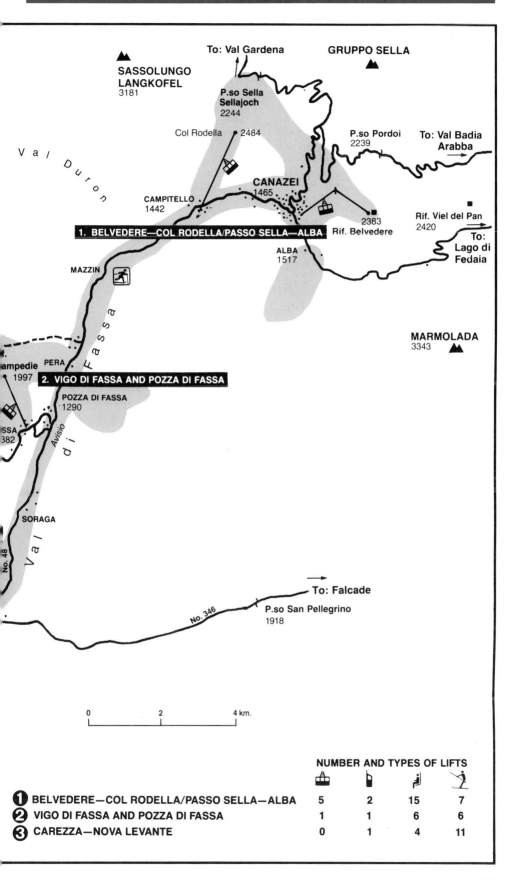

To: Val Gardena

GRUPPO SELLA

▲▲ **SASSOLUNGO
LANGKOFEL**
3181

**P.so Sella
Sellajoch**
2244

Col Rodella ● 2484

P.so Pordoi
2239

To: **Val Badia
Arabba**

V a l   D u r o n

CANAZEI
1465

Rif. Viel del Pan
2420

CAMPITELLO
1442

■ 2383

To:
**Lago di
Fedaia**

1. BELVEDERE—COL RODELLA/PASSO SELLA—ALBA   Rif. Belvedere

MAZZIN

ALBA
1517

F a s s a

MARMOLADA
3343 ▲▲

ampedie **PERA**
1997

2. VIGO DI FASSA AND POZZA DI FASSA

POZZA DI FASSA
1290

Avisio

SSA
382

d i

SORAGA

V a l

No. 48

To: **Falcade**

No. 346

P.so San Pellegrino
1918

```
0        2        4 km.
```


NUMBER AND TYPES OF LIFTS

	🚠	🚡	🪑	🎿
❶ BELVEDERE—COL RODELLA/PASSO SELLA—ALBA	5	2	15	7
❷ VIGO DI FASSA AND POZZA DI FASSA	1	1	6	6
❸ CAREZZA—NOVA LEVANTE	0	1	4	11

VAL DI FASSA

ALPINE SKIING

The Val di Fassa region is primarily for beginners and intermediates including some smaller ski areas that are very pleasant for families. All facilities have snow-making machines. Slopes are near the main villages but you cannot ski from one ski area to the next. However, the excellent local bus service connects all the important villages and ski areas. Transportation to the Passo Pordoi, for off-piste skiing on the Gruppo Sella, can be easily arranged.

CROSS-COUNTRY SKIING

This is one of the more popular regions for track skiing in the Dolomites. Skiing beside the river is pleasant, with an opportunity for leisurely stops in the villages to enjoy an espresso and to browse in shops. You can tour the entire length of the valley and even continue south through the Val di Fiemme. There are bus stops along the way so returning or changing plans is easily done. The Marcialonga, a well-known race (70 km), takes place here every January.

GENERAL PISTE INFORMATION
Longest: About 5½ km, Belvedere to Canazei.
Most vertical: 2383m-1465m, Belvedere to Canazei.
Ranking
  Beginner: Many
  Intermediate: Extensive
  Advanced: Nil
Slope Exposures: All
Region is on the Dolomiti Superski pass.

Belvedere seen from high on Gruppo Sella

SKI AREAS

❶ **Belvedere-Col Rodella/Passo Sella-Alba:** Served by lifts from Canazei, Campitello, and Alba.

The Belvedere section is at the north end of the Val di Fassa below Passo Sella and Passo Pordoi. On the higher part there is intermediate open bowl skiing. The piste then narrow down, winding through trees to Canazei. The slopes can be crowded, with long lift lines as the area is part of the Sella Ronda circuit. The Col Rodella, reached by a cable car from Campitello, connects the Val di Fassa with the vast lift network of Passo Sella and the Val Gardena. Alba, a small area near Canazei, has a pleasant beginner bowl above and a good intermediate pista down to the village. It is usually not crowded and is especially nice for young families.

VAL DI FASSA

❷Vigo di Fassa and Pozza di Fassa:
Two small villages that face each other across the valley. The ski areas adjacent to each have only a few lifts.

Vigo is quite popular as it is sunny and below the dramatic vertical walls of the Catinaccio. Skiing here is for beginners and intermediates on open slopes. Pozza has westerly-facing slopes with sweeping views across the valley to the Catinaccio.

❸Carezza-Nova Levante: Access by lifts from near the Passo Costalunga and Nova Levante.

A collection of lifts serve these open slopes, a scenic area for beginners and intermediates. It is set below the southwest walls of the Catinaccio and there are also sweeping views of the Latemar and the hills and valleys surrounding Nova Levante.

Above Vigo di Fassa, Catinaccio in background

OTHER WINTER ACTIVITIES
Ice skating • Public and private indoor swimming • Bowling • Cleared footpaths •
Back-country skiing with guides • and more.

ALTA BADIA

Central Alta Badia, Corvara and Passo Campolongo

HIGHLIGHTS

The Alta Badia exudes Tyrolean charm and is steeped in the Ladin culture. Less crowded and quieter than neighboring regions, it nevertheless has a complete range of winter recreation facilities and you can easily tour by taxi or ski to Arabba, Cortina and the Val Gardena. This region is set in a wide open sunny hollow, completely surrounded by mountains, so it is generally protected from the wind.

VILLAGES

Corvara, the largest of the Tyrolean villages, spreads out along the valley floor at the western base of the Pralongia plateau. The main shops and hotels are close to a small central piazza. You can walk to many important lifts in the region and the village is on the Sella Ronda circuit.

Colfosco (Kolfuschg) is smaller than Corvara and is located above the town, on the way to the Passo Gardena. It is very sunny, has a quaint old world charm and offers a large selection of tourist accommodations. The Edelweisstal ski area is above the village while lifts and piste between the Passo

Gardena and Corvara pass a few hundred meters in front of the village. You can ski from here to Corvara and join most of the skiing in the Alta Badia.

San Cassiano (St. Kassian), located between La Villa and Passo Valparola, is a sparkling Tyrolean village with many hotels and pensioni on both sides of the road. The excellent lift system nearby takes you up to the Pralongia plateau.

La Villa (Stern) is quite small but right at the base of the large cable car to Piz La Villa, a high point on the Pralongia plateau. One of the most challenging piste in the region curves its way steeply down through woods from the top lift station. Accommodation is plentiful and the nearby villages of Corvara and San Cassiano also have a wide selection.

Pedraces (Pedratsches) and its neighbor **San Leonardo** are two small villages just a few kilometers north of La Villa; both have a good selection of tourist accommodations. The lift from San Leonardo takes you east over homes and farms to a gentle ski area which has splendid mountain and valley views.

MAJOR VILLAGES

	Population	Elevation
Corvara	700	1568m
Colfosco (Kolfuschg)	500	1645m
San Cassiano (St. Kassian)	650	1550m
La Villa (Stern)	850	1450m
Pedraces (Pedratsches)	1,150	1400m

ALTA BADIA

High above La Villa, San Cassiano below

ALTA BADIA

ALPINE SKIING

There is a range of skiing opportunities in this region—from the gentle open slopes on the Pralongia plateau to the more challenging piste above La Villa and below the Gruppo Sella. Lifts connect a number of neighboring regions such as Arabba, Val Gardena, and Val di Fassa. A large part of the Sella Ronda circuit routes its way through the Alta Badia so you can join it at several different points. All skiers—from beginner to advanced—enjoy skiing into the pretty villages. There are many attractive restaurants and rifugi well located for a snack or drink while you marvel at the wide panoramas.

CROSS-COUNTRY SKIING

Groomed tracks are on the valley floor and in both the villages of La Villa and Pedraces. A pleasant circuit takes you through trees between Corvara and Colfosco.

Refreshments above Colfosco

SKI AREAS

❶ Passo Gardena and Colfosco: Lift access from Passo Gardena, Colfosco, Corvara. A series of lifts take you from Corvara to Passo Gardena.

Wide beginner piste descend gently from the passo to Corvara. The final leg from Colfosco to Corvara is so flat that skiers use the chairlift down. These piste tend to become crowded as people make their way around the Sella Ronda. Ski slopes above Colfosco in the Edelweisstal are less crowded and more relaxing, with inviting rifugi positioned to enjoy the sun and lovely views.

❷ Pralongia Plateau: Broad, undulating slopes reached by lifts from Corvara, La Villa, San Cassiano, and Passo Campolongo.

This wide-open plateau is ideal for beginner and intermediate skiers, with views of giant

Rifugio Pralongia

Dolomite peaks such as Civetta and the Marmolada. The generally short piste are served by a network of surface and chairlifts. Be sure to study your map to minimize poling between piste. The area is well-marked but, as much of it looks the same, you can be enjoying the pista and view and ski past an important linking lift. Two dramatic north-facing piste leave from Piz La Villa and arch their way through trees, ending at La Villa. Additional tree-lined piste take you from the top down to San Cassiano. Otherwise, the slopes are wide open.

❸ East side of Gruppo Sella-Boè: South of Corvara; west and above Passo Campolongo. Lift access from Corvara and the passo.

There is one short advanced pista at the top, otherwise, piste here are for beginners and intermediates. From the highest point you can see the Marmolada and distant peaks. As you ski down to Corvara you weave your way through woods with occasional glimpses of the Pralongia and much of the Alta Badia.

Note: There is also pleasant skiing above **Pedraces.**

GENERAL PISTE INFORMATION

Longest: About 5 km,
   Vallon to Corvara.

Most vertical: 2530m-1568m,
   Vallon to Corvara.

Ranking
   Beginner: Extensive
   Intermediate: Extensive
   Advanced: A few

Slope Exposures: All

Region is on the Dolomiti Superski
   pass.

ALTA BADIA

Skiing high on Boè overlooking Pralongia plateau

ALTA BADIA ~ ARABBA

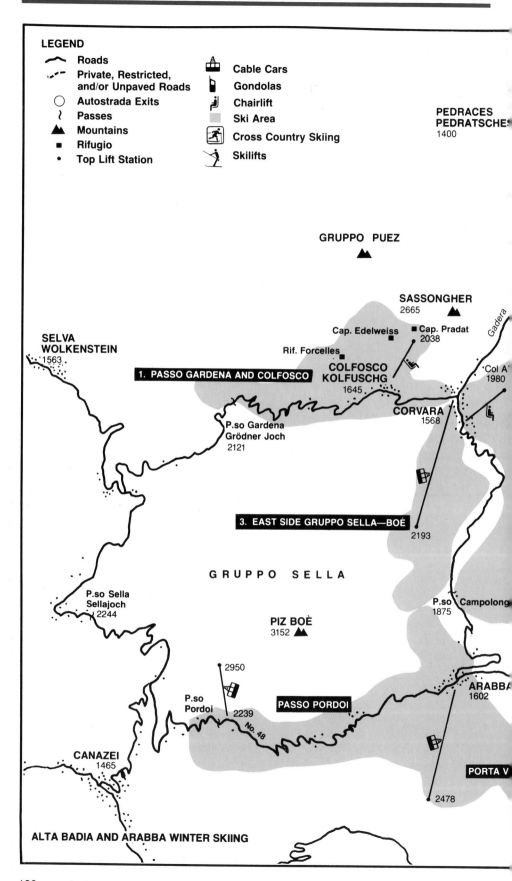

LEGEND

Roads		Cable Cars	
Private, Restricted, and/or Unpaved Roads		Gondolas	
Autostrada Exits		Chairlift	
Passes		Ski Area	
Mountains		Cross Country Skiing	
Rifugio		Skilifts	
Top Lift Station			

PEDRACES PEDRATSCHES
1400

GRUPPO PUEZ

SASSONGHER
2665

Cap. Edelweiss · Cap. Pradat
2038

Rif. Forcelles

SELVA WOLKENSTEIN
1563

1. PASSO GARDENA AND COLFOSCO

COLFOSCO KOLFUSCHG
1645

Col A
1980

CORVARA
1568

P.so Gardena
Grödner Joch
2121

3. EAST SIDE GRUPPO SELLA—BOÈ

2193

G R U P P O   S E L L A

P.so Sella
Sellajoch
2244

P.so Campolong
1875

PIZ BOÈ
3152

2950

P.so Pordoi
2239

PASSO PORDOI

No. 48

ARABBA
1602

CANAZEI
1465

PORTA V

2478

ALTA BADIA AND ARABBA WINTER SKIING

198

ALTA BADIA ~ ARABBA

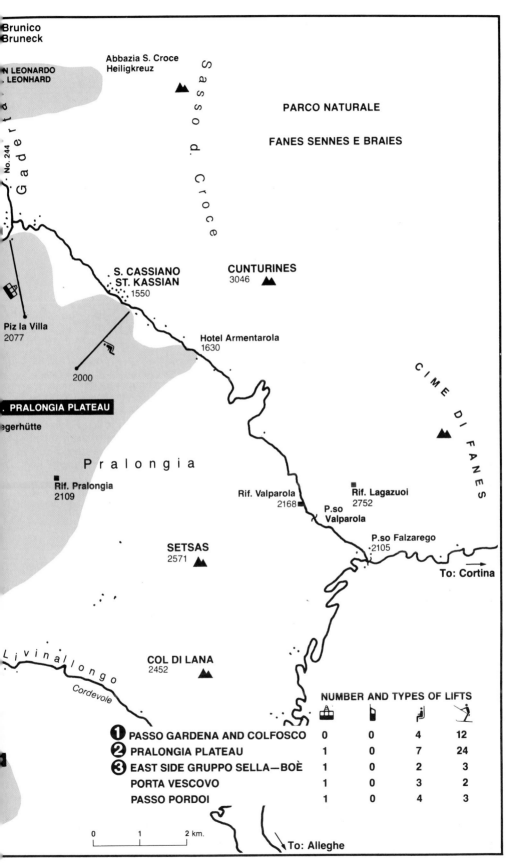

Brunico
Bruneck

N LEONARDO
. LEONHARD

Abbazia S. Croce
Heiligkreuz

S a s s o   d.   C r o c e

PARCO NATURALE

FANES SENNES E BRAIES

No. 244

G a d e r t a

S. CASSIANO
ST. KASSIAN
1550

CUNTURINES
3046

Piz la Villa
2077

Hotel Armentarola
1630

2000

C I M E   D I   F A N E S

. PRALONGIA PLATEAU

egerhütte

P r a l o n g i a

Rif. Pralongia
2109

Rif. Valparola
2168

Rif. Lagazuoi
2752

P.so
Valparola

SETSAS
2571

P.so Falzarego
2105

To: Cortina

L i v i n a l l o n g o

Cordevole

COL DI LANA
2452

	NUMBER AND TYPES OF LIFTS			
	🚠	🚡	🚡	⛷
❶ PASSO GARDENA AND COLFOSCO	0	0	4	12
❷ PRALONGIA PLATEAU	1	0	7	24
❸ EAST SIDE GRUPPO SELLA—BOÈ	1	0	2	3
PORTA VESCOVO	1	0	3	2
PASSO PORDOI	1	0	4	3

0   1   2 km.

To: Alleghe

ARABBA

Village of Arabba

HIGHLIGHTS

Arabba is a tiny, somewhat isolated village surrounded by steep slopes and a vast network of lifts and piste—perfect for the avid alpine skier. It is also on the Sella Ronda circuit and is near the off-piste skiing on the Gruppo Sella. Since it is quite small, accommodation is limited.

ALPINE SKIING

Arabba has truly outstanding skiing for every ability on mostly open slopes that face all exposures. The region is connected to the Alta Badia. Beginners can also ski on piste near the Passo Pordoi and those on the Pralongia plateau in the Alta Badia. Intermediate piste abound, and the advanced skier will spend his time on the steep north-facing slopes of Porta Vescovo, above the village. You can easily ski to another region and back on the same day, such as to the Val Gardena, Val di Fassa, Alta Badia, or the Marmolada.

CROSS COUNTRY SKIING: Limited.

MAJOR VILLAGE

	Population	Elevation
Arabba	350	1602m

HOW TO ARRIVE

By Air:
International airports at Munich, Milan, Venice or smaller airports in Verona and Innsbruck.

By Rail:
Nearest stations: Brunico (Bruneck), then transfer by bus or car.

By Car:
If using the A22: Exit at Bressanone. Take No. 49, following signs to the Val Pusteria. Near Brunico turn right (south) on No. 244 to the Val Badia and Corvara, then continue to Arabba. Bressanone exit to Arabba: about 1½ hrs.

PUBLIC TRANSPORTATION
Taxis and buses are available.

PRINCIPAL LANGUAGE: Italian.

OTHER WINTER ACTIVITIES
Ice skating • Indoor private swimming • and more.

GENERAL PISTE INFORMATION
Longest: About 6 km, Passo Pordoi to Arabba.
Most vertical: 2478m-1602m, Porta Vescovo to Arabba.
Ranking
    Beginner: Many
    Intermediate: Extensive
    Advanced: Several
Slope Exposures: Mainly north and east—some south.
Region is on the Dolomiti Superski pass.

View from Porta Vescovo

SKI AREAS
(See map pp. 198-199 for ski areas)

Porta Vescovo: Lift access from Arabba.

Below this serrated ridge is a wonderful selection of intermediate and advanced piste. Some are very steep, and a few are for those who enjoy "bump" or mogul skiing. Northerly views towards the Alta Badia and beyond are unobstructed from most piste. One popular excursion is skiing from here to Malga Ciapela where you can take the cable car to the top of the Marmolada for the extraordinary view and the thrilling pista down.

Passo Pordoi: West and above Arabba. Lifts from Arabba.

This beginner area has only a few slopes, and they are sometimes crowded. There is a large restaurant and shopping complex at the passo. Expert skiers note that you can take the Sass Pordoi lift from the passo and enjoy the off-piste skiing on the Gruppo Sella.

View from Passo Pordoi towards Arabba

PLAN DE CORONES (KRONPLATZ)

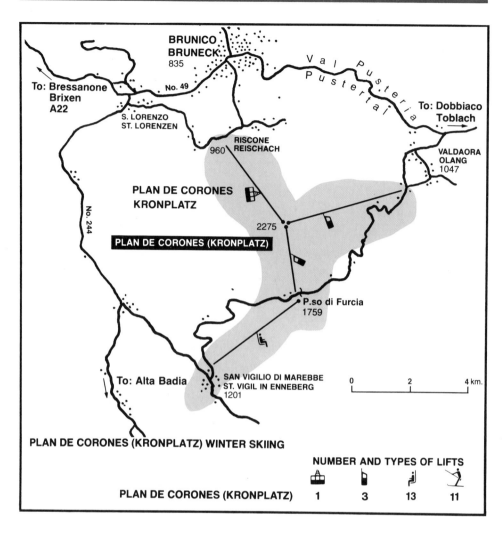

PLAN DE CORONES (KRONPLATZ) WINTER SKIING

NUMBER AND TYPES OF LIFTS			
PLAN DE CORONES (KRONPLATZ)	1	3	13	11

Tuning skis, Plan de Corones

HIGHLIGHTS

Plan de Corones is a bald, round mountain with modern lift facilities. The vast summit is a favorite meeting place for skiers arriving from all sides to enjoy the restaurants and 360° views. There are several small Tyrolean villages in the region and cross-country skiing in the surrounding valleys.

Located in the Val Pusteria, the mountain is easy to reach from the A22 and the large town of Brunico. A car is desirable if you wish to tour outside the region.

MAJOR VILLAGES

	Population	Elevation
Brunico (Bruneck)	12,100	835m
San Vigilio di Marebbe (St. Vigil in Enneberg)	1,200	1201m
Valdaora (Olang)	2,400	1047m

202

PLAN DE CORONES (KRONPLATZ)

HOW TO ARRIVE
By Air:
International airports at Munich, Milan, or Venice or smaller airports in Verona and Innsbruck.

By Rail:
Nearest station: Brunico (Bruneck).

By Car:
If using A22: Exit at Bressanone. Take No. 49, following signs to the Val Pusteria and continue to Brunico. Bressanone exit to Brunico: about 45 min.

PUBLIC TRANSPORTATION
Taxis are available and there is a local bus system.

PRINCIPAL LANGUAGES: German and Italian (Ladin also in San Vigilio).

Village of San Vigilio di Marebbe

OTHER WINTER ACTIVITIES
Indoor and outdoor ice skating • Cleared footpaths • Horse-drawn sleighs • Curling • Private and public indoor swimming • Back-country skiing with guides • Hockey • Cinema • and more.

PLAN DE CORONES (KRONPLATZ)

Skiing down to Valdaora, Plan de Corones

VILLAGES

Brunico (Bruneck) is a large commercial town on the main road through the Val Pusteria. It has many hotels and shops and is just a few minutes drive to **Riscone** where there is lift access to Plan de Corones.

San Vigilio di Marebbe (St. Vigil in Enneberg) is a sunny quaint Tyrolean village at the southern base of Plan de Corones. It is rather isolated yet has a number of small attractive hotels, inns, cafés and many shops. Cross-country tracks and back-country skiing are near the village.

Valdaora (Olang) is a tiny Tyrolean village just off the main road through the Val Pusteria. There are a few shops and small hotels. It has good lift access to Plan de Corones, and for the cross-country enthusiast the vast Val Pusteria track system is nearby.

ALPINE SKIING

Plan de Corones (Kronplatz) has a modern and efficient lift system that disperses crowds well over a complete range of piste. The north-facing piste towards Brunico are wooded and challenging; those facing east down to Valdaora are more gentle, broad, and open. There are a number of ways down to San Vigilio; some on open slopes, others are tree-lined. The huge summit buzzes with activity; there are ski repair stations and restaurants with decks for sunning and viewing. Although the area receives less precipitation than many other regions, the slopes are well-maintained with snow-making equipment.

CROSS-COUNTRY SKIING

A network of tracks from San Vigilio extends for a long spectacular tour into the Fanes area—an immense mountain wilderness. There are also tracks around Valdaora that join the famous long trail network of the Val Pusteria.

GENERAL PISTE INFORMATION

Longest: About 6 km, Plan de Corones to Valdaora.

Most vertical: 2275m-960m, Plan de Corones to Riscone.

Ranking
  Beginner: Many
  Intermediate: Extensive
  Advanced: A few

Slope Exposures: All

Region is on the Dolomiti Superski pass.

PLAN DE CORONES (KRONPLATZ)

Gondola from San Viglio di Marebbe

BRESSANONE (BRIXEN)

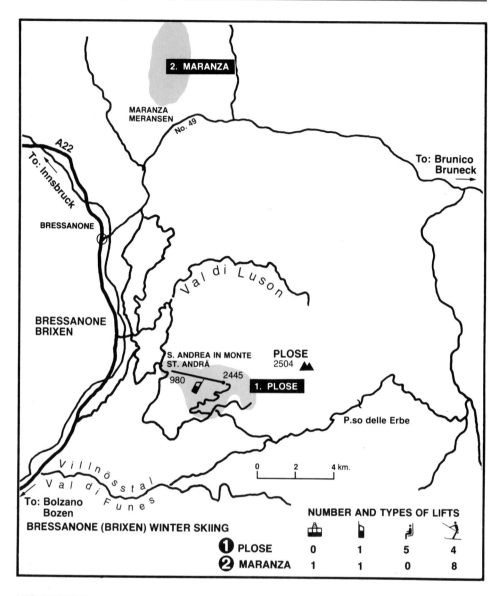

2. MARANZA

MARANZA
MERANSEN

No. 49

A22

To: Innsbruck

To: Brunico
Bruneck

BRESSANONE

BRESSANONE
BRIXEN

Val di Luson

S. ANDREA IN MONTE
ST. ANDRÄ

PLOSE
2504

980   2445

1. PLOSE

P.so delle Erbe

Villnösstal
Val di Funes

To: Bolzano
Bozen

0   2   4 km.

BRESSANONE (BRIXEN) WINTER SKIING

NUMBER AND TYPES OF LIFTS

		🚡	🚠	🚟	⛷
❶	PLOSE	0	1	5	4
❷	MARANZA	1	1	0	8

HIGHLIGHTS

For those with only limited time for skiing, this winter region is an excellent choice for a day's outing as it is a short distance from the autostrada. Both ski areas are near the picturesque medieval town of Bressanone which has a wide range of tourist accommodations, wonderful shopping, and much to do and see. Plose is the principal skiing area and is reached by car in 15 minutes from the town center. From the top there are panoramic views of the Valle Isarco and many of the Dolomite peaks bordering the Val Gardena.

GENERAL PISTE INFORMATION

Longest: About 8 kilometers from Plose to S. Andrea.
Most Vertical: 2445m to 980m, Plose to S. Andrea.
Ranking
  Beginner: A few
  Intermediate: A few
  Advanced: One
Slope Exposures: Northwest and south.
Region is on the Dolomiti Superski pass.

MAJOR VILLAGE

	Population	Elevation
Bressanone (Brixen)............................	16,500	559m

206

BRESSANONE (BRIXEN)

Lift at Maranza

ALPINE SKIING

Plose is a wide-open gentle mountain above Bressanone, with a modern and efficiently arranged lift system. It is best to drive or take a bus to the lower lift station near the hamlet of S. Andrea where a long gondola ride takes you to the summit ski area. Beginner and intermediate skiing predominate but there is a long, tree-lined advanced pista down to S. Andrea. In stormy weather, wind and visibility can be a problem on top as there is little tree cover; however, the advanced pista is somewhat protected. Plose can be crowded on weekends because of its proximity to the autostrada and many local villages. It is not possible to ski to other ski areas or regions from here.

Maranza (Meransen), a 30-minute drive north of Bressanone, is a ski area worth visiting. The slopes are generally south-facing, good for beginner and intermediate skiers, with pleasant vistas and a relaxed ambiance.

CROSS-COUNTRY SKIING

A scenic trail leads into the Val di Funes and there are tracks around Maranza.

OTHER WINTER ACTIVITIES
Indoor and outdoor ice skating • Cleared foot paths • Horse drawn sleighs • Indoor public and private swimming • Indoor tennis • Hockey • Curling • and more.

207

SOUTHWEST

Winter sunlight, San Martino di Castrozza

SOUTHWEST

The three winter regions of the Southwest district have a considerable variety of skiing with outstanding valley and mountain scenery. They are easy to reach from the A22 or by local roads from Feltre or Belluno. If you are already in the Dolomites it is fairly easy to visit any of the three regions. **San Martino di** **Castrozza-Passo Rolle** is a popular resort below the Pale di San Martino and has skiing for all abilities. **Val di Fiemme-Obereggen** has a modern and efficient ski area, Obereggen-Pampeago, and cross-country skiing in valleys and over rolling alps. **Moena-Falcade** has sunny open bowl piste that are seldom crowded, with spectacular panoramic vistas.

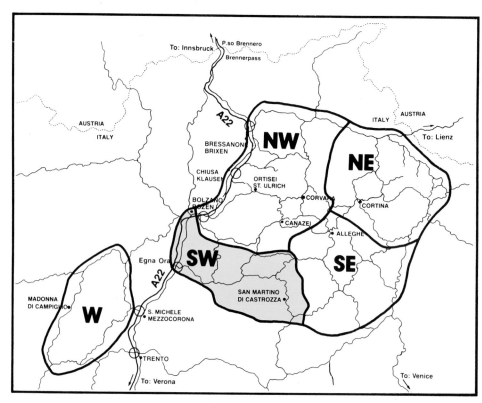

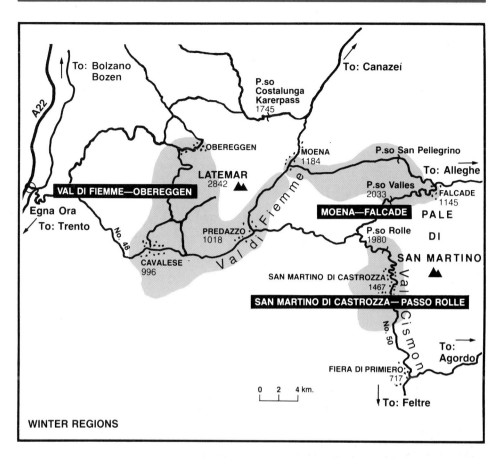

WINTER REGIONS

To: Bolzano Bozen

A22

To: Canazei

P.so Costalunga Karerpass 1745

OBEREGGEN

MOENA 1184

P.so San Pellegrino

To: Alleghe

LATEMAR 2842

VAL DI FIEMME—OBEREGGEN

P.so Valles 2033

FALCADE 1145

Egna Ora
To: Trento

No. 48

Val di Fiemme

MOENA—FALCADE

PALE

PREDAZZO 1018

P.so Rolle 1980

DI

SAN MARTINO

CAVALESE 996

SAN MARTINO DI CASTROZZA 1467

Val Cismon

SAN MARTINO DI CASTROZZA—PASSO ROLLE

No. 50

To: Agordo

FIERA DI PRIMIERO 717

0   2   4 km.

To: Feltre

The grandeur of the Pale di San Martino from Tognola

SAN MARTINO DI CASTROZZA

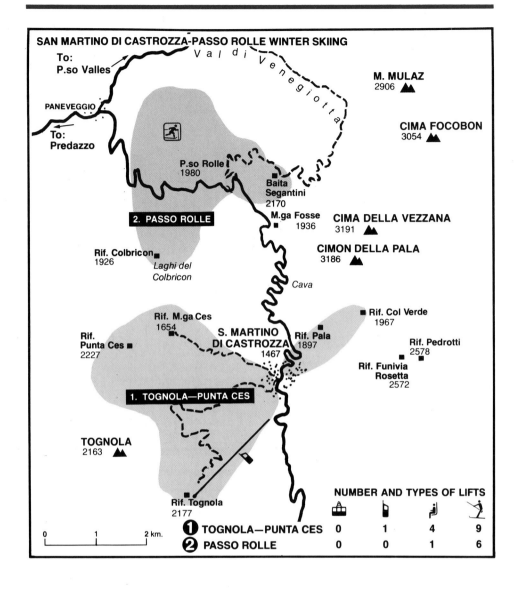

SAN MARTINO DI CASTROZZA–PASSO ROLLE WINTER SKIING

To:
P.so Valles

Val di Venegiotta

M. MULAZ
2906 ▲▲

PANEVEGGIO

To:
Predazzo

CIMA FOCOBON
3054 ▲▲

P.so Rolle
1980

Baita
Segantini
2170

2. PASSO ROLLE

M.ga Fosse
1936

CIMA DELLA VEZZANA
3191 ▲▲

Rif. Colbricon
1926

*Laghi del
Colbricon*

CIMON DELLA PALA
3186 ▲▲

Cava

Rif. M.ga Ces
1654

**S. MARTINO
DI CASTROZZA**
1467

Rif. Pala
1897

■ **Rif. Col Verde**
1967

Rif.
Punta Ces ■
2227

Rif. Pedrotti
2578 ■

**Rif. Funivia
Rosetta**
2572

1. TOGNOLA—PUNTA CES

TOGNOLA
2163 ▲▲

Rif. Tognola
2177

	NUMBER AND TYPES OF LIFTS			
	🚡	🚠	🚟	🎿
❶ TOGNOLA—PUNTA CES	0	1	4	9
❷ PASSO ROLLE	0	0	1	6

0   1   2 km.

HIGHLIGHTS

San Martino is popular with Italian skiers. It exudes ambiance and is an excellent choice for a few days of alpine skiing. The scenery is some of the most stupendous in the Dolomites—the towering spires of the Pale rise dramatically above the village and are constantly in view whether you are skiing or strolling. The gondola ride up the Tognola is a delightful experience and you can join the multitude of Italians, many of whom take the ride to the top simply to sit in the sun, have lunch and marvel at the view. There are plans to connect the region to Moena-Falcade but at the moment San Martino is isolated and a car is helpful if you want to visit other regions.

MAJOR VILLAGE

San Martino stretches along a curving, slightly pitched, main road. In the center is a pretty church and ancient campanile. A river meanders through the village; streets above and below are lined with cafés, bars, and small hotels. There is an amazing selection of tourist accommodations, shops, and boutiques for such a small village. You can walk from the village to the lower lift stations but most people use the local bus.

MAJOR VILLAGE	Population	Elevation
San Martino di Castrozza	600	1467m

SAN MARTINO DI CASTROZZA

Village center, San Martino di Castrozza

ALPINE SKIING

San Martino has virtually every caliber of pista—from gentle beginner to challenging advanced slopes. These piste are wide open or tree-lined and always with the spectacular Pale as a backdrop. Presently, there is no significant snow-making capability and there is only a minimum number of "snow-cats" for grooming the piste. However, there are enough slopes to minimize these needs. Storms often come from the south and west into the Dolomites, so San Martino usually receives adequate snow, but fog and clouds from the Venetian plain can sometimes be a problem.

OTHER WINTER ACTIVITIES
Ice skating • Bowling • Private and public indoor swimming • Cinema • Hockey • and more.

SAN MARTINO DI CASTROZZA

Tognola ski area above San Martino

❶**Tognola-Punta Ces** is west and above San Martino.

Lift access to the Tognola is just below the village. The Punta Ces side is reached by a small chairlift near the village center. (Weather permitting, it is also possible to drive part way up the Punta Ces side on an unpaved road.) Lifts in the higher parts connect these two areas so you can ski in the large bowl and down to either the Tognola or Punta Ces lower lift stations.

At the top of the Tognola lift there are easy open slopes, ideal for families. On clear days views of the Pale and San Martino are magnificent. The advanced skier will be challenged by several varied and interesting piste that descend towards the village. Skiers and non-skiers keep the main uphill lift busy. Piste, however, are not generally crowded.

Adjoining Tognola is the Punta Ces area. The lower slopes are good for novices and families. Beginning at the top, a fine intermediate pista and an interesting advanced pista curve down through trees to the beginner area.

❷ **Passo Rolle:** Lifts leave from here.

A small complex of chair and surface lifts serve piste over open treeless terrain— good for beginners and intermediates. Views to the north and west of the Pale di San Martino and distant peaks are expansive. In bad weather, however, visibility can be a problem.

CROSS-COUNTRY SKIING

There are some tracks in the Passo Rolle area but San Martino has very few.

SAN MARTINO DI CASTROZZA

Dramatic peaks above Passo Rolle

VAL DI FIEMME ~ OBEREGGEN

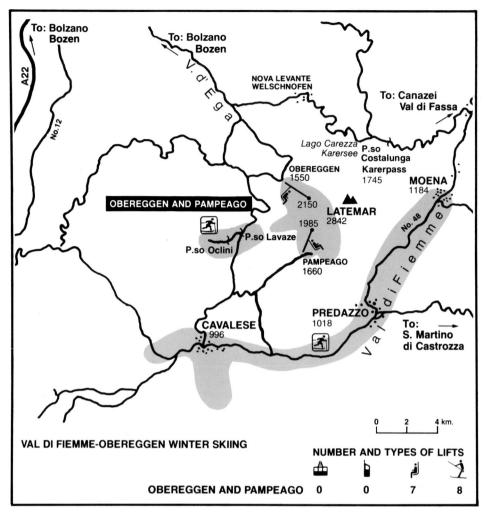

VAL DI FIEMME-OBEREGGEN WINTER SKIING

OBEREGGEN AND PAMPEAGO

NUMBER AND TYPES OF LIFTS			
0	0	7	8

HIGHLIGHTS

The important Val di Fiemme, with its large villages of Cavalese and Predazzo, is near the A22. Alpine skiing is concentrated high above the Val di Fiemme, at the base of the Latemar, where an efficient lift system connects the small winter resorts of Obereggen and Pampeago. Nearby, in the vicinity of the Passo di Lavaze and Passo di Oclini, there is an extensive track system for the cross-country skier. There is also a famous cross-country track running through the Val di Fiemme connecting with the tracks of the Val di Fassa enabling you to ski all the way to Canazei.

It is a good idea to have a car since most tourist accommodations are in the major villages about a half-hour drive from the ski area. It is also possible to drive to other nearby winter regions.

VILLAGES

Cavalese is a thriving, typically Italian, village that straddles both sides of the main road. You will need a car, taxi or local bus to reach the Obereggen-Pampeago ski area from here.

Predazzo is located in a flat basin at an important Dolomite road junction. Shops and accommodations line both the main roads.

Obereggen and **Pampeago,** about a 30-minute drive from Cavalese or Predazzo, are two small modern tourist complexes serving the ski area.

MAJOR VILLAGES

	Population	Elevation
Cavalese	3,600	996m
Predazzo	4,200	1018m

VAL DI FIEMME~OBEREGGEN

ALPINE SKIING

The modern Obereggen-Pampeago ski area is interconnected by lifts so you can easily ski all of it in one day. This area, with pleasant bowl skiing on beginner and intermediate piste, is a good one for families. Obereggen has more tree cover and "vertical." It is easy to reach by car from near Nova Levante. Pampeago can be reached by car or bus from Cavalese and Predazzo.

Since the area is easily accessible from the autostrada, it can be crowded on weekends; however, the lift system does a good job of dispersing crowds. It is not possible to alpine ski to other areas or regions from here. Future plans call for lift connections from Predazzo to Pampeago.

Note: Cermis is a ski area south of Cavalese and not connected to the Obereggen-Pampeago area. It is served by lifts from Cavalese.

CROSS-COUNTRY SKIING

You can ski all the way to Canazei, from village to village, and stop wherever you wish. If you are tired take a bus to cover part of the distance. Not far from the Obereggen-Pampeago ski area is an interesting network of tracks that surround and connect the Passo di Lavaze and Passo di Oclini. This is a completely different experience over gently rolling, thinly wooded terrain.

GENERAL PISTE INFORMATION

Longest: About 6 km, Pala to Obereggen.
Most Vertical: 2460m-1530m, Pala to Obereggen.
Ranking
  Beginner: Many
  Intermediate: Many
  Advanced: Nil
Slope Exposures: All
Region is on the Dolomiti Superski pass.

Enjoying the pista, Obereggen

215

MOENA ~ FALCADE

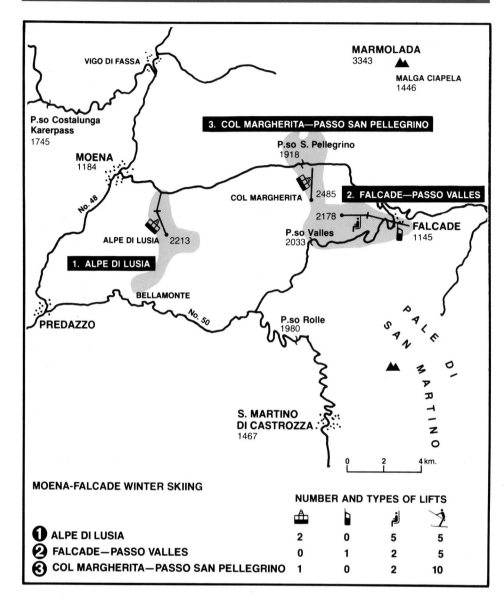

VIGO DI FASSA

MARMOLADA
3343

MALGA CIAPELA
1446

P.so Costalunga
Karerpass
1745

3. COL MARGHERITA—PASSO SAN PELLEGRINO

P.so S. Pellegrino
1918

MOENA
1184

COL MARGHERITA   2485

2. FALCADE—PASSO VALLES

No. 48

2178

FALCADE
1145

ALPE DI LUSIA   2213

P.so Valles
2033

1. ALPE DI LUSIA

BELLAMONTE

P
A
L
E

No. 50

PREDAZZO

P.so Rolle
1980

D
I

S
A
N

M
A
R
T
I
N
O

S. MARTINO
DI CASTROZZA
1467

0   2   4 km.

MOENA-FALCADE WINTER SKIING

	NUMBER AND TYPES OF LIFTS			
❶ ALPE DI LUSIA	2	0	5	5
❷ FALCADE—PASSO VALLES	0	1	2	5
❸ COL MARGHERITA—PASSO SAN PELLEGRINO	1	0	2	10

HIGHLIGHTS

This region offers a complete variety of alpine skiing, fantastic views of many of the most dramatic peaks of the Dolomites, and some famous tracks for cross-country skiing. The two main villages of the region, Moena and Falcade, are on either end of the Passo San Pellegrino. A car is an advantage here as you can tour into other regions from these villages.

VILLAGES

Moena is an attractive village located in a flat sunny bowl where the Val di Fassa joins the Val di Fiemme. The Avisio river meanders through the village and on both sides are many shops and tourist accommodations. The Alpe di Lusia ski area is only a

few kilometers away and the other ski areas of the region are within a 30 to 45 minute drive. You can also take part in the Val di Fassa winter recreational activities from here. The cross-country tracks of the Val di Fassa and Val di Fiemme pass right through the village.

Falcade is one of several small villages in the central Dolomites and has some spectacular views of Civetta, Pelmo, and the Pale di San Martino. While the main part of the village is on the valley floor there is a pleasing mixture of new and old houses and tourist facilities located on the slopes above. The main lift system of the Falcade-Passo Valles ski area is accessible from the village. From Falcade you can make day trips to enjoy the winter activities in San Martino, Alleghe, and the Marmolada.

MOENA~FALCADE

MAJOR VILLAGES

	Population	Elevation
Moena	2,600	1184m
Falcade	2,400	1145m

HOW TO ARRIVE
By Air:
International airports in Munich, Milan, Venice, or smaller airports in Verona and Innsbruck.

By Rail:
Nearest stations: Bolzano and Ora, then transfer by bus or car.

By Car:
If using the A22: Exit at Bolzano Nord and follow signs to the Val d'Ega (which is east of the autostrada). Take the road through this valley to the Passo Costalunga, then to Vigo where it connects with road No. 48. Turn south and drive to Moena. Bolzano Nord exit to Moena: about 1 hr. To continue to Falcade, drive from Moena over the Passo San Pellegrino. Moena to Falcade: about 45 min.

PUBLIC TRANSPORTATION
Taxis are available in the major villages. Local bus service connects the ski areas.

PRINCIPAL LANGUAGES: Italian, German, and Ladin.

Village of Falcade, Civetta in background

ALPINE SKIING

This region is ideal for families; it is rarely crowded, and the scenery is magnificent. There is a wide range of skiing for beginners and intermediates in open treeless bowls plus a few steep piste for the advanced skier. There are three ski areas. Two of them, Falcade-Passo Valles and Col Margherita-Passo San Pellegrino, are interconnected by an extensive network of lifts and piste. You need a car or bus to reach the third area, Alpe di Lusia, as it is a few kilometers from Moena and the other two ski areas.

CROSS-COUNTRY SKIING

The track systems of the Val di Fiemme and Val di Fassa join at Moena giving you extensive touring possibilities on interesting valley terrain. There are other pleasant track systems in the Passo San Pellegrino area and near Caviola, a small village just east of Falcade. Scenery in these areas makes them well worth including in your plans.

MOENA~FALCADE

Chairlift on Alpe di Lusia, Catinaccio in distance

SKI AREAS

❶ Alpe di Lusia: East of Moena. Lift access from the road along the Valle di San Pellegrino, about two kilometers east of Moena.

The wide, open bowls on the upper portions are ideal for beginners and intermediates with marvelous views of the Catinaccio and Pale di San Martino—even the advanced skier will enjoy cruising in this area. Beginner piste also take you down to the hamlet of Bellamonte. There is a challenging north-facing pista that descends from the upper lift station.

❷ Falcade-Passo Valles: Lift access from Falcade and along the road between Falcade and Passo Valles.

Skiing above Falcade is generally for beginners and intermediates on wide, sunny, treeless piste with spectacular views of Civetta, Pelmo and the Pale di San Martino. There is one advanced pista which becomes narrow and tree-lined as it twists its way down to Falcade. Many of the slopes can be icy at times and visibility could be poor in fog or storms.

Chairlift ascending from Falcade

MOENA ~ FALCADE

❸ Col Margherita-Passo San Pellegrino: There is lift access to both ski networks from the Passo San Pellegrino.

Views from Col Margherita are some of the finest in this part of the Dolomites. Only two piste return from Col Margherita to the lower lift station; these are treeless, north-facing, and fairly steep. (Across the road from the Col Margherita lift are a few beginner piste). A rather complicated lift and piste network connects Col Margherita with the Falcade-Passo Valles area so you can ski these areas interchangeably.

Winter landscape, Col Margherita

NORTHEAST

Early light on snow-covered Cristallo

NORTHEAST

The winter regions of **Cortina** and the **Alta Pusteria (Hochpustertal)—Val di Sesto (Sexten),** in the Northeast district, offer some of the best alpine and cross-country skiing in the Dolomites.

Cortina, set in a spectacular and immense mountain amphitheater, is an international ski resort with every type of winter sport. There are slopes for skiers of all abilities and some of the most challenging long piste found anywhere in the Alps.

The Alta Pusteria includes several Tyrolean villages and the beautiful Val di Sesto. This region is noted for its extensive variety of cross-country tracks; alpine skiing is also available.

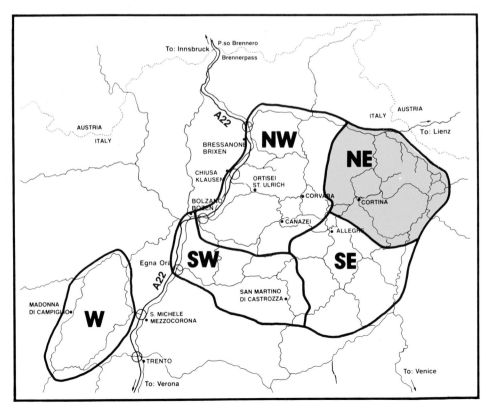

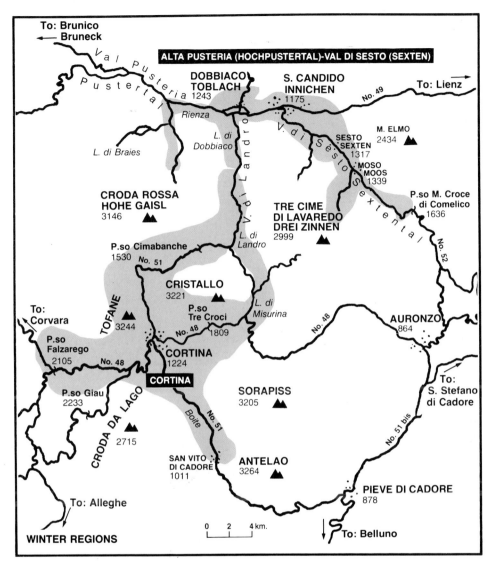

ALTA PUSTERIA (HOCHPUSTERTAL)-VAL DI SESTO (SEXTEN)

To: Brunico
Bruneck

Val Pusteria

Pustertal

To: Lienz

DOBBIACO TOBLACH 1243

S. CANDIDO INNICHEN 1175

No. 49

Rienza

L. di Dobbiaco

L. di Braies

V. di Sesto Sextental

M. ELMO 2434

SESTO SEXTEN 1317

MOSO MOOS 1339

P.so M. Croce di Comelico 1636

CRODA ROSSA HOHE GAISL 3146

V. di Landro

L. di Landro

TRE CIME DI LAVAREDO DREI ZINNEN 2999

No. 52

P.so Cimabanche 1530

No. 51

CRISTALLO 3221

L. di Misurina

No. 48

AURONZO 864

TOFANE 3244

P.so Tre Croci 1809

No. 48

To: Corvara

P.so Falzarego 2105

No. 48

CORTINA 1224

CORTINA

Boite

No. 51

SORAPISS 3205

To: S. Stefano di Cadore

P.so Giau 2233

CRODA DA LAGO 2715

SAN VITO DI CADORE 1011

ANTELAO 3264

No. 51 bis

To: Alleghe

WINTER REGIONS

0 2 4 km.

PIEVE DI CADORE 878

To: Belluno

Tofana ski area above Cortina, Sorapiss in distance

CORTINA

Amphitheater of Cortina

HIGHLIGHTS

Cortina is a world-famous winter resort that rivals any other in the Alps. Magnificently situated in a sunny amphitheater, it is ringed by spectacular peaks which rise nearly 2000 meters above the village. Cortina has offered a complete range of winter sports facilities since hosting the Olympic Games in 1956. Many rewarding winter excursions are within a short drive, including Passo Falzarego, Lago di Misurina, Val di Landro, and Val Boite.

VILLAGES

In **Cortina** life centers around the Corso, a traffic-less, shop-lined street where the late afternoon *passeggiata* proceeds without fail. You can browse and see the latest winter fashions, as well as purchase a gift from one of the many craft and antique shops. At the heart of the Corso is a central piazza, a church with towering campanile, and the interesting Regole Museum. Some large hotels are on the Corso; others, including many smaller ones, can be found on side streets and in the neighborhoods above and below the village. There are also discos to visit after you have dined in one of the many restaurants or hotels.

San Vito di Cadore, a few kilometers south of Cortina, is a small attractive village worth a visit.

On the tracks, Val di Landro

222

HOW TO ARRIVE
By Air:
International airports at Munich, Milan, Venice or smaller airports in Verona and Innsbruck.

By Rail:
Nearest stations: Dobbiaco or Calalzo, then travel by bus or car to Cortina.

By Car:
If using the A22: Exit at Bressanone. Take highway No. 49 to Dobbiaco, then south on No. 51 to Cortina. Bressanone exit to Cortina: about 1½ hrs.

PUBLIC TRANSPORTATION
Taxis are available in Cortina and the larger villages. Local bus service connects Cortina and all ski areas.

APPROXIMATE DRIVING TIME TO MAJOR CENTERS
Milan .... 5 hrs
Munich .... 4 hrs
Innsbruck .... 2½ hrs
Venice .... 2½ hrs
Verona .... 2½ hrs

PRINCIPAL LANGUAGES: Italian and some Ladin.

MAJOR VILLAGE

	Population	Elevation
Cortina d'Ampezzo	8,000	1224m

Village center, Cortina

OTHER WINTER ACTIVITIES
Ice skating stadium • Speed skating rink • Private and public indoor swimming • Indoor tennis • Horse-drawn sleighs • Cinema • Back-country skiing with guides • Hockey • and more.

CORTINA

Challenging pista, Tofana ski area

ALPINE SKIING

For years Cortina's scenic variety and terrain has made it one of Europe's most desirable skiing centers, offering extensive beginner and intermediate slopes as well as some very challenging steep ones for the expert skier. Each of the four major ski areas is large enough to occupy a full day of skiing. The Tofana and Faloria ski areas are reached by cable cars from near the village center; the others require use of cars, buses, or taxis. Since the slopes face all exposures, it is advisable to inquire about the best conditions on any given day. While normally there is sufficient snow in the higher elevations, skiing into the village is not always possible.

The region is so immense that the piste are seldom crowded. There is also a relaxed attitude towards skiing here and on sunny days, the decks of mountain restaurants are filled with skiers and non-skiers enjoying the view while eating and visiting with friends.

SKI AREAS

❶ Tofana: West and above Cortina. Lift access from Cortina (near the skating rink).

The tremendous, mostly east-facing flanks of the Tofana offer a variety of piste for all skiing abilities—some of the most challenging ones begin at the top of the second lift station. Beginners will find a few easy piste in the higher parts, but most are lower and closer to Cortina. Terrain above is open and dramatic with sheer dolomite rock walls beside you. There is some delightful bowl skiing leading to lower piste that curve through woods—eventually ending at the village. The lift system is efficient and disperses crowds quite well. Tofana gets early morning sun and continues to be sunny most of the day. Plans are underway to link this immense area to the Lagazuoi-Col Gallina-Cinque Torri ski area. Once accomplished, Cortina will be connected by lift and piste with the Alta Badia, Arabba and other western regions in the Dolomites.

CORTINA

Looking down on Tofana ski area, Antelao and Pelmo in background

CORTINA

Catching the winter sun, Faloria

❷Faloria: East and above Cortina. Lift access from the central part of the village near the bus station.

These slopes are mostly north-facing From the top there are amazing views of Cristallo and distant peaks of the Sesto including the famous Tre Cime di Lavaredo.

The area is generally beginner and intermediate open-bowl skiing on the higher slopes, with gentle tree-bordered piste below. You can ski down from Faloria and, by walking across the road at Cap. Rio Gere, connect with the Cristallo ski area. You have other alternatives at this point: you can ski the beginner pista back to Cortina, call a taxi or take a bus back to the village, or ride the chairlifts back to the top of Faloria and take the cable car down to Cortina.

❸Cristallo: East and above Cortina with lift access from Cap. Rio Gere on the road to the Passo Tre Croci.

This area may be reached by car, taxi or bus from Cortina or by skiing down from Faloria. The slopes are mostly south-facing. There is a challenging advanced pista at the top and pleasant beginner and intermediate skiing below. The advanced pista is down a steep gully and should only be attempted by an expert skier when conditions are good. After walking across the road at Cap. Rio Gere you can take chairlifts to the top of the Faloria thus combining both areas for a wonderful day of skiing.

❹Lagazuoi-Col Gallina-Cinque Torri: West of Cortina. Lift access to Lagazuoi is from Passo Falzarego. Chairlifts to Col Gallina and Cinque Torri are located near the passo.

Skiers and non-skiers alike go up to Rifugio Lagazuoi to enjoy one of the most dramatic 360° views anywhere in the Dolomites. The advanced pista, from the rifugio down to Passo Falzarego, is one of the favorites in the region. You ski beside towering mountain walls with continual views of valleys and distant peaks. A long intermediate pista from the rifugio into the Alta Badia ends at Armentarola; here there is a popular hotel with excellent cuisine.

On the Cortina side of the Passo Falzarego, are the Col Gallina and Cinque Torri

areas—they can be skied interchangeably. Both have views of the Tofane, are seldom crowded, and are good for beginners and intermediates. The upper piste are wide open, with some tree-lined portions lower on the Cinque Torri.

Note: Near Cortina, at **Lago di Misurina** and the village of **San Vito di Cadore,** are smaller scenic ski areas worth trying.

CROSS-COUNTRY SKIING

More than 74 kilometers of tracks take you through some of the most dramatic Dolomite valley scenery. Just north of Cortina you can ski along portions of abandoned railroad tracks—even through tunnels.

The popular trail from Cortina to Dobbiaco through the Val di Landro is absolutely beautiful. Gigantic mountains border the valley and views of the north walls of Cristallo are particularly majestic. Along the way are cozy restaurants so you can take a break and enjoy the mountain setting.

Pista, Lagazuoi to Passo Falzarego

Rifugio Lagazuoi, Tofana di Rozes in background

227

CORTINA

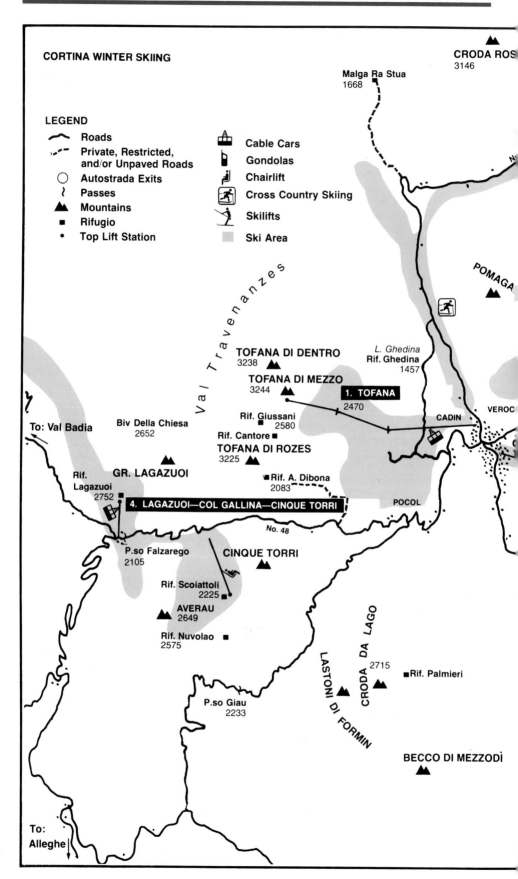

CORTINA WINTER SKIING

LEGEND

- 〰 Roads
- –·– Private, Restricted, and/or Unpaved Roads
- ◯ Autostrada Exits
- ⌇ Passes
- ▲▲ Mountains
- ■ Rifugio
- • Top Lift Station

- 🚠 Cable Cars
- 🚡 Gondolas
- 🚡 Chairlift
- 🎿 Cross Country Skiing
- 🎿 Skilifts
- Ski Area

CRODA ROS
3146

Malga Ra Stua
1668

POMAGA

V a l   T r a v e n a n z e s

TOFANA DI DENTRO
3238 ▲

TOFANA DI MEZZO
3244 ▲

L. Ghedina
Rif. Ghedina
1457

1. TOFANA
2470

CADIN

VEROC

Biv Della Chiesa
2652

Rif. Giussani
2580

Rif. Cantore ■

TOFANA DI ROZES
3225 ▲

To: Val Badia

GR. LAGAZUOI

Rif.
Lagazuoi
2752

■ Rif. A. Dibona
2083

4. LAGAZUOI—COL GALLINA—CINQUE TORRI

POCOL

No. 48

P.so Falzarego
2105

CINQUE TORRI ▲

Rif. Scoiattoli
2225 ■

AVERAU
2649 ▲

Rif. Nuvolao ■
2575

P.so Giau
2233

LASTONI DI FORMIN

CRODA DA LAGO
2715 ▲
■ Rif. Palmieri

BECCO DI MEZZODÌ ▲

To:
Alleghe

CORTINA

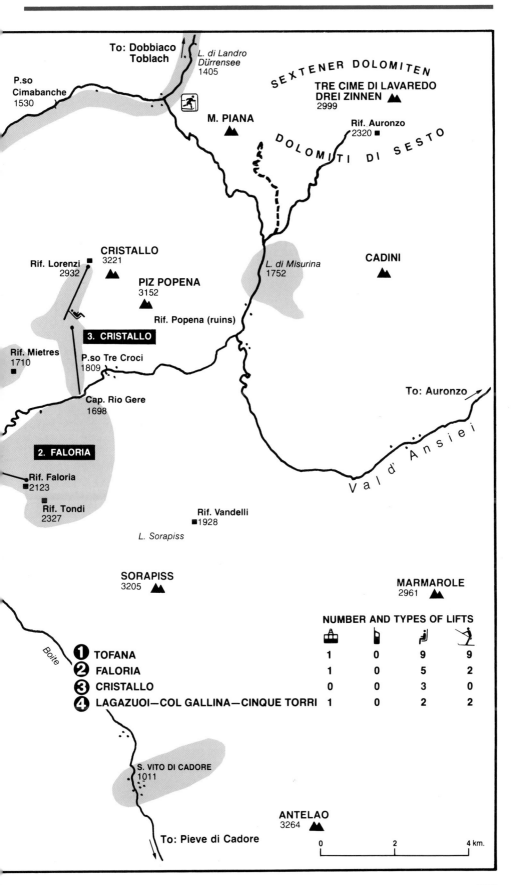

To: Dobbiaco Toblach

L. di Landro Dürrensee 1405

P.so Cimabanche 1530

SEXTENER DOLOMITEN

TRE CIME DI LAVAREDO DREI ZINNEN 2999

M. PIANA

Rif. Auronzo 2320

D O L O M I T I   D I   S E S T O

CRISTALLO 3221

Rif. Lorenzi 2932

PIZ POPENA 3152

L. di Misurina 1752

CADINI

Rif. Popena (ruins)

3. CRISTALLO

Rif. Mietres 1710

P.so Tre Croci 1809

Cap. Rio Gere 1698

To: Auronzo

V a l   d'   A n s i e i

2. FALORIA

Rif. Faloria 2123

Rif. Tondi 2327

Rif. Vandelli 1928

L. Sorapiss

SORAPISS 3205

MARMAROLE 2961

NUMBER AND TYPES OF LIFTS

Boite

❶	TOFANA	1	0	9	9
❷	FALORIA	1	0	5	2
❸	CRISTALLO	0	0	3	0
❹	LAGAZUOI—COL GALLINA—CINQUE TORRI	1	0	2	2

S. VITO DI CADORE 1011

ANTELAO 3264

To: Pieve di Cadore

0   2   4 km.

ALTA PUSTERIA ~ VAL DI SESTO

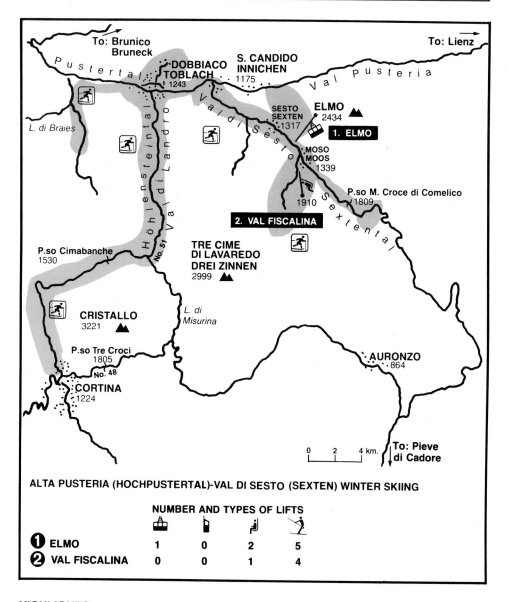

ALTA PUSTERIA (HOCHPUSTERTAL)-VAL DI SESTO (SEXTEN) WINTER SKIING

NUMBER AND TYPES OF LIFTS

	🚠	📱	🚡	🎿
1 ELMO	1	0	2	5
2 VAL FISCALINA	0	0	1	4

HIGHLIGHTS

This peaceful and uncrowded winter region is a haven for the cross-country skier, although there is also alpine skiing on Elmo and above Moso. Charming Tyrolean villages offer comfortable accommodation. The two largest villages, Dobbiaco and San Candido in the Val Pusteria and the two small villages of Sesto and Moso in the Val di Sesto are excellent places to stay. A car is a definite advantage as it is an easy drive to Cortina for the day.

VILLAGES

Dobbiaco (Toblach) is a quiet, attractive Tyrolean village with an impressive main piazza and a pretty onion-domed church. Accommodation is plentiful. It is a conve-

nient base for cross-country skiing in the Val Pusteria and the Val di Landro.

San Candido (Innichen) is located where the Val Pusteria and Val di Sesto meet. There is a good selection of tourist facilities around the charming old village center with newer accommodations along the side streets. Lift access to Elmo is a few kilometers east of San Candido at Versciaco in the Val Pusteria.

Sesto (Sexten) and its small neighbor **Moso (Moos)** are quaint Tyrolean villages with attractive shops, quiet hotels and spectacular views of the Sesto Dolomites. A cable car leaves from Sesto taking skiers to the upper slopes of Elmo. There is lift access to the Val Fiscalina area from Moso.

ALTA PUSTERIA ~ VAL DI SESTO

HOW TO ARRIVE
By Air:
International airports at Munich, Milan, Venice, or smaller airports in Verona and Innsbruck.

By Rail:
Nearest stations: Dobbiaco or Calalzo.

By Car:
If using the A22: Exit at Bressanone. Take highway No. 49 to Dobbiaco. Bressanone exit to Dobbiaco: about 1 hr.

PUBLIC TRANSPORTATION
Taxis are available in the major villages. Local bus service connects the villages and ski areas.

PRINCIPAL LANGUAGES: German and Italian.

MAJOR VILLAGES

	Population	Elevation
Dobbiaco (Toblach)	2,700	1243m
San Candido (Innichen)	3,000	1175m
Sesto (Sexten)	1,800	1317m

Village center, San Candido

OTHER WINTER ACTIVITIES
Outdoor ice skating • Indoor public and private swimming • Indoor tennis • Horse-drawn sleighs • Curling • Hockey • Cleared footpaths • Back country skiing with guides • and more.

ALTA PUSTERIA ~ VAL DI SESTO

ALPINE SKIING

The major area for alpine skiing is at Elmo, a rounded non-dolomitic mountain rising above Sesto and San Candido. There is also a small ski area several kilometers southeast of San Candido in the Val di Sesto above Moso.

SKI AREAS

❶ Elmo is the largest alpine ski area in this region with lift access from Versciaco in the Val Pusteria and also from the village of Sesto.

The area is good for beginners and intermediates. Panoramic views of the Sesto and Val Pusteria from the summit are outstanding. The north-facing piste are tree-bordered while the west and south facing slopes have little tree cover and can become icy.

CROSS-COUNTRY SKIING

This is an exceptional region for cross-country skiing that includes the famous track from Dobbiaco south to Cortina, all the east-west tracks in the Val Pusteria, and tracks extending through the Val di Sesto into the Val Fiscalina. Excursions on these tracks are not difficult and are thoroughly enjoyable because of the spectacular and varied scenery. The track to Cortina routes you between towering mountain massifs with views ahead of the north walls of Cristallo and Popena. On the other hand, an outing in the Val Pusteria is generally along flat and sunny terrain. The Val di Sesto and Val Fiscalina are two of the most beautiful valleys in the Dolomites—as you glide along well-groomed tracks, you have continual views of the Sesto Dolomites.

Moso and Val Fiscalina from Elmo ski area

❷ Val Fiscalina. Lift access is near the end of the Val Fiscalina (which branches off the Val di Sesto at Moso).

There is pleasant uncrowded skiing on beginner and intermediate piste. One steep advanced pista descends down the north side to the lower lift station.

Note: A small ski area, with beginner skiing for families, is a few kilometers from Moso, at the **Passo M. Croce di Comelico.** There are trail-type piste that connect this area to the Val Fiscalina. Skiing is also possible near **San Candido** and **Dobbiaco.**

GENERAL PISTE INFORMATION

Longest: About 5 km, Elmo to Versciaco.

Most Vertical: 2199m-1130m, Elmo to Versciaco.

Ranking
  Beginner: Many
  Intermediate: Several
  Advanced: Nil

Slope Exposures: All

Region is on the Dolomiti Superski pass.

Cross-country skiing, Val Fiscalina

SOUTHEAST

Snow-carpeted Colle Santa Lucia

SOUTHEAST

In the Southeast district, skiing is primarily beginner and intermediate against a backdrop of three of the most magnificent Dolomite peaks: Civetta, Pelmo and the Marmolada. There are two winter regions, **Civetta-Pelmo** and the **Marmolada.** Skiing in the Civetta-Pelmo region is a delightful experience. You are surrounded by giant peaks, small uncrowded valleys and villages—some new, others old and charming. The Marmolada, the highest mountain in the Dolomites, has a magnificent long pista that thrills both intermediate and advanced skiers. Cross-country skiing is at present rather limited.

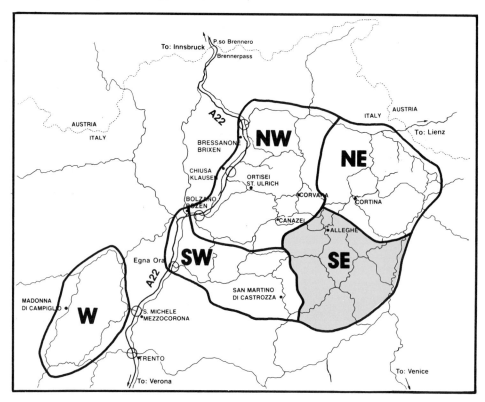

SOUTHEAST

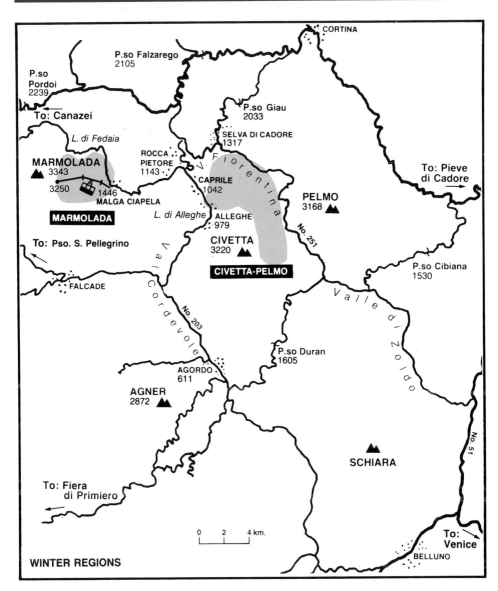

WINTER REGIONS

P.so Falzarego
2105

CORTINA

P.so
Pordoi
2239

To: Canazei

P.so Giau
2033

SELVA DI CADORE
1317

To: Pieve
di Cadore

L. di Fedaia

ROCCA
PIETORE
1143

MARMOLADA
▲ 3343

3250

1446

MALGA CIAPELA

MARMOLADA

CAPRILE
1042

PELMO
3168 ▲▲

L. di Alleghe

ALLEGHE
979

To: Pso. S. Pellegrino

CIVETTA
3220 ▲▲

CIVETTA-PELMO

No. 251

P.so Cibiana
1530

FALCADE

V a l   C o r d e v o l e

V a l l e   d i   Z o l d o

No. 203

P.so Duran
1605

AGORDO
611

AGNER
2872 ▲▲

To: Fiera
di Primiero

SCHIARA ▲▲

0   2   4 km.

To:
Venice

BELLUNO

V. Fiorentina

Exciting pista, Marmolada

235

CIVETTA~PELMO

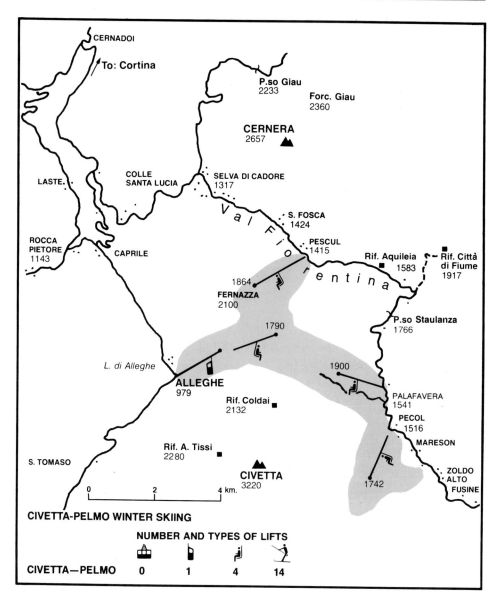

CIVETTA-PELMO WINTER SKIING

NUMBER AND TYPES OF LIFTS

	🚡	🚠	🚡	⛷
CIVETTA—PELMO	0	1	4	14

HIGHLIGHTS

This is a delightful uncrowded winter region with small Italian villages. The recently developed lift system offers excellent skiing for beginners and intermediates. The area has magnificent closeup views of Civetta and Pelmo. A car is a definite advantage as tourist facilities are spread out between the villages and it is also an easy drive to Cortina, the Marmolada and Moena-Falcade regions.

MAJOR VILLAGES

Alleghe is splendidly positioned on Lago di Alleghe at the foot of the great north wall of Civetta. It is a small village with a number of nice hotels, restaurants and shops. A major lift leaves conveniently from the village to the ski area. Alleghe is surrounded by mountains, so it tends to lose the sun by mid-afternoon.

Caprile is an older Italianate village, centrally located for skiing in both this region and the Marmolada—it takes about 30 minutes to drive to the ski areas. The village has tourist accommodations, including a popular small hotel.

Selva di Cadore is in a lovely, sunny setting with dramatic views of Pelmo and is only a few kilometers from the lift at Pescul. It has a small selection of tourist accommodations.

Pescul and **Pecol** have small clusters of modern tourist facilities that have been developed as the ski area has expanded. Lifts leave from both Pescul and Pecol and other nearby points.

CIVETTA~PELMO

MAJOR VILLAGES

	Population	Elevation
Alleghe	1,600	979m
Selva di Cadore	1,500	1317m
Caprile	800	1042m

HOW TO ARRIVE

By Air:
International airports at Munich, Milan, Venice, or smaller airports in Verona and Innsbruck.

By Rail:
Nearest station: Belluno. Then transfer by car or bus to Alleghe.

By Car:
If using the A22: Exit at Bressanone, drive through the Val Pusteria. Turn south near Brunico and continue to La Villa. Branch left towards Passo Falzarego. Turn right (south) at the passo and continue to Alleghe. Bressanone exit to Alleghe: about 2 hrs.

PUBLIC TRANSPORTATION

Taxis in major villages. Local bus service connects villages.

PRINCIPAL LANGUAGE: Italian.

Village of Selva di Cadore

OTHER WINTER ACTIVITIES
Outdoor ice skating • Private indoor swimming • Hockey • and more.

CIVETTA~PELMO

Pelmo from Fernazza ski area

ALPINE SKIING

The ski area encompasses Fernazza (above and between Alleghe and Pescul) and Zoldo Alto (above Pecol). Together, they form a long, slightly S-shaped ridge. The slopes in the Fernazza area are more open, while those on the Zoldo Alto side have more tree cover. Lift access is convenient from Alleghe, Pescul, Palafavera and Pecol.

Skiing here is a pleasant experience as the lift system has been well planned and the pista layout allows you to ski the entire area interchangeably without poling. Beginners and intermediates will enjoy skiing on the undulating ridge and open bowls as well as skiing down to the small villages. While the piste are generally short, they are interesting and the views of giant peaks are breathtaking. There is one long advanced pista with a good "vertical" that twists its way down from the top to Alleghe. The lower part can become icy at times so it may be closed. The region is not on the Dolomiti Superski pass so you will need to purchase an area pass, but the price is reasonable and the region itself is generally not expensive.

CROSS-COUNTRY SKIING

There are some tracks around Caprile, Pescul, and near Pecol.

MARMOLADA

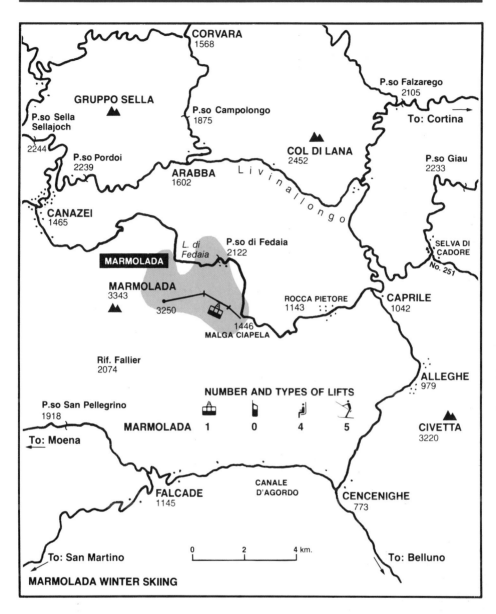

MARMOLADA WINTER SKIING

HIGHLIGHTS

Alpine skiing on the Marmolada—the highest mountain in the Dolomites with the largest glacier—is a uniquely thrilling winter or summer experience. The summit and glacier bustle with skiers and visitors; everyone thrills when taking the three-stage cable car to the summit for the extraordinary 360° views. You can ski to Malga Ciapela from the Arabba region and enjoy a day of skiing on the Marmolada with plenty of time for your return by ski. You can also drive from other nearby regions such as Civetta-Pelmo and Moena-Falcade.

The main Marmolada cable car lifts, and certain other lifts in this region, are not on the Dolomiti Superski pass so you must buy a separate ticket to take the cable car.

Check at the first lift station about snow conditions as they can vary throughout the year. Also verify which lifts are operating on or near the summit.

VILLAGES

The tiny village of **Malga Ciapela** is conveniently located right at the base of the Marmolada, at the lowest lift station. It consists of a few modern small hotels and restaurants. **Rocca Pietore,** near Malga Ciapela, has tourist facilities, and buses connect it to the lift system at Malga Ciapela. Less than a half-hour's drive away are Alleghe and Caprile (see the Civetta-Pelmo region) where you can find additional tourist facilities.

MARMOLADA

Summit lift station, Marmolada

ALPINE SKIING

There is one long fantastic pista (experts vary as to whether it is 12 or 14 kilometers) from the top of the Marmolada down to Malga Ciapela. The pista is steep off the summit but fine for intermediates and always well-groomed. Towards the bottom, the slope becomes quite easy and flattens out near Malga Ciapela. The ever-changing panoramic views are spell-binding and you will hardly believe you have descended some 2,000 meters. Since the best skiing is on the higher part, you may choose to repeat this portion by using the upper lifts; but do keep checking conditions as wind and snow quality can change rapidly.

MARMOLADA

Skiing down the Marmolada

GENERAL PISTE INFORMATION
Longest: About 12 km, from the summit to Malga Ciapela.
Most vertical: 3265m to 1446m, from the summit to Malga Ciapela.
Ranking: The lower slopes, near Malga Ciapela, are for beginners; upper slopes are good for intermediate skiers.
Slope Exposures: North and east

WEST

Winter in the Dolomiti di Brenta

WEST

The West district, conveniently centered around the popular **Madonna di Campiglio,** offers a complete range of winter recreation. This winter region takes somewhat longer to reach by car, compared with many of the others, but once there everything is close at hand to assure a delightful winter holiday. There is extensive alpine skiing for all abilities, with long piste surrounded by wonderful scenery. The Italian resort village of Madonna di Campiglio has plentiful accommodations, excellent shopping and several discos. Its neighbor to the south, **Pinzolo,** is especially noted for an annual 24-hour cross-country marathon.

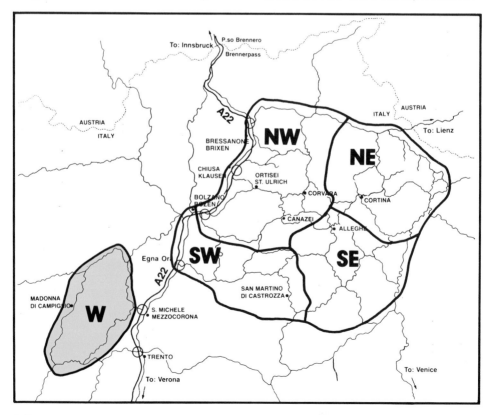

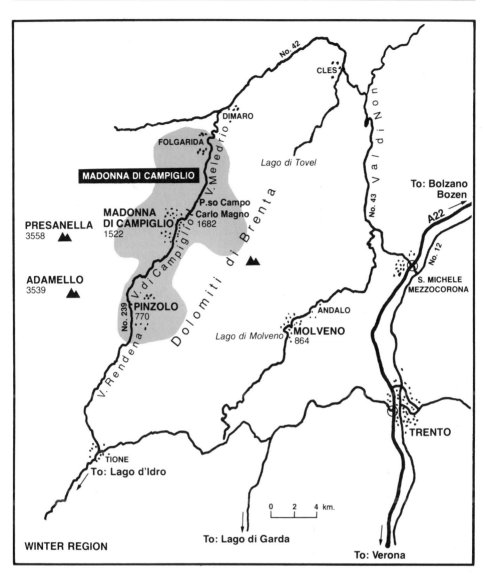

PRESANELLA
3558

ADAMELLO
3539

MADONNA DI CAMPIGLIO

MADONNA
DI CAMPIGLIO
1522

PINZOLO
770

No. 42

CLES

DIMARO

FOLGARIDA

Lago di Tovel

V. Meledrio

P.so Campo
Carlo Magno
1682

Dolomiti di Brenta

V. di Campiglio

V. Rendena

No. 239

TIONE
To: Lago d'Idro

Lago di Molveno

ANDALO

MOLVENO
864

No. 43 Val di Non

To: Bolzano
Bozen

A22

No. 12

S. MICHELE
MEZZOCORONA

TRENTO

0   2   4 km.

To: Lago di Garda

To: Verona

WINTER REGION

Village of Madonna di Campiglio

MADONNA DI CAMPIGLIO

HIGHLIGHTS

The Madonna di Campiglio region is one of Italy's most popular winter resorts. Many young people, as well as families, return here year after year for a "white week", or just a short week-end holiday, amidst the splendor of the Brenta ridge and the Adamello and Presanella massifs. While it requires a 1 to 1½ hour drive to Madonna from the autostrada, once you arrive you will find a completely self-contained winter recreational area. All the ski areas, other sports activities, and tourist accommodations are convenient to the village. Special wintertime opportunities are available, such as evening rides in horse-drawn sleighs to mountain restaurants, and parachute skiing for the adventuresome.

VILLAGES

Madonna di Campiglio is a bustling village with an international flavor. Since the 1930s it has gradually developed from its earlier popularity as a mountaineering center into a world-class winter resort. Boutiques, shopping arcades, cafés and hotels are in the town center, while smaller pensioni are found on the side streets. The lifts are either

Race training, Cinque Laghi ski area

within walking distance of the village or can be reached by a short bus or taxi ride. In the afternoon the *passeggiata* begins, continuing through the dinner hour and into the evening when lively discos open their doors.

Pinzolo, a year-round Italian village below Madonna, is a busy place. Lifts are located near the village but, since it is 800 meters lower in elevation than Madonna, alpine skiing is somewhat limited. However, cross-country skiing is noteworthy here—particularly the annual 24-hour marathon which draws more entrants each year.

MAJOR VILLAGES

	Population	Elevation
Madonna di Campiglio	1,000	1522m
Pinzolo	2,300	770m

HOW TO ARRIVE
By Air:
International airports at Munich, Milan, Venice, or smaller airports in Verona and Innsbruck.

By Rail:
Nearest stations: Trento, Mezzocorona, then travel by bus or car.

By Car:
If using the A22: Exit at San Michele (north of Trento), then follow No. 43 past Cles where it joins No. 42. Follow No. 42 to Dimaro where you turn south towards Madonna di Campiglio. A22 exit to Madonna: about 1½ hrs.

PUBLIC TRANSPORTATION
Taxis are available in the villages. There is a good local bus service connecting all the villages and important lift facilities.

APPROXIMATE DRIVING TIME TO MAJOR CENTERS
Milan	3 hrs
Munich	5 hrs
Innsbruck	3¼ hrs
Venice	3½ hrs
Verona	2½ hrs

PRINCIPAL LANGUAGE: Italian.

MADONNA DI CAMPIGLIO

High on Grostè ski area above Madonna di Campiglio

MADONNA DI CAMPIGLIO

Dolomiti di Brenta from Cinque Laghi ski area

ALPINE SKIING

This region offers interesting skiing for all abilities on piste that vary greatly in length as well as terrain. You can try four ski areas on the same day, with little need for local transportation, although you should consider the weather in your planning. Crowds are well-dispersed because the skiing covers such a vast area. Also, the lift system is efficient, and is continually being updated. This region is not included on the Dolomiti Superski pass but the lifts in Madonna are under one ownership and the area-wide pass affords convenient skiing between all the ski areas.

SKI AREAS

❶ Spinale-Grostè: East and above Madonna with lift access from the village.

These two vast areas are well-connected by lifts and can be skied interchangeably all day. Skiing ranges from the long gently-sloping piste at the top of Grostè to some very steep west-facing piste off Spinale. Grostè is wonderful for the beginner as the

slopes are wide and you have a sense of being on a glacier. Spinale is a small mountain adjacent to the Grostè lift network and has piste with all exposures. The north-facing piste are gentle with some trees; those facing the other directions are more challenging. You may find lift lines when everyone is getting started in the morning.

❷ Cinque Laghi: Above Madonna on the west with access from the village.

This area has some very exciting piste for the accomplished skier. An annual World Cup slalom race, the traditional "Tre-Tre," takes place just above the village. The slopes face southeast and are wide and sparsely wooded at the higher elevations but as you descend thick forests border the piste. This area never seems to become crowded, possibly because there are fewer piste here and it is not directly linked to the other areas. There is an attractive large restaurant at the top lift station and a small cozy one midway down the piste where skiers enjoy sitting in the sun and marveling at the Brenta ridge across the valley.

MADONNA DI CAMPIGLIO

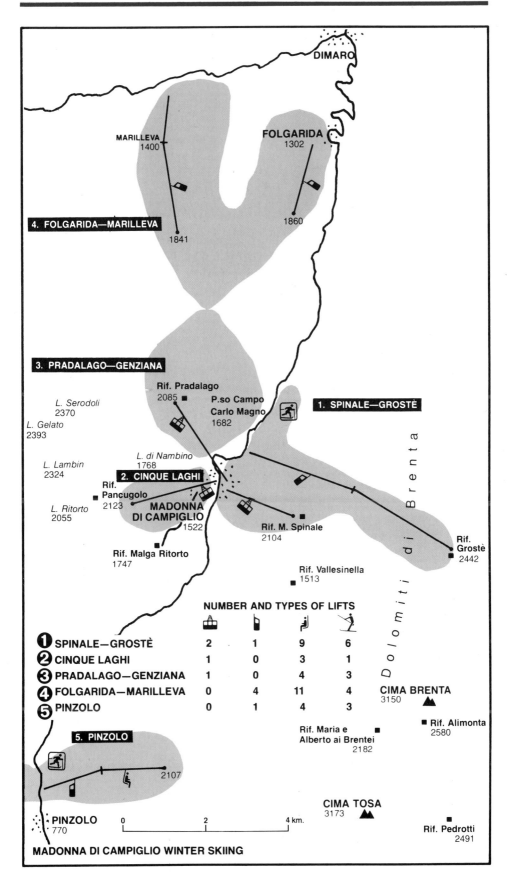

DIMARO

MARILLEVA
1400

FOLGARIDA
1302

1860

4. FOLGARIDA—MARILLEVA

1841

3. PRADALAGO—GENZIANA

Rif. Pradalago
2085

P.so Campo
Carlo Magno
1682

1. SPINALE—GROSTÈ

L. Serodoli
2370

L. Gelato
2393

L. di Nambino
1768

L. Lambin
2324

2. CINQUE LAGHI

Rif.
Pancugolo
2123

L. Ritorto
2055

**MADONNA
DI CAMPIGLIO**
1522

Rif. M. Spinale
2104

Rif.
Grostè
2442

Rif. Malga Ritorto
1747

Rif. Vallesinella
1513

B
r
e
n
t
a

D
o
l
o
m
i
t
i

d
i

NUMBER AND TYPES OF LIFTS

❶	SPINALE—GROSTÈ	2	1	9	6
❷	CINQUE LAGHI	1	0	3	1
❸	PRADALAGO—GENZIANA	1	0	4	3
❹	FOLGARIDA—MARILLEVA	0	4	11	4
❺	PINZOLO	0	1	4	3

CIMA BRENTA
3150

Rif. Alimonta
2580

5. PINZOLO

Rif. Maria e
Alberto ai Brentei
2182

2107

CIMA TOSA
3173

PINZOLO
770

0   2   4 km.

Rif. Pedrotti
2491

MADONNA DI CAMPIGLIO WINTER SKIING

MADONNA DI CAMPIGLIO

Ski tour destination, Rifugio Malghette

❸Pradalago-Genziana: Above and west of Madonna with lift access from the village.

This is a very good area for the beginner as there are numerous long easy slopes. The intermediate skier will also enjoy wide piste in treeless bowls. The lift system connects with that of Folgarida and Marilleva.

❹Folgarida-Marilleva: Access to Folgarida is a few kilometers north of Madonna. Marilleva is a considerable distance northwest of Madonna. However, both of these ski areas can be reached by lifts and skiing from the Genziana area.

These two modern complexes can be skied interchangeably. Marilleva has won design awards for integrating its lodge, restaurant, parking and lift complex with the natural surroundings. Weekends can be crowded with local residents who come by car from all the nearby villages. The piste are nearly all beginner and are somewhat narrow.

Most of the slopes face north so you cannot see the Brenta.

❺ Pinzolo: The ski area is above and east of the village with lift access from the village.

This small area has beginner and intermediate skiing. From the top there are sweeping views of the Brenta, Adamello and Presanella.

CROSS-COUNTRY SKIING

A number of fine opportunities are available here. In the Campo Carlo Magno area a lovely network of tracks undulates over open rolling terrain, in and out of forests. There are also some track excursions into small valleys above Madonna—some even over frozen lakes. One excursion to Lago Malghette is well worth the effort as the Rifugio Malghette, on the edge of the lake, has a delightful atmosphere.

MADONNA DI CAMPIGLIO

Back-country skiing high in the Dolomiti di Brenta

OTHER WINTER ACTIVITIES
Ice skating • Indoor tennis • Indoor swimming • Cleared footpaths • Back-country skiing with guides • and more.

ITINERARIES

1. Pastoral Valley—1 to 2 hours from A22 exit: Val di Funes

A brief, rewarding trip through a lush, peaceful valley watched over by the dramatic peaks of the Odle group.

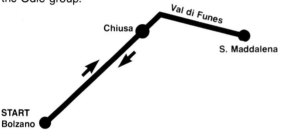

2. Alpine Splendor—3 to 4 hours: Alpe di Siusi

The route from the Val Gardena leads up to the largest alp in Europe with its breathtaking vistas of the Sassolungo, Sciliar, and Gruppo Sella.

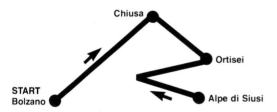

3. Two Valleys—3 to 4 hours: Val di Fassa and Val Gardena

Neighboring valleys demonstrate the dramatic contrasts in architecture and scenery within the Dolomites. The Catinaccio, Gruppo Sella and Sassolungo provide background for the tour.

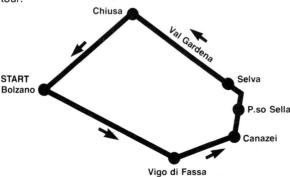

ITINERARIES

4. Classic Valley Tour—6 to 7 hours

This classic route, through the western and eastern Dolomites, gives you the opportunity to see the varied geology of these awesome mountains. The itinerary travels through picturesque valleys with a wealth of villages and hamlets to explore, and also goes by lovely Lago di Misurina.

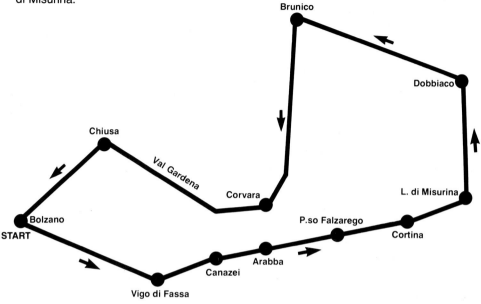

5. Grand Tour—12 to 14 hours: two days with a night on route

This is a leisurely exploration of the majesty of the Dolomites showing the variety of scenic beauty that sets these mountains apart. The route offers a loop to the lovely Val di Sesto on the first day, with a suggested overnight stop in or near Cortina. The return is via smaller valleys with charming hamlets.

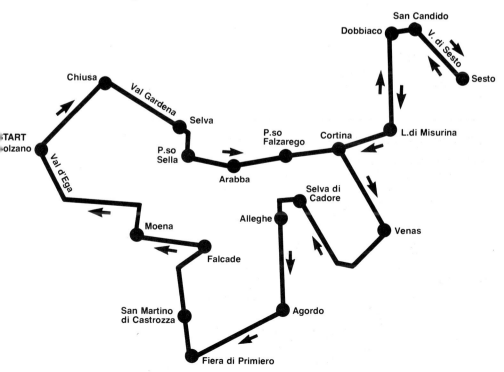

253

ITINERARIES

6. The Brenta—5 to 6 hours

This route highlights the special scenery in the most westerly area of the Dolomites: gentle hills, imposing mountains, lush meadows, hospitable villages and a lovely lake.

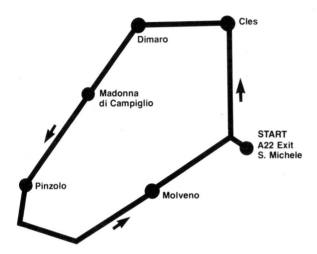

7. Cortina Giant Mountain Tour—4 to 5 hours

The grandeur of many of the giant massifs of the central Dolomites, including the Marmolada, Gruppo Sella, Civetta, Pelmo, and Antelao, are the highlights of this trip.

ITINERARIES

Pelmo from near Selva di Cadore

8. Highlights from Belluno—7 to 8 hours

This route begins in the southern part of the Dolomites but can be started at any point. It encompasses most of the major peaks in the eastern and western areas including the Tofane and Pale di San Martino.

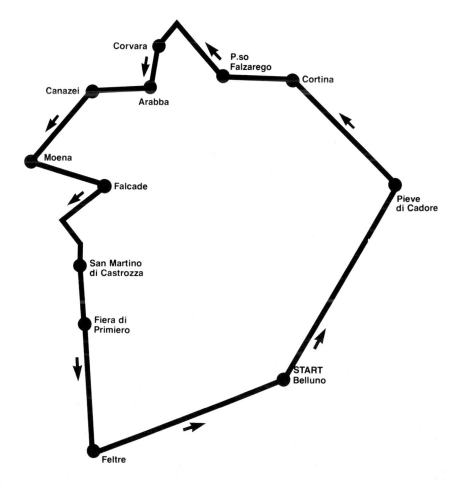

ITINERARIES

10-DAY WALKING ITINERARY
Walkers will enjoy this program which requires little ground transportation. It also offers challenging opportunities for the more ambitious hikers and climbers.

Note: Walking and hiking routes for the Val Gardena and Cortina, along with helpful maps, can be found in the Summer section of this book.

Part I—The Val Gardena—3 nights
Day 1: Arrival in Val Gardena. Time to get oriented, relax, and explore. Walk on the Alpe di Siusi, in the villages, or meander between San Pietro and Lajon.

Day 2: Val Gardena. Take a village ramble, walking loop, or a day hike. Enjoy shopping in the villages. You may choose to spend this night in a hotel on the Alpe di Siusi.

Day 3: Val Gardena. Time for a vigorous hike—a 4 to 6 hour itinerary.

Part II—Hike to Cortina—3 nights
Day 4: To the Val di Fassa. Take the chairlift from Santa Cristina to Monte Pana. Hike to Zallinger Hütte. Have lunch and walk to Col Rodella where the cable car takes you down to Campitello. Spend the night here or in Canazei—there should be time for village exploring.

Day 5: To the Val Badia. Bus or taxi from the Val di Fassa to Passo Pordoi. Ride Sass Pordoi cable car to the summit plateau of the Sella. Hike across the plateau, then descend the Val Mezdì to Colfosco. Spend the night in Colfosco or Corvara. You will have ample time to shop and wander through the villages.

Day 6: To Rifugio Lagazuoi. Ride the Col Alto chairlift to the Pralongia plateau. Hike across the undulating terrain and descend to Armentarola for lunch. A ten-minute taxi ride will take you to Passo Falzarego. Ride the cable car up to Rifugio Lagazuoi and enjoy the late afternoon sunset. Spend the night in this comfortable rifugio. (Phone 0436-867-303)

Part III: Cortina—4 nights
Day 7: From Rifugio Lagazuoi to Cortina. Rise early to watch the spectacular sunrise (weather permitting) from the rifugio deck. Following breakfast, start hiking past World War I battle zones, then continue beneath the Tofane walls to Rifugio Dibona. Have lunch here and either walk or take a taxi to Cortina. Night in Cortina.

Day 8: Cortina. Day hikes of your choice, or sight-seeing. In the late afternoon and early evening join the *passeggiata* on the Corso.

Day 9: Cortina. There are many hikes to choose from including, perhaps, a visit to the Tre Cime di Lavaredo.

Day 10: Depart by car or bus from Cortina. Drive by the serene Lago di Misurina on the way to the Val di Sesto. Time permitting, stroll into the Val Fiscalina—a final thrill before leaving the Dolomites.

A 3-DAY HIKER'S ITINERARY—OVERNIGHTS IN RIFUGI
This trek is for strong hikers on Intermediate grade routes. An average of about six hours of hiking is required per day.

Note: The course follows portions of hikes described in the Cortina and Cordevole and Fiorentina-Zoldo sections of the book.

Suggested Maps: 1:50,000: Tabacco #1: 1:25,000 Tabacco #03.

Day 1: Rifugio Dibona to Rifugio Lagazuoi. You walk along a magnificent trail beneath the Tofana di Rozes walls and through World War I battle zones. While this is an uphill trek, the rewards along the way are worth the ascent. If you prefer not to walk, you may take a taxi or bus to Passo Falzarego and ride the cable car up to Rifugio Lagazuoi. Spend the night at Rifugio Lagazuoi. (Telephone 0436-867-303)

Day 2: Rifugio Lagazuoi to Passo Giau. Take the cable car down to Passo Falzarego. Cross the road and take the trail southeast up to Rifugio Averau. From here take a round-trip detour up and back to Rifugio Nuvolau, then take trail #452 to Passo Giau. This hike undulates through varied terrain with panoramic views of many of the major peaks of the central Dolomites. Spend the night at Rifugio Enrosadira (Telephone 0437-720-109).

ITINERARIES

Day 3: Passo Giau to Rifugio Aquileia. Take Alta Via #1 from the passo and proceed first to Forcella Giau. Continue on Alta Via #1 all the way to the Rifugio Città di Fiume. From the rifugio, it is an hour's descent to Rifugio Aquileia. This is a popular route with ever-changing vistas and increasingly dramatic views of two of the Dolomite giants, Pelmo and Civetta. Spend the night in Rifugio Aquileia. (Telephone 0437-720-269).

3-DAY HIKER'S ITINERARY

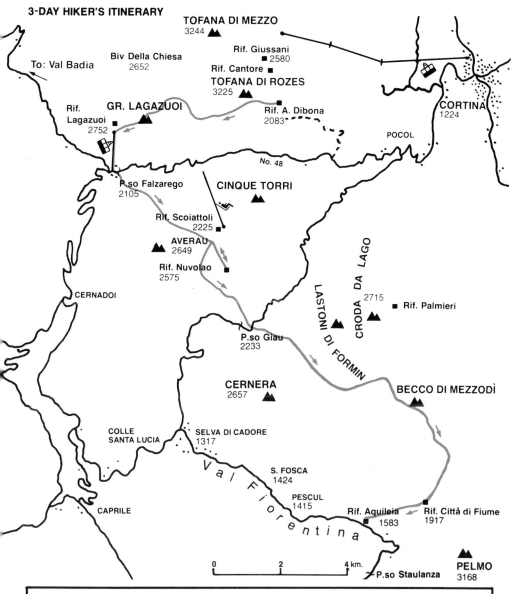

SUGGESTED ONE, TWO, OR THREE WEEK STAYS IN THE DOLOMITES
One Week:
You can spend one week in either the Val Gardena or Cortina, or you can divide your time between them.
Alternatively, divide your week between San Martino di Castrozza and Madonna di Campiglio in the Brenta.
Two Weeks:
Six days in Cortina and the Sesto, five in the Val Gardena (or vice versa), and three days divided between San Martino di Castrozza and Cordevole and Fiorentina-Zoldo areas.
Three Weeks:
Four days in the Brenta, six in the Val Gardena, six in Cortina and the Sesto, and five divided between San Martino di Castrozza and Cordevole and Fiorentina-Zoldo areas.

TRAVEL TIPS

TRAVEL TIPS
Information in this section is specifically for travel in the Dolomites; see also the Bibliography. You may also wish to refer to one of the many excellent general guides to Italy.

LANGUAGES
Both Italian and German are spoken by local people in many parts of the Dolomites—Italian more in the eastern and southern parts. English will be understood in the larger villages, hotels, tourist offices, and shops. Local people are friendly and try to assist you but it is useful to carry a phrase book.

OFFICE HOURS
Check in advance for opening times of shops, banks, tourist offices, etc., as schedules vary according to season and location. Stores may be open from 8:30 to 12:30 in the morning and 3:30 to 7:30 in the afternoon. Banking hours do not always coincide with store schedules.

HEALTH TIPS
Local tourist offices can be helpful in suggesting doctors and dentists. There are hospitals in the major towns bordering the Dolomites such as Bolzano and Bressanone. The tap water in the Dolomites is generally excellent.

BANKS AND CREDIT CARDS
Banks cash travelers' checks in foreign currencies and in any denomination—passports are required for identification. Exchange rates are better in banks than in the major hotels. Most shops and restaurants will not want to cash travelers' checks in foreign currencies. Credit cards are not always accepted except in the larger villages.

AZIENDA DI SOGGIORNO AND HOTELS
Major villages referred to in this book are listed below. The address, phone number and telex of the local tourist office, *Azienda di Soggiorno,* is given for each of these villages. The Azienda can assist with reservations and has a complete list of all types of accommodation including apartments, rooms to rent, rifugi, etc. The more deluxe hotels in each village are listed with their telephone numbers. A total count of more economical accommodation, which may include garni and pensioni, is also included. No recommendation is implied by either inclusion or omission from this list.

AGORDO
Telephone Code 0437
Postal Code 32021 (BL)
Azienda di Promozione Turistica
Address Piazza Libertà 33, 32021 Agordo
Telephone 62105
● **Hotels**
  ★★ – 2 Lodgings
   ★ – 4 Lodgings

ALLEGHE
Telephone Code 0437
Postal Code 32022 (BL)
Azienda di Promozione Turistica
Address Piazza Kennedy 17, 32022 Alleghe
Telephone 723333
Telex 440053
● **Hotels**
  ★★★
  Centrale; phone 723476
  Sporthotel Europa; phone 723362
  ★★ – 8 Lodgings
   ★ – 2 Lodgings

ALPE DI SIUSI (SEISERALM)
Telephone Code 0471
Postal Code 39040 (BZ)
Azienda di Soggiorno
Address 39040 Schlern
Telephone 71333

● **Hotels**
  ★★★★
  Eurotel Sciliar; phone 72928; Telex 400181
  Floralpina; phone 72907
  Plaza; phone 72973; Telex 400877
  ★★★
  Bellavista; phone 72972
  Icaro; phone 76389
  Paradiso; phone 72905
  Piccolo Hotel Sciliar; phone 72957
  Saltria; phone 72966
  Sole-Sporthotel Sonne; phone 76377
  Steger-Dellai; phone 72964
  ★★ – 6 Lodgings
   ★ – 14 Lodgings

ARABBA
Telephone Code 0436
Postal Code 32020 (BL)
Azienda di Promozione Turistica
Address Via Pieve 41, Arabba 32020
Telephone 79130
Telex 440823
Telefax 0436/78300
● **Hotels**
  ★★★★
  Sporthotel Arabba; phone 79321
  ★★★
  Porta Vescovo; phone 79139
  Hotel Olympia; phone 79135
  ★★ – 4 Lodgings
   ★ – 9 Lodgings

HOTELS, PENSIONI, AND GARNI

Nearby Arabba
Passo Campolongo
★★★
Boè; phone 79144
Monte Cherz; phone 79133

AURONZO
Telephone Code 0435
Postal Code 32041 (BL)
Azienda di Promozione Turistica Cadore
Address Viale Roma 22, 32041 Auronzo
Telephone 9359 or 9426
● **Hotels**
  ★★ – 11 Lodgings
    ★ – 26 Lodgings

BRESSANONE (BRIXEN)
Telephone Code 0472
Postal Code 39042 (BZ)
Azienda di Soggiorno
Address 39042 Bressanone/Brixen
Telephone 36401
Telex 400638
● **Hotels**
  ★★★★
Dominik; phone 30144; Telex 401524
Elefant; phone 32750; Telex 400491
Temlhof; phone 36658
  ★★★
Albero Verde-Grüner Baum; phone 32732;
    Telex 401643
Alpenrose; phone 32191
Brixnerhof; phone 34404
Chiavi d'Oro-Goldener Schlüssel; phone 36379
Corona d'Oro-Goldene Krone; phone 35154
Croce d'Oro-Goldenes Kreuz; phone 34255
Edith; phone 51307
Gasser; phone 36105
Gasserhof; phone 34697
Hofstatt; phone 35420
Jarolim; phone 33155
Mirabel; phone 36058
Orso Grigio-Grauer Bär; phone 36472
Posta-Post; phone 36062
Senoner; phone 32525
Sole-Sonne; phone 36271
Sporthotel; phone 51329
Tourist; phone 31545
  ★★ – 24 Lodgings
    ★ – 43 Lodgings

BRUNICO (BRUNECK)
Telephone Code 0474
Postal Code 39031 (BZ)
Azienda di Soggiorno
Address 39031 Brunico
Telephone 85722
Telex 400350 Crontour
● **Hotels**
  ★★★★
Royal Hotel Hinterhuber; phone 21221; Telex 400650
Rudolf; phone 21223; Telex 400579
  ★★★
Andreas Hofer; phone 85469
Blitzburg; phone 85723
Bologna; phone 85917
Corso; phone 85434
Krondlhof; phone 21080
Majestic; phone 84887
Olympia; phone 84657
Petrus; phone 84263
Posta-Post; phone 85127
Reischacherhof; phone 85009
Schoenblick; phone 85774
Sporthotel Gisbach; phone 21273
Tirolerhof; phone 84555
  ★★ – 20 Lodgings
    ★ – 33 Lodgings

CAMPITELLO
Telephone Code 0462
Postal Code 38031 (TN)
Azienda di Soggiorno
Address 38031 Campitello di Fassa
Telephone 61137
● **Hotels**
  ★★★
Alaska; phone 61430
Alpi; phone 61148
Gran Paradis; phone 67333
Grohmann; phone 61177
Panorama; phone 67312
Park Hotel Fedora; phone 61597
Salvan; phone 61427
Sellaronda; phone 62525
Sport Hotel Enrosadira; phone 61203
  ★★ – 11 Lodgings
    ★ – 14 Lodgings

CANAZEI
Telephone Code 0462
Postal Code 38032 (TN)
Azienda di Soggiorno
Address 38032 Canazei
Telephone 61113 or 61145
Telex 400012
● **Hotels**
  ★★★
Alla Rosa; phone 61107
Astoria; phone 61302
Bellevue; phone 61104
Cristallo; phone 61317
Croce Bianca; phone 61111
Diana; phone 61477
Dolomiti; phone 61106
Faloria; phone 61118
Hotel Andreas; phone 62106
Il Caminetto; phone 61230
Italia; phone 61120
Jan Maria; phone 62145
La Perla; phone 62453
Tyrol; phone 61156
  ★★ – 19 Lodgings
    ★ – 19 Lodgings
Nearby Canazei
Alba
★★★
Alpe; phone 61357
Giulia; phone 62217
La Cacciatora; phone 61411
  ★★ – 13 Lodgings
    ★ – 7 Lodgings
Passo Pordoi
★★★
Gonzaga; phone 62121
    ★ – 2 Lodgings

CAPRILE
Telephone Code 0437
Postal Code 32023 (BL)
Azienda di Promozione Turistica
Address Piazza Kennedy 17, 32022 Alleghe
Telephone 723333
Telex 440053
● **Hotels**
  ★★★
Alla Posta; phone 721171; Telex 440136
  ★★ – 3 Lodgings
    ★ – 1 Lodging

CASTELROTTO (KASTELRUTH)
Telephone Code 0471
Postal Code 39040 (BZ)
Azienda di Soggiorno
Address 39040 Castelrotto
Telephone 71333
Telex 400110   *(continued)*

HOTELS, PENSIONI, AND GARNI

CASTELROTTO (KASTELRUTH) (continued)
- **Hotels**
  ★★★★
  Posthotel Lamm; phone 71343
  ★★★
  Alpen Royal; phone 71350
  Cavallino d'Oro-Golden Roessl; phone 71337
  Kastelruth; phone 71308
  Madonna; phone 71194
  Oswald von Wolkenstein; phone 71639
  Savoy; phone 71707
  Silbernagl; phone 71699
  Solaia-Haus Am Sonnenhang; phone 71444
  St. Anna-Jaegerhuett; phone 71314
  Tyrol; phone 71397
  ★★ - 18 Lodgings
  ★ - 4 Lodgings

CAVALESE
Telephone Code 0462
Postal Code 38033 (TN)
Azienda di Soggiorno
Address 38033 Cavalese
Telephone 30298
Telex 400096
- **Hotels**
  ★★★
  Bellavista; phone 30205
  Cavalese; phone 30306
  Coronelle; phone 30436
  Eurotel Cermis; phone 30572
  Excelsior; phone 31315
  Gruenwald; phone 30369
  Hotel Garden; phone 30483
  Hotel Trunka Lunka; phone 30233
  Lagorai; phone 30454
  Orso Grigio; phone 31481
  Panorama; phone 31636
  Park Hotel Azalea; phone 30109
  San Valier; phone 31285
  Sporting; phone 31650
  ★★ - 7 Lodgings
  ★ - 11 Lodgings

COLFOSCO (KOLFUSCHG)
Telephone Code 0471
Postal Code 39033 (BZ)
Azienda di Soggiorno
Address 39033 Corvara in Badia
Telephone 836145
Telex 401555
- **Hotels**
  ★★★★
  Cappella; phone 836183; Telex 400643
  Kolfuschgerhof; phone 836188
  ★★★
  Centrale; phone 836118
  Gran Ciasa; phone 836138
  Mezdi; phone 836079
  Salvan; phone 836015
  ★★ - 22 Lodgings
  ★ - 28 Lodgings

CORTINA D'AMPEZZO
Telephone Code 0436
Postal Code 32043 (BL)
Azienda di Promozione Turistica
Address Piazzetta S. Francesco 8, 32043
    Cortina d'Ampezzo
Telephone 3231
Telex 440004
- **Hotels**
  ★★★★★
  Cristallo; phone 4281; Telex 440090
  Miramonti Majestic Grand Hotel; phone 4201;
    Telex 440069
  ★★★★
  Ambra; phone 867344; Telex 440066
  Ancora; phone 3261; Telex 440004
  Cortina; phone 4221; Telex 440004

De La Poste; phone 4271; Telex 440044
Europa; phone 3221; Telex 440043
Lajadira; phone 5746; Telex 440066
Mirage; phone 867827; Telex 433217
Savoia Grand Hotel; phone 3201; Telex 440810
Splendid Venezia; phone 3291; Telex 440817
Sporting Hotel Villa Blu; phone 867541; Telex 440066
★★★
Ampezzo; phone 4241; Telex 440004
Capannina; phone 2950; Telex 440066
Columbia; phone 3607; Telex 440066
Concordia Park Hotel; phone 4251; Telex 440004
Corona; phone 3251; Telex 440004
Fanes; phone 3427; Telex 440066
Franceschi Park Hotel; phone 867041; Telex 440066
Impero; phone 4246
Majoni; phone 866945
Menardi; phone 2400; Telex 440066
Miriam; phone 2665; Telex 440066
Motel Agip; phone 861400; Telex 440066
Natale; phone 867730
Olimpia; phone 3256; phone 440066
Parc Hotel Victoria; phone 3246; Telex 440004
Pontechiesa; phone 2523; Telex 440066
Principe; phone 2872; Telex 440066
Regina; phone 2797; Telex 440066
Royal; phone 867045; Telex 440066
San Marco; phone 866941; Telex 440066
Serena; phone 2604; Telex 440066
Villa Neve; phone 2228; Telex 440066
Villa Oretta; phone 866741; Telex 440066
★★ - 27 Lodgings
★ - 4 Lodgings
Nearby Cortina
Misurina
★★★
Lavaredo; phone 39127
Passo Tre Croci
★★★★
Tre Croci; phone 867141; Telex 440004
Pocol
★★★
Argentina; phone 5641; Telex 440066
Sport Tofana; phone 3281; Telex 440004
★★ - 2 Lodgings

CORVARA
Telephone Code 0471
Postal Code 39033 (BZ)
Azienda di Soggiorno
Address 39033 Corvara in Badia
Telephone 836176
Telex 401555
- **Hotels**
  ★★★★
  La Perla; phone 836132; Telex 401685
  Panorama; phone 836083; Telex 401220
  Posta Zirm; phone 836175; Telex 400844
  Sassonger; phone 836085
  ★★★
  Arlara; phone 836146
  Chalet Madrisa; phone 836042
  Ciasa de Munt; phone 836213
  Col Alto; phone 836129
  Greif; phone 836101
  La Plaza; phone 836011
  Ladinia; phone 836010
  Marmolada; phone 836139
  Martagon; phone 836129
  Miramonti; phone 836030
  Planac; phone 836210
  Tablé; phone 836144
  Veneranda; phone 836127
  Villa Eden; phone 836041
  ★★ - 31 Lodgings
  ★ - 9 Lodgings

DOBBIACO (TOBLACH)
Telephone Code 0474
Postal Code 39034 (BZ)

HOTELS, PENSIONI, AND GARNI

Azienda di Soggiorno
Address 39034 Dobbiaco
Telephone 72132
Telex 400569; Telefax 72730
● **Hotels**
★★★
Alpengasthof Ratsberg; phone 72213
Cristallo-Walch; phone 72138
Gratschwirt; phone 72293; Telex 400595
Hubertushof; phone 72276
Parkhotel Bellevue; phone 72101
Post; phone 72104
Santer; phone 72142
Serles; phone 72512
Toblacherhof; phone 72217
Union; phone 72146
Urthaler; phone 72241
   ★★ – 21 Lodgings
      ★ – 11 Lodgings

FALCADE
Telephone Code 0437
Postal Code 32020 (BL)
Azienda di Promozione Turistica
Address Piazza Municipio 1, 32020 Falcade
Telephone 59241 or 59242
Telex 440821
● **Hotels**
★★★★
Molino; phone 590970
★★★
Arnica; phone 599523
Focobon; phone 599244
Nigritella; phone 599319
San Giusto; phone 599041
Stella Alpina; phone 599046
   ★★ – 6 Lodgings
      ★ – 1 Lodging

FIERA DI PRIMIERO
Telephone Code 0439
Postal Code 38054 (TN)
Azienda di Soggiorno
Address 38054 Fiera di Primiero
Telephone 62407
Telefax 62992
● **Hotels**
★★★
Aurora; phone 62386
Belvedere; phone 62414
Eden; phone 62664
Isola Bella; phone 62404
La Perla; phone 62115
Mirabello; phone 64241
Park Hotel Iris; phone 62848
Primiero; phone 62077
Tressane; phone 62205
Villa Giulia; phone 62848
   ★★ – 10 Lodgings
      ★ – 10 Lodgings

LA VILLA (STERN)
Telephone Code 0471
Postal Code 39030 (BZ)
Azienda di Soggiorno
Address 39030 La Villa
Telephone 847037
Telex 401005
Telefax 847277
● **Hotels**
★★★★
Christiania; phone 847016
★★★
Aurora; phone 847173
Bel Sit; phone 836001
Dolasilla; phone 847006
Dolomiti; phone 847143
La Villa; phone 847035
Ladinia; phone 847044

Savoy; phone 847088
   ★★ – 10 Lodgings
      ★ – 16 Lodgings

MADONNA DI CAMPIGLIO
Telephone Code 0465
Postal Code 38084 (TN)
Azienda di Soggiorno
Address 38084 Madonna di Campiglio
Telephone 42000
Telefax 40404
● **Hotels**
★★★★
Alpina; phone 41075
Carlo Magno Zeledria Hotel; phone 41010;
   Telex 401158
Cristallo; phone 41132
Dahu; phone 40242
Edith; phone 41533
Golf Hotel; phone 41003; Telex 400882
Grifone; phone 42002
Miramonti; phone 41021
Relais Club des Alpes; phone 40000; Telex 401365
Savoia Palace Hotel; phone 41004
★★★
Ambiez Residencehotel; phone 42110
Ariston; phone 41070
Arnica; phone 40377
Bertelli; phone 41013
Bonapace; phone 41019
Catturanino; phone 40123
Chalet dei Pini; phone 41489
Cime d'Oro; phone 42113
Cozzio; phone 41083
Cristiania; phone 41470
Crozzon; phone 41217
Des Alpes 2; phone 41002; Telex 401365
Diana; phone 41011
Erika; phone 41022
Europa; phone 41036
Grazia; phone 41104
Ideal; phone 41016
Il Caminetto; phone 41242
La Baita; phone 41066
Laura; phone 41246
Lorenzetti; phone 41404
Majestic; phone 41080
Milano; phone 41210
Oberosler; phone 41136
Palu; phone 41280
Posta; phone 41006; Telex 401365
Roch; phone 40100
Spinale; phone 41116
Splendid; phone 41141
Sport Campiglio; phone 40311
St. Hubertus; phone 41144
St. Raphael; phone 41570
Touring; phone 41051
Vidi; phone 41174
   ★★ – 14 Lodgings
      ★ – 5 Lodgings

MALGA CIAPELA
Telephone Code 0437
Postal Code 32020 (BL)
Azienda di Promozione Turistica
Address 32022 Malga Ciapela-Rocca Pietore
Telephone 722138
● **Hotels**
★★★
Principe Marmolada; phone 722041
Roy; phone 722027
Tyrolia; phone 722054
   ★★ – 11 Lodgings
      ★ – 1 Lodging

MOENA
Telephone Code 0462
Postal Code 38035 (TN)

(continued)

MOENA *(continued)*
Azienda di Soggiorno
Address 38035 Moena
Telephone 53122 or 53340
Telex 400677
● **Hotels**
★★★
Alpi; phone 53194
Belvedere; phone 53233
Catinaccio; phone 53235
Cavalletto; phone 53164
Centrale; phone 53228
Ciampian; phone 53186
De Ville; phone 53350
Dolce Casa; phone 53126
Dolomiti-Garber; phone 53218
Europa; phone 53161
Faloria; phone 53149
Garden Hotel; phone 53314
La Romantica; phone 53298
La Serenella; phone 53236
La Soldanella; phone 53201
Laurino; phone 53238
Leonardo; phone 53355
Maria; phone 53265
Monti Pallidi; phone 53221
Monza; phone 53205
Piedi bosco; phone 53389
Post Hotel; phone 53760
Sport Hotel; phone 53239
Stella; phone 53215
Villa Patrizia; phone 53185
★★ – 16 Lodgings
★ – 13 Lodgings
Nearby Moena
Forno
★★★
Valsorda; phone 53460
★★ – 1 Lodging
Passo di San Pellegrino
★★★★
Monzoni; phone 53352
★★★
Arnika; phone 53491
Costabella; phone 53326
Cristallo; phone 53342
San Marco; phone 53475

MOLVENO
Telephone Code 0461
Postal Code 38018 (TN)
Azienda di Soggiorno
Address 38018 Molveno
Telephone 586924
Telex 401385
● **Hotels**
★★★
Alexander Hotel Cima; phone 586928
Ariston; phone 586907
Aurora; phone 586946
Bellariva; phone 586952
Belvedere; phone 586933; Telex 401310
Des Alpes; phone 586983
Du Lac; phone 586965
Fontanella; phone 586955
Gloria; phone 586962
Ischia Alle Dolomiti di Brenta; phone 586057
Lido; phone 586932
Londra; phone 586943
Milano; phone 586909
Miralago; phone 586935
Miramonti; phone 586923
Molveno; phone 586934
Negritella; phone 586942
Nevada; phone 586970
Olimpia; phone 586961
Paganella; phone 586925
Panorama; phone 586929
Stella Alpina; phone 586918

Venezia; phone 586920
★★ – 7 Lodgings
★ – 4 Lodgings

MOSO (MOOS)
Telephone Code 0474
Postal Code 39030 (BZ)
Azienda di Soggiorno
Address 39030 Sesto
Telephone 70310
Telex 400196
● **Hotels**
★★★★
Rainer; phone 70366
Sporthotel Fischleintal; phone 70365
★★★
Alpi; phone 70378
Berghotel Tyrol; phone 70386
Dolomitenhof; phone 70364
Drei Zinnen-Tre Cime; phone 70321
Holzer; phone 70340
Royal; phone 70423
Schoenblick; phone 70332
Moso and Sesto
★★ – 19 Lodgings
★ – 33 Lodgings

OBEREGGEN
Telephone Code 0471
Postal Code 39050 (BZ)
Azienda di Soggiorno
Address 39050 Nova Ponente
Telephone 616567
Telefax 616592
● **Hotels**
★★★★
Sporthotel Obereggen; phone 615797; Telex 401205
★★★
Cristal; phone 615627
★★ – 4 Lodgings
★ – 1 Lodging

ORTISEI (ST. ULRICH)
Telephone Code 0471
Postal Code 39046 (BZ)
Azienda di Soggiorno
Address 39046 Ortisei
Telephone 76328
Telex 400305
Telefax 76749
● **Hotels**
★★★★
Aquila-Adler; phone 76203
Grien; phone 76340
Hell; phone 76785
★★★
Alpenheim; phone 76515
Angelo-Engel; phone 76336
Cosmea; phone 76464
Gardena-Groednerhof; phone 76315
Genziana-Enzian; phone 76246
Hartmann; phone 76270
LaPerla; phone 76421
La Rodes; phone 76108
Lersc; phone 76541
Luna-Mondschein; phone 76214
Miraurtijei; phone 76384
Piciuel; phone 77351
Posta Cavallino Bianco; phone 76392
Pra'Palmer; phone 76710
Rainell; phone 76145
Regina; phone 76329
Ronce; phone 76383
Stettneck; phone 76563
Villa Emilia; phone 76171
Villa Luise; phone 76498
★★ – 43 Lodgings
★ – 18 Lodgings

PAMPEAGO
Telephone Code 0462
Postal Code 38038 (TN)
Azienda di Soggiorno
Address 38038 Tesero
Telephone 83032
- **Hotels**
  ★★★
  Pampeago; phone 83167
  ★ - 1 Lodging

PECOL
Telephone Code 0437
Postal Code 32010 (BL)
- **Hotels**
  ★★ - 5 Lodgings
  Nearby Pecol
  Mareson (Zoldo Alto)
  ★★ - 4 Lodgings
  ★ - 1 Lodging

PEDRACES (PEDRATSCHES)
Telephone Code 0471
Postal Code 39036 (BZ)
Azienda di Soggiorno
Address 39036 Badia
Telephone 839695
- **Hotels**
  ★★★★
  Sporthotel Teresa; phone 839623
  ★★★
  Lec da Sompunt; phone 847015
  Miramonti; phone 839661
  Serena; phone 839664
  ★★ - 5 Lodgings
  ★ - 9 Lodgings
  Nearby Pedraces
  San Leonardo
  ★★ - 3 Lodgings
  ★ - 2 Lodgings

PESCUL
Telephone Code 0437
Postal Code 32020 (BL)
Proloco Val Fiorentina
Address 32020 Selva di Cadore
Telephone 720243
- **Hotels**
  ★★★ - 1 Lodging
  ★★ - 3 Lodgings
  ★ - 1 Lodging

PIEVE DI CADORE
Telephone Code 0435
Postal Code 32044 (BL)
Azienda di Promozione Turistica
Address Via XX Settembre 18, 32044 Pieve di Cadore
Telephone 31644 or 31645
- **Hotels**
  ★★ - 7 Lodgings
  ★ - 2 Lodgings

PINZOLO
Telephone Code 0465
Postal Code 38086 (TN)
Azienda di Soggiorno
Address 38086 Pinzolo
Telephone 51007
Telex 401342
- **Hotels**
  ★★★
  Centro Pineta; phone 52758
  Corona; phone 51030
  Cristina; phone 51620
  Edelweiss; phone 51223
  Europeo; phone 51115
  Ferrari; phone 52624
  Funivia; phone 51266
  Hotel Canada; phone 52062

Olympic; phone 51505
Pinzolo-Dolomiti; phone 51024
  ★★ - 13 Lodgings
  ★ - 11 Lodgings

POZZA DI FASSA
Telephone Code 0462
Postal Code 38036 (TN)
Azienda di Soggiorno
Address 38036 Pozza di Fassa
Telephone 64136; 64117
- **Hotels**
  ★★★
  Anda; phone 64283
  Arnika; phone 64149
  Buffaure; phone 64287
  Chalet Alaska; phone 64091
  Gran Baita; phone 64284; Telex 401379
  Ladinia; phone 64201
  Laurino; phone 64125
  Mater Dei; phone 64148
  Meida; phone 64283
  Milena; phone 64190
  Monzoni; phone 64280
  Rene; phone 64258
  Trento; phone 64279
  ★★ - 10 Lodgings
  ★ - 11 Lodgings

PREDAZZO
Telephone Code 0462
Postal Code 38037 (TN)
Azienda di Soggiorno
Address 38037 Predazzo
Telephone 51237 or 51477
Telex 401329
- **Hotels**
  ★★★★
  Ancora; phone 51651
  ★★★
  Bellaria; phone 51648
  Liz; phone 51264
  Touring; phone 51212
  Vinella; phone 51151
  ★★ - 4 Lodgings
  ★ - 1 Lodging

ROCCA PIETORE
Telephone Code 0437
Postal Code 32020 (BL)
Azienda di Promozione Turistica
Address Piazza Kennedy 17, 32022 Rocca Pietore
Telephone 721319
Telex 440053
- **Hotels**
  ★★ - 1 Lodging
  ★ - 3 Lodgings

SAN CANDIDO (INNICHEN)
Telephone Code 0474
Postal Code 39038 (BZ)
Azienda di Soggiorno
Address 39038 San Candido (Innichen)
Telephone 73149
Telex 400329
Telefax 73377
- **Hotels**
  ★★★★
  Cavallino Bianco; phone 73135
  ★★★
  Brandi; phone 73393
  Helmhotel; phone 76742
  San Candido-Innichen; phone 73102
  Panorama Leitlhof; phone 73440
  Parkhotel Sole Paradiso; phone 73120; Telex 400329
  Pojaufer; phone 76759
  Posta-Post; phone 73355; Telex 400328
  Rainer; phone 76724
  Sporthotel Tyrol; phone 73198
  ★★ - 18 Lodgings
  ★ - 7 Lodgings   *(continued)*

SAN CASSIANO (ST. KASSIAN)
Telephone Code 0471
Postal Code 39036 (BZ)
Azienda di Soggiorno
Address 39030 San Cassiano
Telephone 849422
Telex 401005
● **Hotels**
★★★★
Ciasa Salares; phone 849445
Diamant; phone 849499
Rosa Alpina; phone 849377; Telex 400552
★★★
Fanes-Pitscheiderhof; phone 849470
La Stüa; phone 849456
Tirol; phone 849531; Telex 450433
★★ - 16 Lodgings
★ - 18 Lodgings
Nearby San Cassiano
Armentarola
★★★
Armentarola; phone 849522
★★ - 1 Lodging

SAN MARTINO DI CASTROZZA
Telephone Code 0439
Postal Code 38058 (TN)
Azienda di Soggiorno
Address 38058 San Martino di Castrozza
Telephone 68101 or 68352
Telex 401543
● **Hotels**
★★★★
Grand des Alpes; phone 68518
Hotel Savoia; phone 68094
★★★
Alpino; phone 68193
Belvedere; phone 68440
Cimone; phone 65261
Colbricon; phone 68063
Colfosco; phone 68224
Cristallo; phone 68134
Europa; phone 68575
Hotel Orsingher; phone 68544
Jolanda; phone 68158
Letizia; phone 68615
Madonna; phone 68296
Majestic Dolomiti; phone 68033
Margherita; phone 68140
Montanara; phone 68183
Nevada; phone 68078
Paladin; phone 68680
Panorama; phone 68667
Plank; phone 68403
Regina; phone 68017
Rosetta; phone 68622
San Martino; phone 68011
Sayonara; phone 68174
★★ - 13 Lodgings
★ - 6 Lodgings
Nearby San Matino di Castrozza
Passo Rolle
★★★
Venezia; phone 68315
★★ - 2 Lodgings
★ - 2 Lodgings

SAN VIGILIO DI MAREBBE (ST. VIGIL IN ENNEBERG)
Telephone Code 0474
Postal Code 39030 (BZ)
Azienda di Soggiorno
Address 39030 San Vigilio di Marebbe
Telephone 51037
● **Hotels**
★★★
Almhof; phone 51043
Clara; phone 51026
Condor; phone 51017

Corona-Krone; phone 51038
Emma; phone 51133
Floralp; phone 51115
Gran Pré; phone 51065
La Stöa; phone 51055
Les Alpes; phone 51080
Monte Sella; phone 51034
Olympia; phone 51028
Parc Posta; phone 51010
Sport; phone 51030
Teresa; phone 51001
★★ - 23 Lodgings
★ - 15 Lodgings

SAN VITO DI CADORE
Telephone Code 0436
Postal Code 32046 (BL)
Azienda di Promozione Turistica
Address Via Nationale 9, 32046 San Vito Di Cadore
Telephone 9405 or 9119
● **Hotels**
★★★★
Marcora; phone 9101
★★★
Cima Belpra; phone 9118
Ladinia; phone 9562
★★ - 15 Lodgings
★ - 8 Lodgings

SANTA CRISTINA (ST. CHRISTINA)
Telephone Code 0471
Postal Code 39047 (BZ)
Azienda di Soggiorno
Address Via Chemun 25b, 39047 Santa Cristina
Telephone 73046
Telex 400025
● **Hotels**
★★★★
Hotel Uridl; phone 73215
Touring; phone 73119
★★★
Carmen; phone 76440
Cristallo; phone 76499
Dosses; phone 73326
Interski; phone 73460
Posta; phone 76678
Villa Martha; phone 76628
Villa Pallua; phone 73366
★★ - 15 Lodgings
★ - 24 Lodgings
Nearby Santa Cristina
Monte Pana
★★★★
Sporthotel Diamant; phone 76780
Sporthotel Monte Pana; phone 76128; Telex 401689
★★★
Cendevaves; phone 76562

SELVA DI CADORE
Telephone Code 0437
Postal Code 32020 (BL)
Azienda di Promozione Turistica
Address 32020 Selva di Cadore
Telephone 720243
● **Hotels**
★ - 2 Lodgings
Nearby Selva di Cadore
Santa Fosca
★★★
Nigritella; phone 720041
★★ - 3 Lodgings
★ - 3 Lodgings

SELVA (WOLKENSTEIN)
Telephone Code 0471
Postal Code 39048 (BZ)
Azienda di Soggiorno
Address 39048 Selva di Val Gardena
Telephone 75122
Telex 400359

HOTELS, PENSIONI, AND GARNI

● **Hotels**
★★★★
Aaritz; phone 75011
Alpenroyal; phone 75178
Antares; phone 75400; Telex 400580
Genziana; phone 75187
Oswald; phone 75151
Piccolo; phone 75186
Sporthotel Gran Baita; phone 75210; Telex 401432
Tyrol; phone 75270
★★★
Alaska; phone 75298
Alpino; phone 75134
Armin; phone 75347
Astor; phone 75207
Bel Mont; phone 76714
Chalet Portillo; phone 75205
Condor; phone 75055
Continental; phone 75411
Des Alpes; phone 75184
Dorfer; phone 75204
Gardenia; phone 76353
Granvara; phone 75250
Jaegerheim; phone 76216
Kristiania; phone 76847
Laurin; phone 75105
Linder; phone 75242
Malleier; phone 75296
Meisules; phone 75200
Mignon; phone 75359
Miravalle; phone 75166
Olympia; phone 75145
Posta al Cervo; phone 75174
Pralong; phone 75370
Savoy; phone 75343
Sochers Club; phone 76601
Soel; phone 74147
Solaia; phone 75104
Sporthotel Maciaconi; phone 76229
Sun Valley; phone 75152
Villa Prinoth; phone 75269
★★ - 80 Lodgings
　★ - 48 Lodgings

SESTO (SEXTEN)
Telephone Code 0474
Postal Code 39030 (BZ)
Azienda di Soggiorno
Address 39030 Sesto
Telephone 70310
Telex 400196
Telefax 70318
● **Hotels**
★★★
Monika; phone 70384
Parkhotel; phone 70305
Sextnerhof; phone 70314
St. Veit; phone 70390
Strobl; phone 70371
Waldheim; phone 70316
★★ - 20 Lodgings
　★ - 30 Lodgings
Nearby Sesto
Passo Monte Croce
★★★
Kreuzberg-Passo Monte Croce; phone 70328

SIUSI (SEIS)
Telephone Code 0471
Postal Code 39040 (BZ)
Azienda di Soggiorno
Address 39040 Siusi
Telephone 71124
Telex 400110
● **Hotels**
★★★★
Diana; phone 71129; Telex 400110
Edelweiss; phone 71130
Seiserhof; phone 71125

★★★
Bad Ratzes; phone 71131
Dolomiti-Dolomitenhof; phone 71128
Europa; phone 71174
Genziana-Enzian; phone 71150
Pranti; phone 71430
Ritterhof; phone 71522
Schlosshotel Mirabell; phone 71134
Waldrast; phone 71117
★★ - 12 Lodgings
　★ - 4 Lodgings

VALDAORA (OLANG)
Telephone Code 0474
Postal Code 39030 (BZ)
Azienda di Soggiorno
Address 39030 Valdaora
Telephone 46277
Telex 400652
● **Hotels**
★★★
Aichner; phone 46286
Berghotel Zirm; phone 46054
Christoph; phone 46426
Hubertus; phone 46104
Kristall; phone 46477
Markushof; phone 46250
Messnerwirt; phone 46178
Mirabell; phone 46191
Posta-Post; phone 46127; Telex 400350
Scherer; phone 46174
Villa Tirol; phone 46422
★★ - 18 Lodgings
　★ - 16 Lodgings

VIGO DI FASSA
Telephone Code 0462
Postal Code 38039 (TN)
Azienda di Soggiorno
Address 38039 Vigo di Fassa
Telephone 64093 or 64094
Telex 400540
● **Hotels**
★★★★
Park Corona; phone 64211; Telex 400180
★★★
Alla Rosa; phone 64286
Cima Dodici; phone 64175
Crescenzia; phone 64112
Genzianella; phone 64151
Hotel Andes; phone 64575
La Grotta; phone 64047
Piccolo; phone 64217
Vigo; phone 64180
★★ - 10 Lodgings
　★ - 14 Lodgings
Nearby Vigo di Fassa
Passo di Costalunga
Telephone Code 0471
★★★
Savoy; phone 616-824
S. Giovanni di Fassa
★★★
Dolomiti; phone 64131
Tamion
★★★
Gran Mugon; phone 64208
Vallonga
★★★
Fontana; phone 64140

HOTELS, PENSIONI, AND GARNI

ITALIAN PROVINCES OF THE DOLOMITES

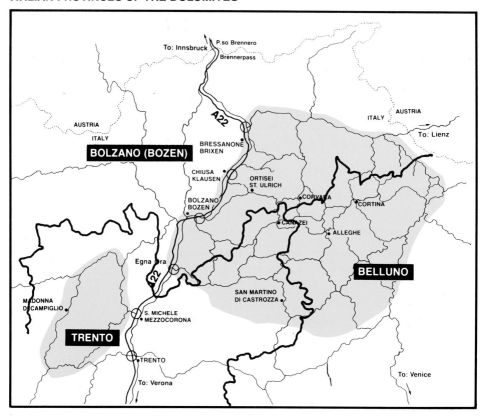

The Dolomites lie in the north Italian regions of Trentino-Alto Adige and Veneto, and within the provinces of Bolzano, Trento, and Belluno.

Bolzano (Bozen) . . . . BZ
Trento . . . . TN
Belluno. . . . . BL

The hotels, pensioni, and garni in this book are in these provinces.

GLOSSARY

DOLOMITE GLOSSARY

English — *Italian*

above — *sopra*
accident — *incidente*
ahead — *avanti*
ahead (straight) — *diritto*
all — *tutto*
alone — *solo*
altitude, difference in — *dislivello*
always — *sempre*
arrival — *arrivo*
avalanche — *valanga*
bad — *cattivo*
bed — *letto*
behind — *dietro*
bill (in a restaurant) — *il conto*
breakfast — *prima colazione*
bridge — *ponte*
bus stop — *fermata*
busy — *occupato*
cable car — *funivia*
cable (fixed) — *cavo fisso*
to call — *chiamare*
car — *automobile*
car park — *parcheggio*
cashier — *cassa*
chairlift — *seggiovia*
to change — *cambiare*
clear weather — *sereno*
to climb — *scalare*
closed — *chiuso*
cloudy — *nuvoloso*
cold — *freddo*
to continue — *continuare*
correct — *giusto*
cost — *costo*
crampons — *ramponi*
crossing — *traversata*
daily — *giornaliero*
danger — *pericolo*
dark — *scuro*
day — *giorno*
departure — *partenza*
descent — *discesa*
difficult — *difficile*
direction — *direzione*
distance — *distanza*
to do — *fare*
doctor — *medico*
dormitory — *dormitorio*
down — *giù*
early, soon — *presto*
east — *est*
eastern — *orientale*
easy — *facile*
emergency — *emergenza*
emergency exit — *uscita di sicurezza*
entrance — *entrata*
example — *esempio*
exit — *uscita*
expert — *esperto*
exposed — *esposto*

fall — *caduta*
far — *lontano*
fast — *veloce*
first — *primo*
first aid — *pronto soccorso*
flat or level — *piano*
fog — *nebbia*
forest — *bosco*
free — *libero*
full — *pieno*
glacier — *ghiacciaio*
to go down — *scendere*
to go up — *salire*
guide — *guida*
half — *mezzo*
help — *aiuto*
here — *qui*
high — *alto*
hill — *colle*
hospital — *ospedale*
hot — *caldo*
hour — *ora*
hut (mountain) — *rifugio*
ice — *ghiaccio*
ice axe — *piccozza*
ice skates — *pattini*
ice stadium — *stadio del ghiaccio*
intermediate — *medio*
itinerary — *itinerario*
key — *chiave*
lake — *lago*
last — *ultimo*
left — *sinistra*
line (for ski lift) — *coda*
long — *lungo*
to lose — *perdere*
map — *mappa*
mechanic — *meccanico*
mountain hut — *rifugio*
narrow — *stretto*
near — *vicino*
north — *nord*
not permitted — *vietato*
one way — *senso unico*
open — *aperto*
pass — *passo*
pass or saddle, (small) — *forcella*
please — *per favore, or prego*
question — *domanda*
railway station — *stazione ferroviaria*
rain — *pioggia*
ready — *pronto*
reservation — *prenotazione*
ride, last down — *ultima discesa*
ride, last up — *ultima salita*
right — *destra*
river — *fiume*
road — *strada*
room — *camera*
    room (single) — *camera singola*
    room (two bed) — *camera a due letti*
    room (with bath) — *camera con bagno*
    room (with shower) — *camera con doccia*

GLOSSARY

rope — *corda*
route — *via or percorso*
safe — *sicuro*
same — *stesso*
sandwich — *panino*
schedule — *orario*
school — *scuola*
scree — *ghiaione*
service — *servizio*
sickness (mountain) — *mal di montagna*
short — *corto*
sign — *segno*
ski — *sci*
to ski — *sciare*
ski (cross country) — *sci di fondo*
ski instructor — *maestro di sci*
ski lift network — *rete di impianti*
ski poles — *bastoncini da sci*
ski rental —*noleggio*
ski repair — *riparazioni*
ski run — *pista*
small — *piccolo*
snow — *neve*
south — *sud*
steep — *ripido*
storm — *temporale*
summit — *cima*
swimming pool — *piscina*
ticket — *biglietto*
ticket office — *biglietteria*
ticket (round trip) — *andata e ritorno*
time — *tempo*
tire chains, — *catene da neve*
tiring — *faticoso*
toilet — *W.C.*
tourist office (local) — *azienda di soggiorno*
trail — *sentiero*
uphill — *in salita*
valley — *val, valle*
view — *vista, panorama*
to walk — *camminare*
walk — *passeggiata*
wall — *parete, muro*
water — *acqua*
weather — *tempo*
west — *ovest*
western — *occidentale*
wide — *largo*
wind — *vento*
within — *dentro*
wounded — *ferito*
wrong — *sbagliato* —

Italian — English

acqua — *water*
aiuto — *help*
alpe — *large upland meadow*
alta via — *multi-day high-level hiking route*
alto — *high*
andata e ritorno — *round trip ticket*
aperto — *open*
arrivo — *arrival*

automobile/macchina — *car*
autostazione — *bus station*
avanti — *ahead*
azienda di soggiorno — *local tourist office*
baita — *small mountain hut*
bastoncini da sci — *ski poles*
biglietteria — *ticket office*
biglietto — *ticket*
bivacco — *small metal hut*
bosco — *forest*
cabinovia — *gondola*
caduta — *fall*
caldo — *hot*
cambiare — *to change*
camera — *room*
    a due letti — *two bed room*
    con bagno — *room with bath*
    con doccia — *room with shower*
    singola — *single room*
camminare — *to walk*
canalone — *gully*
cassa — *cashier*
catene da neve — *tire chains*
cattivo — *bad*
cavo fisso — *fixed cable*
cengia — *ledge*
chiamare — *to call*
chiave — *key*
chiuso — *closed*
cima — *summit*
Club Alpino
    Italiano (C.A.I.) — *Alpine Club*
coda — *line (for ski lift)*
col, colle — *hill*
confine — *border*
continuare — *to continue*
corda — *rope*
corto — *short*
costo — *cost*
dentro — *within*
destra — *right*
dietro — *behind*
difficile — *difficult*
direzione — *direction*
diritto — *straight ahead*
discesa — *descent, downhill skiing*
dormitorio — *dormitory*
dislivello — *difference in altitude*
distanza — *distance*
domanda — *question*
emergenza — *emergency*
entrata — *entrance*
esperto — *expert*
esposto — *exposed*
est — *east*
facile — *easy*
faticoso — *tiring*
ferito — *wounded*
fermata — *bus stop*
fiume — *river*
forcella — *small pass or saddle*
freddo — *cold*
funivia — *cable car*
fuori pista — *off-piste*

GLOSSARY

garni — *bed and breakfast inn*
ghiacciaio — *glacier*
ghiaccio — *ice*
ghiaione — *scree*
giorno — *day*
giù — *down*
giusto — *right (correct)*
guida — *guide*
hütte (German) — *mountain hut*
il conto — *the bill (in a restaurant)*
impianti, rete di — *ski lift network*
incidente — *accident*
in salita — *uphill*
itinerario — *itinerary*
joch (German) — *pass*
lago — *lake*
largo — *wide*
letto — *bed*
libero — *free*
lontano — *far*
maestro di sci — *ski instructor*
mal di montagna — *mountain sickness*
malga — *mountain farm house*
meccanico — *mechanic*
medio — *intermediate*
medico — *doctor*
meuble — *bed and breakfast inn*
mezzo — *half*
molto — *much*
montagna — *mountain*
nebbia — *fog*
neve — *snow*
noleggio — *ski rental service*
nord — *north*
nuvoloso — *cloudy*
occidentale — *western*
occupato — *busy*
ora — *hour*
orario — *schedule*
ovovia — *gondola*
orientale — *eastern*
ospedale — *hospital*
ovest — *west*
panino — *sandwich*
parcheggio — *car park*
parete — *wall*
partenza — *departure*
passeggiata — *walk*
passo — *pass*
pattini — *ice skates*
pensione — *hotel accommodation*
    completa — *all meals included*
    mezza — *breakfast and one other meal*
percorso — *path, route by foot, ski, etc.*
perdere — *to lose*
per favore, prego — *please*
pericolo — *danger*
piano — *flat, level*
piccolo — *small*
piccozza — *ice axe*
a piedi — *by foot*
pieno — *full*
piscina — *swimming pool*
pista, piste — *ski run, ski runs*

piz — *summit*
pioggia — *rain*
ponte — *bridge*
prenotazione — *reservation*
presto — *early, soon*
prima colazione — *breakfast*
primo — *first*
pronto — *ready*
pronto soccorso — *first aid*
ramponi — *crampons*
rifugio — *mountain hut*
ripido — *steep*
salire — *to go up*
scalare — *to climb*
scendere — *to go down*
sci — *ski*
sciare — *to ski*
sci di fondo — *cross-country skiing*
sci riparazioni — *ski repair service*
scuro — *dark*
seggiovia — *chairlift*
segno — *sign*
sempre — *always*
senso unico — *one way*
sentiero — *trail*
sereno — *clear (weather)*
servizio — *service*
sfondo — *background*
sicuro — *safe*
sinistra — *left*
skilift — *T bar or pomalift*
solo per esperti — *only for experts*
solo — *alone*
sopra — *above*
sbagliato — *wrong*
scuola — *school*
stadio del ghiaccio — *ice stadium*
stazione ferroviaria — *railway station*
std. (German) — *hour*
stesso — *same*
strada — *road*
sud — *south*
tal (German) — *valley*
temporale — *storm in summer*
tempo — *weather, time*
traversata — *crossing*
ultima discesa — *last ride down*
ultima salita — *last ride up*
ultimo — *last*
uscita — *exit*
uscita di sicurezza — *emergency exit*
valanga — *avalanche*
val, valle — *valley*
veloce — *fast*
vento — *wind*
via — *route*
via ferrata — *steep hike, climb*
    with fixed cables
vicino — *near*
vietato — *not permitted*
vista — *view*
W.C. — *toilet*
weg (German) — *trail*

PROFILES

AUTHORS

James and Anne Goldsmith, Mill Valley, California, U.S.A.

In researching this book, the Goldsmiths spent the better part of four summers and three winters in the Dolomites. Both are experienced mountain hikers, climbers, skiers, and backpackers.

Jim organized and produced the book. He wrote most of the text and took a majority of the summer and winter photos. Anne edited and wrote many sections and coordinated the additional editing, design and production.

The Goldsmiths' mountain experience has been in California's Sierra Nevada, Grand Teton and Yellowstone National Parks, and the Wind River and Beartooth ranges of Wyoming and Montana. They have also spent time in Switzerland, Austria, and the Lake District of England. Two treks to Nepal have taken them to the Kali Gandaki and Solo Khumbu.

The Goldsmiths live in Mill Valley, California, and have four grown children.

CONTRIBUTING AUTHORS

Giovanni Rizzardi, Rome and Selva di Val Gardena, Italy.

Giovanni inspired us from the beginning to attempt this project and consulted with us every step of the way. He was especially helpful with design ideas and translations as well as providing technical translators for important background material. He helped us gather and interpret information on geology and history, and accompanied us on many hikes and skiing excursions.

Giovanni is a professional architect in Rome, specializing in historic preservation.

Gernot Mussner, Ortisei, Italy.

Gernot was an invaluable contributor, gathering cultural, statistical, and travel information throughout the Dolomites. He joined us in California to assist in organizing the initial text. He aided with many translations, and in writing and verifying information on the Ladins, Land Ownership, and the Legend.

Gernot was born and raised in the Val Gardena where he is a professional ski instructor. His fluency in Italian, German, Ladin, English and French also involves him in all aspects of the media. He is a free-lance writer for magazines, newspapers and the Ladin radio station.

PROFILES

Paolo Pompanin, Cortina d'Ampezzo, Italy.

Paolo assisted with all aspects of Cortina and the Sesto, as well as the mapping. During two working trips to California, he helped develop the scope, design, and terminology for the maps including the geography, summer excursion and winter ski diagrams. He provided resources and specific help for much of the Cortina information such as history, the Regole, walks, hikes and skiing. He also worked in preparing and editing the glossary.

A native of Cortina, Paolo is an Alpine Guide, a noted climber, and on the Cortina mountain rescue team.

BOOK DESIGNER

George Charles Hampton, Mill Valley, California, U.S.A.

George conceived and executed the overall design and production of the book, and has embellished it with his illustrations and original map-diagrams. His enthusiasm and energy were an unending source of support. Both George and his wife, Jacqueline, joined us in the Dolomites during one of our summer research sessions, traveling the back roads and taking many photographs.

George is part owner and creative director of a San Francisco advertising agency. He is a talented illustrator and professional photographer as well.

RESEARCH TEAM — ITALY

Franz and Carmen Perathoner, Selva di Val Gardena, Italy.

Franz assisted with the Winter section of the book, helping us delineate the winter regions and ski areas and obtain statistical information on the recreational facilities. For nearly three years he provided helpful suggestions on design, mapping, and editing.

A lawyer by profession, Franz is an executive with Dolomiti Superski.

Carmen made us feel at home while staying in Selva. The Risaccia apartments (owned and managed by Carmen and Franz) became our home and office most of the months we spent working on the project. She helped edit and proof the Village Life, Food and Wine sections and made valuable comments on the text and design.

Ugo Pompanin, Cortina d' Ampezzo, Italy.

A noted mountain guide, Ugo has tirelessly supported the project since the summer of 1986. He suggested and critiqued all the Cortina and Sesto walks, excursions and hiking itineraries, provided introductions to local experts in various fields, and guided us on several hikes in the Sesto.

Ugo is active in the Regole of Cortina as well as many civic organizations.

Norbert Mussner, Ortisei, Italy.

For nearly three years Norbert was our summer and winter guide. Together we hiked many routes in San Martino, Cortina, and Cordevole and skied in the Val Gardena, Val di Fassa, Moena-Falcade and San Martino regions. He edited and critiqued our hikes in the Val Gardena and Val di Fassa.

Norbert taught for 30 years in the trilingual schools of the Val Gardena. He is a professional photographer and nature guide.

Edi Stuflesser, Ortisei, Italy.

Since February, 1986, Edi has been involved in the project and always encouraged us. He helped define the geographical boundaries for the book. In three winters he guided us through nearly all the winter regions and ski areas of the Dolomites including Alta Badia, Arabba, Plan de Corones, the Marmolada, Civetta-Pelmo, Val di Fiemme-Obereggen, and Bressanone. He introduced us to the exciting off-piste skiing on the Gruppo Sella.

Edi is one of the most popular and respected mountain guides in the Dolomites. Since 1952, he has been a member of the mountain rescue party of the Val Gardena.

PROFILES

Willy Dondio, Bolzano, Italy.

Willy spent hours meeting with us. He wrote detailed explanations of history and geology, provided us with maps and graphics on these subjects and was particularly helpful in the preparation of the history map. He also suggested small out-of-way hamlets to see and unusual driving excursions.

For 30 years Willy was employed by the Tourist Board of the South Tyrol in Bolzano. He is the author of several textbooks about the South Tyrol and the Dolomites.

Prof. Dott. Alfonso Bosellini, Ferrara, Italy.

Alfonso graciously wrote the geology essay for us and provided the necessary information for the geology chart.

Alfonso is Professor of Geology at the University of Ferrara. For years he has specialized on the geology of the Dolomites and has written many scientific articles and lectured worldwide on the subject.

ADDITIONAL RESEARCH

Robert Striffler, Ettlingen, West Germany.

Robert reviewed and critiqued the World War I section of our book. He gave us much needed information on the mine explosions in the mountains during the war.

Robert is a mechanical engineer by profession but his avocation is the study of World War I military history. For more than 15 years he has researched the mine explosions on the Italian front. He is the author of *Der Minenkrieg in Tirol.*

Jacqueline Hampton, Mill Valley, California, U.S.A.

Jacqueline was an invaluable aid. She helped us with the Food and Wine section, proofing of text, and researching the driving excursions throughout the Dolomites.

Wayne and Lee Hanson, Bozeman, Montana, U.S.A.

Wayne helped with the winter research — skiing with us throughout the Dolomites in the winter of 1986. He and Lee traveled on foot around many of the Dolomite massifs exploring hikes and excursions.

For years, Wayne was an instructor with Outward Bound, a mountain climbing guide, and a professional ski instructor. He currently is in business in Bozeman, Montana.

Peter Whitfield — London, England.

Peter is the manager of a book and map store. He originally consulted with us about the need for a travel guide to the Dolomites.

SPECIAL ACKNOWLEDGEMENTS — DOLOMITES

Bolzano — Giuseppe Richebuono
Cortina — Rinaldo Zardini, Stefano Zardini, the Hotel Menardi, the Regole di Cortina d'Ampezzo
Madonna di Campiglio — Bruno Detassis, Cesare Maestri
Ortisei — Helmut Schmalzl
San Martino di Castrozza — Antonio Lott
Aziende di Soggiorno — and offices of **DOLOMITI SUPERSKI**

PRODUCTION ASSISTANTS — U.S.A.

Phil Diamond — Advisor and Legal Consultant
Bea Seidler — Editorial and Copy Consultant
Elizabeth Robinson, Cynthia Roby — Copy Editing
Donald Robertson — Production Coordination
Jane Divel, Lisa Irons — Mechanical Production
Cari Goldsmith — Hike Research Assistant

PHOTOGRAPHY

James Goldsmith, George Charles Hampton, Wayne Hanson

Additional Photo Credits
Roberto Vecellio — Camosci p. 17
Norbert Mussner — Ladin p. 28
Published under license of Oesterreichiche National Bibliothek — Piccolo Lagazuoi p. 22
Archives of Rinaldo Majoni — Cortina Alpine Guides p. 118
Paolo Pompanin — Civetta-Pelmo pp. 234-237

272

BIBLIOGRAPHY

SELECT BIBLIOGRAPHY

ALBRECHT, FLORENCE CRAIG. "Austro - Italian Mountain Frontiers." *The National Geographic Magazine* (April, 1915): 321-376.

ARDITO, STEFANO. "Deodat de Dolomieu: L'aventuriero Che Inciampo Nelle Dolomiti." *Alp* - Speciale: 200 Anni di Dolomiti (April, 1988): 36-38.

BATTAGLIA, FRANCO. *Gruppo di Brenta*. Bologna: Nicola Zanichelli, 1982.

BELLI, MARIO FERRUCCIO. *Storia di Cortina d'Ampezzo*. 3rd ed. Agenzia Distribuzione Dolomiti Inc. di Pancera e Sovilla, 1982. *Cortina d'Ampezzo: Guida Storia, All'arte ed al Turismo*. Cortina, Italy: Edizioni Dolomiti, 1987.

The Classic Walks of the World. Walt Unsworth, ed. London: Oxford, 1985.

COLLINS, MARTIN. *Alta - Via: High Level Walks in the Dolomites*. Cumbria: Cicerone Press, 1986.

CORNELL, TIM, AND JOHN MATTHEWS. *Atlas of the Roman World*. London: Phaidon, 1982.

DELLAGO, EDMUND. *The Priceless Tradition of Anri*. Italy: Fotolito Longo, 1985.

DONDIO, WILLY. *I Rifugi Alpini Dell'Alto Adige*. Trento: Manfrini, 1982.

EDWARDS, AMELIA. *Untrodden Peaks and Unfrequented Valleys*. London: Virago, 1986.

FINI, FRANCO. *Cadore e Ampezzano*. Bologna: Nicola Zanichelli, 1981.

FRASS, HERMANN. *Volto e Anima Dell'Alto Adige: Natura - Storia - Arte*. Bolzano: Athesia, 1978. *Dolomiti Genesi e Fascino*. Bolzano: Athesia, 1983.

GERHARDINGER, ELISABETTA, AND ANTONIO GUERRESCHI. "Mondeval De Sora." *Archeologia Viva* (1988): 49-64.

HUXLEY, ANTHONY. *Mountain Flowers in Colour*. London: Blanford, 1967.

Il Museo Della Val Gardena. Photos by Robert Moroder and Luis Piazza.

KOHLHAUPT, PAULA. *I fiori delle Dolomiti*. 3rd ed. Bolzano: Athesia, 1984. *Piccolo flora delle Dolomiti*. 5th ed. Bolzano: Athesia, 1984.

LANGES, GUNTHER. *La Guerra Fra Rocce e Ghiacci*. Translated by Generale Aldo Daz. Bolzano: Athesia, 1981.

MORODER, EDGARD. *Gardena Valley in the Dolomites*. 5th ed. Trento: Manfrini, 1985.

MUSSNER, GERNOT. *50 Anni Scuola Sci Ortisei 1935-1985*. Ortisei: Typak for Scuola di Sci Ortisei, 1985.

ORTNER, PETER. *Animali delle Nostre Alpi*. 2nd ed. Bolzano: Athesia, 1982.

PALMER, R.R., AND JOEL COLTON. *A History of the Modern World*. 4th ed. New York: Alfred A. Knopf, 1971.

PANIZZA, MARIO. RINALDO ZARDINI AND MASSIMO SCAMPARI. *La Grande Frana su cui e sorta Cortina d'Ampezzo*. S. Vito Di Cadore: Edizioni Dolomiti, 1986.

PAULI, LUDWIG. *The Alps: Archaeology and Early History*. Translated by Eric Peters. London: Thames and Hudson, 1984.

PLAUT, S. JAMES. *The House of Anri: A Popular Account of Woodcarving in the South Tyrol*. Randolf, Mass.: Schmid, 1984.

RICHEBUONO, GIUSEPPE. *Cenni Storici Sulle Regole D'Ampezzo*. Milan: Mursia, 1974. *Storia di Cortina d'Ampezzo: Studi e Documenti Dalle Origini al 1915*. Milan: Mursia, 1974.

ROSSARO, ENRICO. *Dolomites of Cortina D'Ampezzo*. Translated by Bryan Brooks. Trento: Manfrini, 1974.

SCHAUER, THOMAS, AND CLAUS CASPARI. *Flora e Fauna delle Alpi*. Translated by Carlo Pesarini et al. Munich: BLV Verlagsgesellsehaft M.B.H., 1973.

SCHAUMANN, WALTHER. *Monte Piana: Storia, Escursioni e Paesaggio: Museo all'Aperto degli anni 1915/17*. 2nd ed. Translated by Carlo Milesi. Italy: Ghedina e Tassotti Editori 1986.

TRACANELLA, E. *Guide to Geological Field Trips in the Eastern Italian Alps (Dolomites)*. Milan: Centro Stampa AGIP, 1984.

ZARDINI, RINALDO. *Fossili Cassiani*. Cortina d'Ampezzo: Tipografia Ghedina, 1985. *La Flora Montana e Alpina di Cortina d'Ampezzo*. Cortina d'Ampezzo: Cooperativa, 1985. *Geologia e Fossili Attorno a Cortina d'Ampezzo*. Cortina d'Ampezzo: Tipografia Ghedina, 1986.

Pale di San Martino from Tognola

273

INDEX

INDEX

INDEX

NOTES